PHOTOGRAPHY YEAR BOOK
1980

INTERNATIONALES
JAHRBUCH DER FOTOGRAFIE
1980

Photography Year Book 1980

Edited by R. H. Mason FIIP, Hon. FRPS
Designed by John Sanders

**INTERNATIONALES
JAHRBUCH DER FOTOGRAFIE
1980**

FOUNTAIN PRESS

Deutsche Ausgabe: Wilhelm Knapp Verlag, Düsseldorf

Fountain Press,
Argus Books Ltd,
14 St James Road,
Watford, Herts,
England

ISBN 0 85242 694 1

Deutsche Ausgabe:
Wilhelm Knapp Verlag,
Niederlassung der Droste Verlag GmbH
4000 Düsseldorf I

ISBN 3 87420 119 8

© Argus Books Ltd, 1979
Published October 1979

Typesetting by
Ace Engravers Ltd.

Origination by
Sun Litho Ltd.

Printed and bound
in Great Britain by
Morrison & Gibb Ltd,
London and Edinburgh

CONTENTS INHALT

THE PHOTOGRAPHERS

DIE FOTOGRAFEN

Introduction
By R. H. Mason

An annual is, or should be, a reflection of the best of the years' work, although in this case excluding the specialist spheres of photography such as medicine, science and purely commercial applications. There is always a temptation to include a high proportion of photo journalism and news pictures, especially those depicting war or violence because they have a powerful impact. Some reviewers expect to see many such pictures and regard them, together with those having a so-called sociological message, as being the only worthwhile photography, but I have taken a broader view in selecting this year's pictures.

Most pictures of violence and man's inhumanity to man have been seen in the press so they have been omitted this year and, as far as possible, the book reflects the more pleasurable aspects of photography by amateurs and professionals throughout the world. Very few authors have more than one picture reproduced and, as a result, I hope the reader will find more variety and interest. He will certainly find many new names.

It is customary in an annual to draw conclusions about new trends in photography that have been observed during the year. In my view this is too short a period to identify any change or any new movement. For over a century photography has experienced a gradual evolution both in techniques and aesthetic approach and in the last two decades the technical aspect has seen enormous advances, particularly in automated apparatus.

The prestige of photography rises and falls, fashions change and subject matter varies, but one thing that has come to stay in recent years is a sincerity of approach. In the early days photography's devotees were pre-occupied with a difficult and unreliable process and it is not surprising that they attempted to copy painting. Most of the subjects they chose were picturesque or romantic and landscapes dominated exhibition walls for several decades. Then followed a period when formal and static portraiture delighted people by enabling them to see their own images cheaply produced in pseudo-classic studio settings. This period also produced the sickly sentimental, romantic and allegorical pictures which were much to Victorian taste but which were done just as well, and often better, by painters.

It was after the turn of the century that some enlightened amateurs began to exploit the qualities unique to photography – the ability to capture transitory light effects, to tell a story in an instant, to record the fleeting but expressive moment and to see things afresh from an unusual angle or in startling close-up. We owe a lot to those pioneers, who in their way were as original and honest as the French impressionists, but their influence did not last long and there was a reversion to the sentimental and, even worse, to the artifices of table-top and dressed up models. This reached its height before the last war when unshaved models were dressed as fishermen and photographed by studio lighting while others were posed in period costumes without the benefit of stage surroundings to give them authenticity. Shivering nudes on the borders of misty lakes appeared in every Salon and made the title of *"September Morn"* into a joke. H. P. Robinson's *"Fading Away"* at least told a story!

Perhaps it is the harsher reality of modern living, plus the improvements in lenses and fast materials, which have given rise to the refreshing honesty of approach that is thankfully evident in a lot of work today, and especially that of amateurs. An honest approach produces originality because it must reflect the personal view of the author.

Of all the forms of expression of the human mind, pictures are one of the oldest and even those who profess not to understand them cannot escape their influence. They are the first things understood by children, they were one of the first expressions of imagination evinced by ancient cave men and they are still the only universal language; but a picture is not just an ingenious arrangement of objects within a given space – it must also express something of nature – an emotion which will arouse, excite or stimulate others, although not necessarily, as some photographers think, violently. We can liken it to the ancient Aeolian harp which gave music only when placed where the wind could pass through it. Man made the harp but nature made the music and both were dependent on the other. The photographer is like the maker of the harp; nature, the wind which stirs our emotions, is the player and the viewer is like the listener who will react to what he hears according to his own imagination and degree of culture. It is this intimate reaction in each individual viewer that can vary so much according to that viewer's temperament, intelligence, humour and environment that no artist can attempt to control. So, in a sense, he becomes a partner with the viewer in an imaginative experience.

However, that reaction is not necessarily favourable in all cases and it is unlikely that every picture in any annual will please all readers – those who like to be hit with explosive force by powerful subject matter depicted in heavy black contrasts will not appreciate so much the soufflés in high key, the dreamy landscapes or the pastel euphoria of our dust cover, and vice versa, but both can be equally sincere.

It was on this basis that we have made a selection of 227 photographs from the many thousands submitted or, in some cases, invited. Over 160 photographers are featured and they come from 32 different countries. Inevitably, there is a majority from the United Kingdom because the number of prints submitted was overwhelming, but the number reproduced from other countries is in a greater proportion. There were considerably fewer tone separations and other darkroom derivatives than have been seen in recent years. If this indicates a trend, it is a welcome one because there has been a surfeit in the past of prints which used these devices to give an artful distraction to a weak subject.

An interesting aspect of the submissions was that nearly all the black and white photographs were of a high standard and the colour prints were also good, but many panels of transparencies had only one or two reproducable examples and a balance of near duplications that it would be kind to describe as poor. The conclusion is that photographers are much more selective with their black and white work. This is borne out by the fact that most of the black and white submissions averaged about six prints but in colour transparencies the average was nearer twenty – some workers even sending as many as forty! It is pleasing to note that colour print workers seem to be making a more aesthetic use of colour and depending less on impact through the employment of primary colours. On the whole I felt that there was more originality than I have seen in many exhibitions and competitions. Grinning Malaysian children, fishermen casting nets on misty lakes and nudes behind mottled glass – just three of the many hackneyed subjects that have been copied from year to year – were conspicuous by their absence.

Readers are welcome to submit their best work for the 1981 edition, and a leaflet giving details of requirements is enclosed, so these remarks may help in assessing the policy behind the annual. In the final analysis, of course, the selection is a personal one on the part of the Editor but it is hoped that this years' edition of *Photography Year Book* will provide food for thought, even controversy, as well as some pleasurable browsing.

Focus Elsevier Fotojaarboek 1980
Inleiding
door R. H. Mason

Dit fotojaarboek probeert een weergave te zijn van het beste fotografische werk van het afgelopen jaar, alhoewel in dit geval de medische, de wetenschappelijke en commerciële fotografie buiten beschouwing zijn gelaten. Er bestaat altijd de verleiding om veel werk van fotojournalisten en persfoto's op te nemen, vooral als ze een beeld van een oorlog of ander geweld geven, omdat díe foto's altijd veel indruk maken. Er zijn recensenten die vooral dergelijke foto's verwachten en zij beschouwen deze, samen met die welke een zogenaamde sociologische boodschap uitdragen, als de enige belangrijke vorm van fotografie, maar bij het selecteren van de foto's ben ik dit jaar van een breder standpunt uitgegaan.

De meeste foto's waarop diverse soorten geweld te zien zijn verschenen al in de pers en zijn dit jaar daarom weggelaten. Daarentegen hebben we geprobeerd zoveel mogelijk de meer plezierige kanten van de fotografie te belichten, van zowel amateurs als beroepsmensen en afkomstig uit alle delen van de wereld. Er zijn maar weinig fotografen van wie meer dan één foto is afgedrukt, wat tot gevolg heeft dat de lezer/kijker erg veel afwisseling en interesse zal aantreffen. Hij zal zeker een groot aantal nieuwe namen tegenkomen.

Het is gebruikelijk in een fotojaarboek conclusies te trekken omtrent nieuwe trends in de fotografie zoals die zich in het afgelopen jaar hebben ontwikkeld. Naar mijn mening is een jaar veel te kort om een verandering of een nieuwe ontwikkeling te kunnen signaleren. De fotografie heeft gedurende de afgelopen honderd jaar een geleidelijke ontwikkeling ondergaan, zowel wat de techniek als de vormgeving betreft. De techniek heeft de laatste twintig jaar zelfs een stormachtige ontwikkeling doorgemaakt, vooral wat de automatisering betreft, maar voor de toegewijde fotograaf is niets zo belangrijk als de voldoening die hij put uit het tot uitdrukking brengen van zijn ideeën of het uitbeelden van zijn persoonlijke ervaringen.

De invloed van de fotografie mag toe- of afnemen, de stijl en onderwerpen mogen veranderen, de oprechte benadering van het onderwerp is de laatste jaren gebleven. In de beginjaren van de fotografie waren haar beoefenaars bezig met een moeilijk en onbetrouwbaar procédé en het is dan ook niet verwonderlijk dat ze het schilderen imiteerden. Meestal kozen ze schilderachtige of romantische onderwerpen en vele tientallen jaren lang domineerden landschapsopnamen de wanden van de tentoonstellingsruimten. Toen volgde er een periode waarin de mensen in de ban raakten van vormelijke en statische portretten en van de manier om van zichzelf goedkoop foto's te laten maken in de pseudo-klassieke omgeving van een fotostudio. Deze periode leverde ook de oer-sentimentele, romantische en allegorische afbeeldingen op die zo goed bij de Victoriaanse smaak pasten, maar die met hetzelfde resultaat beter door een schilder gemaakt hadden kunnen worden.

Het was eerst na de eeuwwisseling dat een aantal verlichte amateurs de unieke eigenschappen van de fotografie begon te gebruiken: de mogelijkheid kortstondige lichteffecten vast te leggen, het in een seconde iets duidelijk kunnen maken, een expressief maar snel voorbijgaand gebeuren vastleggen en bepaalde dingen uit een totaal nieuwe hoek of via een opzienbarende close-up zien. We hebben erg veel aan die pioniers te danken, die op hun manier even origineel en eerlijk waren als de Franse impressionisten, maar hun invloed was niet van lange duur want opnieuw greep men terug naar de sentimentaliteit met zijn kunstgrepen en starre, opgedofte modellen. Deze wijze van fotograferen bereikte juist voor de Tweede Wereldoorlog haar hoogtepunt; bebaarde modellen werden als visser aangekleed en in de studio gefotografeerd terwijl anderen met het oog op echtheid zonder achtergrond werden opgenomen. Van de kou bibberende naakten aan de rand van nevelige meren maakten in iedere salon hun opwachting en gaven aan titels als Septemberochtend een humoristisch effect.

In Fading Away van H. P. Robinson zat tenminste nog een soort verhaal.

Misschien komt het omdat het leven tegenwoordig zoveel harder is geworden en door het gebruik van sneller materiaal en de sterk verbeterde objectieven dat alles mowenteel zoveel eerlijker wordt benaderd. Een benadering die gelukkig in erg veel werk is terug te vinden, vooral in dat van amateurs. Een eerlijke benadering levert originaliteit op omdat het de persoonlijke kijk van de maker weergeeft. Portretten zijn openhartiger en laten meer van het karakter zien, landschappen worden even vrijpostig gepresenteerd en zelfs de zogenaamde studies, zoals naakten en stillevens, worden als fotografie aangekondigd en proberen tegenwoordig niet meer met de andere grafische technieken te wedijveren.

Ik heb het nu natuurlijk over het fotografisch werk zoals dat op de belangrijke tentoonstellingen ingen en in de goede fotoboeken te zien is.

Helaas zijn er (reeds veel) mensen die tegenwoordig rasters en separatietechnieken gebruiken in de hoop een ongeïnspireerd negatief nog in een foto met een boodschap te kunnen veranderen maar over het algemeen groeit men er wel overheen en uiteindelijk gebruiken ze dit soort attributen alleen maar als het bij het onderwerp past en ze de nadruk willen leggen op de boodschap slechts.

Van alle uitdrukkingsvormen van de menselijke geest behoren afbeeldingen tot de oudste en zelfs zij die beweren ze niet te begrijpen, kunnen zich toch niet wapenen tegen hun invloed. Het zijn de eerste dingen die door kinderen worden begrepen. Ze waren de uitdrukkingsmogelijkheden van rotsbewoners en zijn nog steeds de enige universele taal die over de hele wereld wordt verstaan; maar een foto is niet alleen een opstelling van verschillende voorwerpen binnen een gegeven kader, zij dient ook een bepaalde geaardheid uit te drukken: een emotie die andere kan opwekken, uitlokken of stimuleren, hoewel dit echt niet, zoals sommige fotografen wel denken, op een schokkende manier hoeft te gebeuren. We kunnen het vergelijken met de aeolusharp die alleen muziek maakte als hij op een plaats werd gezet waar de wind erdoorheen kon spelen. De mens maakte de harp maar de natuur maakte de muziek en beide stonden los van elkaar. De fotograaf is als de maker van de harp; natuur, die onze ontroering opwekt, is de harpspeler en de toeschouwer is als de luisteraar die op datgene wat hij hoort volgens zijn eigen gevoelens en geaardheid reageert. Het is deze innerlijke reactie in ieder afzonderlijke beschouwer die zo kan variëren al naar gelang zijn temperament, intelligentie, gevoel voor humor en milieu; geen enkele kunstenaar heeft hier greep op. Op deze manier wordt hij samen met de toeschouwer deelgenoot in een fantasierijke ervaring.

Die reactie is echter niet in alle gevallen even gunstig en het is nauwelijks aannemelijk dat alle foto's in dit jaarboek de kijker zullen bevallen. Zij die door een explosieve kracht met een indrukwekkend onderwerp geconfronteerd willen worden, zullen de fijnzinnige hoogstandjes, de dromerige landschappen en de pastelachtige euforie op ons stofomslag nauwelijks weten te waarderen, en omgekeerd natuurlijk, en beide meningen zijn even oprecht.

Op deze basis zijn we gekomen tot een selectie van 227 foto's uit vele duizenden ingezonden en een aantal op uitnodiging gemaakte foto's.

Er is werk van meer dan 160 fotografen uit 32 verschillende landen. Onvermijdelijk komt een groot deel uit Groot-Brittannië omdat het aanbod uit dat land het grootst was, maar het aantal uit andere landen afkomstige foto's neemt niet langer een ondergeschikte plaats in. Er zaten aanzienlijk minder toonseparaties en andere dokatrucs bij de inzendingen dan vroeger. Als dit een bepaalde tendens aanduidt, dan is het er een die wij van harte toejuichen omdat er in het verleden een vloed van afdrukken bij ons is binnengekomen die door middel van deze kunstgrepen op kunstige manier de aandacht van een zwakke opname wisten af te leiden.

Een interessant aspect aan de inzendingen was dat bijna alle zwartwitopnamen op een bijzonder hoog peil stonden en de kleurenfoto's ook goed waren terwijl er van hele series dia's soms slechts enkele reproduceerbaar waren, terwijl de rest vaak de kwaliteit bezat waarvoor het predikaat 'zwak' nog te gunstig was. De conclusie is dat fotografen wat betreft hun zwartwitwerk veel selectiever zijn. Dit blijkt wel uit het feit dat de gemiddelde inzending zes zwartwitafdrukken omvatte, terwijl de gemiddelde dia-inzending zo'n twintig dia's groot was – sommige fotografen stuurden er zelfs veertig in! Het is plezierig te merken dat de kleurenfotografen een zeer esthetisch gebruik van kleur gaan maken en dat ze minder op schokeffecten, verkregen door het gebruik van primaire kleuren, vertrouwen. In het algemeen geloof ik dat er sprake is van een grotere originaliteit dat in het verleden op tentoonstellingen en wedstrijden werd getoond.

Grinnikende Maleisische kinderen, vissers die hun netten boven nevelige meren uitwierpen en naakten achter matglas – drie van de vele afgezaagde onderwerpen die van jaar tot jaar overgenomen werden – schitteren nu door afwezigheid.

Lezers worden hierbij uitgenodigd hun beste werk voor onze editie van 1981 in te zenden. Hiertoe is een formulier met bijzonderheden en voorwaarden bijgevoegd, bijzonderheden die er weer toe bijdragen dat de gedragslijn van dit jaarboek nog duidelijker komt vast te staan. Natuurlijk is deze selectie een persoonlijke keuze van de samensteller, maar ik hoop dat deze editie van ons Fotojaarboek voldoende stof tot nadenken en zelfs tot controverses zal geven, maar tegelijkertijd ook een plezierig doorbladeren zal betekenen.

Einführung
von R. H. Mason

Ein Jahrbuch spiegelt die besten Leistungen des Jahres wider, oder sollte dies zumindest tun, obgleich in dieser Sammlung die spezialisierten Bereiche medizinischer, wissenschaftlicher und rein kommerzieller Fotografie nicht vertreten sind. Man fühlt sich stets versucht, viele journalistische und aktuelle Aufnahmen zu bringen, besonders wenn sie Krieg oder Gewalttaten darstellen, da solche Bilder sehr eindrucksvoll sind. Manche Rezensenten bestehen darauf, daß ein Jahrbuch viele solche Bilder enthalte, und vertreten sogar den Standpunkt, daß allein zeitgenössische und "soziologisch interessante" Vorgänge lohnende Gegenstände der Fotografie seien, doch ich habe meine Wahl der diesjährigen Aufnahmen nach weniger beschränkten Grundsätzen getroffen.

Die meisten Aufnahmen, die Gewalttaten und unmenschliches Verhalten behandeln, sind bereits aus den Zeitungen bekannt und wurden daher dieses Jahr wenn irgend möglich ausgeschlossen. Das Buch spiegelt vielmehr die angenehmeren Aspekte der Kunst von Amateur- und Berufsfotografen in allen Teilen der Welt wider. Nur in sehr wenigen Fällen ist ein Künstler durch mehr als eine Aufnahme vertreten, und ich hoffe, daß dies zu der Vielfalt und dem Interesse des Werkes beiträgt. Eines ist sicher: Der Leser wird in dieser Ausgabe gar manchen neuen Namen finden.

Es ist üblich, in einem Jahrbuch über neue Strömungen zu berichten, die während des Jahres in Erscheinung getreten sind. Meiner Ansicht nach kann sich eine Änderung oder eine neue Bewegung in einer so kurzen Zeitspanne nicht deutlich abzeichnen. Seit mehr als einem Jahrhundert entwickelt sich die Fotografie allmählich sowohl in technischer als auch in ästhetischer Hinsicht, und in den beiden letzten Jahrzehnten wurden auf technischer Ebene – besonders im Zusammenhang mit automatischen Geräten – enorme Fortschritte erzielt. Für den Fotografen "mit Leib und Seele" bedeutet die Mechanik im Vergleich mit der Genugtuung, die der Ausdruck seiner Ideen oder die Darstellung seiner persönlichen Erlebnisse bedingt, jedoch nur wenig.

Das Prestige der Fotografie nimmt zu und ab, die Moden ändern sich und es werden immer wieder neue Themen bevorzugt, doch eine Norm – das Bestehen auf absoluter Aufrichtigkeit – hat in den letzten Jahren festen Fuß gefaßt. Als die Fotografie noch in den Kinderschuhen steckte, galt es, eines schwierigen und unzuverlässigen Prozesses Herr zu werden, und es ist daher nicht erstaunlich, daß die Fotografen versuchten, "mit der Kamera zu malen". Ihre Themen waren meistens bildhaft und romantisch, und an den Wänden der Galerien herrschten mehrere Jahrzehnte lang Landschaftsaufnahmen vor. Dann folgte eine Zeit, in der die Betonung auf förmlichen, posenhaften Porträts lag, die die Möglichkeit zu billiger "Selbstverewigung" in pseudoklassischen Atelierszenen boten. Dies war auch die Blütezeit der saccharinsüßen, sentimentalen, romantischen und allegorischen Bilder, die den Viktorianern so gut gefielen, aber von Malern genau so gut und in vielen Fällen besser ausgeführt werden konnten.

Nach der Jahrhundertwende begannen einige weitblickende Amateure mit der Verwertung der der Fotografie eigenen Eigenschaften – der Möglichkeit vorübergehende Lichteffekte zu erhaschen, einen Vorgang so darzustellen, daß er auf einen Blick verständlich ist, den flüchtigen aber bedeutungsschweren Augenblick zu erfassen und Dinge frisch aus einem ungewöhnlichen Winkel oder in überraschender Nähe zu zeigen. Wir schulden jenen Pionieren viel. Auf ihre Weise waren sie ebenso originell und ehrlich wie die französischen Impressionisten, doch dauerte ihr Einfluß nicht lang, und das Pendel schwang zu sentimentalen und, was noch schlimmer war, zu künstlichen Arrangements auf Tischen und zu verkleideten Modellen zurück. Diese Tendenz erreichte ihren Höhepunkt vor dem letzten Weltkrieg, als "Dressmen" unrasiert und als Fischer verkleidet bei Atelierbeleuchtung oder in historischen Trachten "in natürlicher Umgebung" aufgenommen wurden. In jedem Salon hingen Aufnahmen von vor Kälte bebenden Nackten an nebelverschleierten Seen, so daß der Titel "Septembermorgen" zu einem Scherz wurde. "Fading Away" (im Schwinden begriffen) von H. P. Robinson hatte wenigstens eine Story!

Vielleicht ist die erfrischende Aufrichtigkeit, die heute so viele Aufnahmen – besonders von Amateuren – kennzeichnet, der härteren Realität des modernen Lebens besseren Objektiven und sensitiveren Filmen zu verdanken. Aufrichtigkeit aber geht Hand in Hand mit Originalität, denn sie kann nicht umhin, die persönliche Anschauung des Künstlers zum Ausdruck zu bringen. Porträtaufnahmen sind sachlicher und spiegeln die Persönlichkeit wider, Landschaftsbilder sind im allgemeinen kühn und selbst sogenannte "Studien" wie Akt- und Stilaufnahmen sind eindeutig Fotografien, ohne die geringste Nachahmung anderer Formen darstellender Kunst.

Selbstverständlich spreche ich hier von den Werken, die in führenden Ausstellungen und den guten Sammlungen zu sehen sind. Leider gibt es auch Fotografen, die sich fruchtlos bemühen, minderwertige Negative mit Hilfe von Schirmen und Farbauszugstechniken zu überzeugenden Bildern umzugestalten, doch in der Regel geben sie diese fragwürdigen Methoden wieder auf und verwenden Hilfsmittel nur, wenn sie dem Thema entsprechen und dessen Botschaft wirklich betonen.

Bilder zählen zu den ältesten Ausdrucksformen des menschlichen Geistes, und selbst Menschen, die sie angeblich nicht verstehen, können sich ihrem Einfluß nicht entziehen. Selbst kleine Kinder reagieren auf Bilder, unsere Vorväter malten sie bereits an die Wände ihrer Höhlen und sie sind auch heute noch die einzige universale Sprache. Ein Bild besteht aber nicht nur in einer geistreichen Zusammenstellung von Gegenständen innerhalb einer bestimmten Fläche – es muß vielmehr auch ein Gefühl zum Ausdruck bringen, das den Beschauer anregt oder erregt, obgleich nicht unbedingt auf heftige Weise, wie manche Fotografen meinen. Wir können es mit der alten Äolsharfe vergleichen, die nur dann ertönte, wenn der Wind durch die Saiten strich. Die Harfe war ein Werk von Menschenhand, doch der Wind war eine Naturerscheinung, und ohne Harfe bzw. ohne Wind gab es keine Musik. Der Fotograf ist wie der Harfenmacher, die Natur – der Wind, die unsere Gefühle anspricht – spielt das Instrument, und der Beschauer ist wie der Zuhörer, der je nach seiner eigenen Fantasie und Bildung auf das Gehörte reagiert. Diese ureigene Reaktion des einzelnen Beschauers kann je nach dessen Temperament, Intelligenz, Humor und Umgebung so unterschiedlich sein, daß jeder Versuch sie zu beherrschen fehlschlagen muß. Der Künstler und der Beschauer sind somit auf eine Weise Partner in einem subjektiven Erlebnis.

Diese Reaktion ist jedoch nicht immer positiv, und es ist unwahrscheinlich, daß jedes Bild in einem Jahrbuch allen Lesern gefallen wird. Diejenigen, die "kräftige", kontrastreiche Darstellungen lieben, werden weniger Verständnis für die verfeinerten Stilübungen, die versonnenen Landschaften oder die in Pastelltönen gehaltene Euphorie auf der Schutzhülle unseres Jahrbuchs aufbringen. Andere Leser mögen vielleicht die kräftigen Effekte nicht, doch beide Gruppen können in ihren Urteilen gleich aufrichtig sein.

Dies waren die Gedankengänge, von denem wir uns bei der Wahl der 227 Aufnahmen unter den vielen tausenden, die uns – zum Teil auf Aufforderung – zugingen, leiten ließen. Es sind über 160 Fotografen aus 32 Ländern vertreten. Die meisten Aufnahmen sind natürlich von britischen Künstlern, da die Anzahl der von ihnen unterbreiteten Bilder überwältigend war, doch ist der Anteil von Aufnahmen aus anderen Ländern relativ größer. Es gab bedeutend weniger Farbauszüge und andere Dunkelkammerderivate als in früheren Jahren. Falls dies auf eine Tendenz hindeutet, so kann man sie nur begrüßen, da in früheren Jahren viel zu oft von Mitteln dieser Art Gebrauch gemacht wurde, um einer schwachen Aufnahme ein künstlicheres Interesse zu verleihen.

Interessant war in diesem Zusammenhang auch, daß nahezu alle Schwarz/Weiß-Aufnahmen hochwertig und auch die Farbaufnahmen gut waren. In vielen Dia-Sammlungen dagegen gab es nur ein oder zwei, die zur Reproduktion geeignet waren, und der Anteil an anderen sehr ähnlichen Dias war so hoch, daß man sich nur wundern kann. Der Grund dafür dürfte wohl darin bestehen, daß Fotografen bei ihren Schwarz/Weiß-Aufnahmen viel selektiver sind. Dies geht auch daraus hervor, daß die meisten Fotografen im Durchschnitt etwa sechs Schwarz/Weiß-Aufnahmen an uns sandten, aber nahezu 20 – und in gewissen Fällen sogar 40 – Farbdias! Es ist zu begrüßen, daß Farbfotografen in der Farbenwahl anscheinend mehr Gefühl walten lassen und sich nicht so sehr auf kräftige Primärfarben verlassen. Im allgemeinen schienen mir die Bilder origineller zu sein, als in vielen Ausstellungen und Wettbewerben, die ich gesehen habe. Grinsende malayische Kinder, Fischer mit ihren Netzen auf dunstigen Seen und Aktaufnahmen hinter fleckigen Glasscheiben, um nur drei der zahlreichen abgedroschenen Themen zu nennen, die von einem Jahr zum anderen aufzutauchen pflegten, fehlten glücklicherweise ganz.

Leser können ihre besten Aufnahmen für die Ausgabe 1981 einreichen, und wir fügen eine Druckschrift mit Einzelheiten hinsichtlich der Erfordernisse bei. Die von uns verfolgten Richtlinien dürften aus dieser Einführung hervorgehen. Letzten Endes entscheidet natürlich der Redakteur ganz nach eigenem Empfinden, welche Aufnahmen angenommen werden, doch hoffen wir, daß die diesjährige Ausgabe des Photography Year Book manches enthält, was zum Denken, ja sogar zum Widerspruch, sowie zu entspannendem Genuß anregt.

Introduction
par R. H. Mason

Une publication annuelle est, ou devrait être, le reflet de ce qui s'est fait de mieux au cours de l'année, exception faite, dans le cas présent, des domaines spécialisés de la photographie tels que la médecine, la science et les applications purement commerciales. On est toujours tenté de publier une forte proportion d'images de photojournalisme et d'information pure, en particulier celles qui dépeignent la guerre ou la violence, parce qu'elles ont un impact puissant. Certains espèrent trouver ces images en très grand nombre et les considèrent, au même titre que celles supposées transmettre un message sociologique, comme étant la seule photographie qui vaille, mais, pour ma part, j'ai élargi le champ de sélection des images présentées cette année.

La plupart des images de violence et de l'inhumanité de l'homme à l'égard de l'homme ont été vues dans la presse et c'est pourquoi elles ont été omises cette année, afin que l'album reflète autant que possible les aspects plus agréables de la photographie telle qu'elle est pratiquée par les amateurs et les professionnels du monde entier. Très peu d'auteurs ont plus d'une photographie reproduite. J'espère ainsi que le lecteur trouvera dans l'album une plus grande variété et un intérêt accru. Il y rencontrera en tout cas de nombreux noms nouveaux.

Il est courant, dans une publication annuelle, de tirer des conclusions sur les nouvelles tendances de la photographie qui ont été observées au cours de l'année. Or, à mon avis, c'est là une période trop courte pour déceler un changement ou un mouvement nouveau. Pendant plus d'un siècle, la photographie a subi une évolution progressive tant dans ses techniques que dans son approche esthétique et, au cours des deux dernières décennies, l'aspect technique a connu des progrès considérables, en particulier dans le domaine de l'automatisation des appareils. Mais, pour le photographe convaincu, la mécanique est de peu d'importance en comparaison de la satisfaction que l'on peut attendre de la possibilité d'exprimer ses idées ou de traduire en images ses expériences.

Le prestige de la photographie a ses fluctuations; les modes changent et les sujets varient, mais il une chose qui s'est imposée ces dernières années; la sincérité de l'approche. Au début, les adeptes de la photographie étaient préoccupés par un processus difficile et peu fiable, et il n'est donc pas surprenant qu'ils aient tenté de copier la peinture. La plupart des sujets qu'ils choisissaient étaient pittoresques ou romantiques, et c'est ainsi que les paysages ont, pendant plusieurs décennies, dominé les murs des expositions. Puis vint une période au cours de laquelle les portraits officiels et statiques eurent la vogue, en ce qu'ils permettaient à tout un chacun d'avoir sa propre image reproduite dans des décors pseudo-classiques de studio. Cette période a également engendré les photographies maladivement sentimentales, romantiques et allégoriques, dans le goût victorien, mais dont les peintres s'acquittaient tout aussi bien et même souvent mieux.

C'est après le tournant du siècle que certains amateurs éclairés commencèrent à exploiter les qualités propres à la photographie, à savoir l'aptitude à saisir des effets de lumière transitoires, à raconter des histoires en un instant, à enregistrer le moment fugitif mais expressif et à voir les choses d'un oeil neuf sous un angle inhabituel ou en un gros plan saisissant. Nous devons beaucoup à ces pionniers qui, à leur manière, étaient aussi originaux et aussi honnêtes que les impressionnistes français, mais leur influence fut de courte durée et il se produisit un retour aux modèles sentimentaux et, ce qui est pire, aux artifices des modèles miniature et apprêtés. Cette mode atteignit son point culminant avant la dernière guerre, où l'on vit apparaître des modèles non rasés, habillés en pêcheur et photographiés sous un éclairage de studio, tandis que d'autres posaient en costume d'époque sans le bénéfice de décors de théâtre propres à leur conférer l'authenticité. Des nus grelottants sur les bords de lacs embrumés firent leur apparition dans tous les salons, au point que le titre "September Morn" (Matin de septembre) devint un sujet de plaisanterie. Du moins le "Fading Away" (Évanescence) de H. P. Robinson racontait-il quelque chose!

C'est peut-être la dure réalité de la vie moderne, jointe aux progrès réalisés dans le domaine des objectifs photographiques et des émulsions rapides, qui a donné naissance à cette honnêteté d'approche rafraîchissante qui transparaît dans de nombreuses photographies actuelles, en particulier chez les amateurs. Une approche honnête engendre l'originalité parce qu'elle reflète nécessairement la vision personnelle de l'auteur. Les portraits sont plus candides et reflètent le caractère, les paysages sont généralement hardis dans leur présentation et même les "études" telles que les nus et les photos de mode sont présentés comme étant de la photographie, sans chercher à copier une quelconque autre forme d'art graphique.

Evidemment, je me réfère ici aux oeuvres que l'on trouve dans les grandes expositions et dans les bons livres. Malheureusement, il y a ceux qui emploient des écrans et des techniques de séparation dans une vaine tentative de transformer un négatif non inspiré en une image saisissante, mais ils sont généralement dépassés par la réalité et, finalement, n'utilisent ces artifices que lorsque le sujet s'y prête et lorsqu'ils permettent de préciser le message.

Parmi toutes les formes d'expression de l'esprit humain, les images sont l'une des plus anciennes, et même ceux qui prétendent ne pas les comprendre ne peuvent échapper à leur influence. Ce sont les premières choses que comprennent les enfants, elles sont l'une des premières expressions de l'imagination chez les hommes des cavernes et elles restent le seul langage universel; mais une image n'est pas seulement un arrangement ingénieux d'objets dans les limites d'un espace donné — elle doit également exprimer quelque chose de la nature — une émotion qui soulèvera. excitera ou stimulera d'autres personnes, encore que pas nécessairement, comme le pensent certains photographes, de manière violente. Nous pouvons la comparer à l'ancienne harpe éolienne, qui ne produisait de la musique que lorsqu'elle était placée de manière que le vent pût la traverser. L'homme fabriquait la harpe, mais c'est la nature qui faisait la musique, et ils dépendaient l'un de l'autre. Le photographe est comme le fabricant de la harpe; la nature, le vent qui engendre nos émotions, est le musicien; et l'observateur est comme l'auditeur qui réagit à ce qu'il entend selon sa propre imagination et son niveau de culture. C'est cette réaction intime de chaque observateur qui peut varier dans des proportions si considérables, selon le tempérament, l'intelligence, l'humour et l'environnement de cet observateur, qu'aucun artiste ne peut espérer la dominer. Ainsi, en un sens, il devient un partenaire de l'observateur dans une aventure d'imagination.

Toutefois, cette réaction n'est pas nécessairement favorable dans tous les cas, et il est peu probable que toutes les images d'un album plaisent à tous les lecteurs: ceux qui aiment être frappés par la force explosive de sujets puissants décrits par de lourds contrastes en noir n'apprécieront que modérément les soufflés lumineux, les paysages de rêve ou l'euphorie pastel de notre jaquette, et vice versa, mais ils peuvent être également sincères.

C'est sur cette base que nous avons opéré une sélection de 227 photographies parmi les milliers qui nous ont été envoyées ou que, dans certains cas, nous avons sollicitées. Plus de 160 photographes, originaires de 32 pays différents, sont représentés. Evidemment, la plupart sont originaires du Royaume-Uni parce que le nombre de photographies qui nous ont été envoyées était écrasant, mais le nombre des photographies originaires d'autres pays est, proportionnellement, plus élevé. Il y a beaucoup moins de séparations de tons et autres artifices de chambre noire que ces dernières années. Si cela est l'indice d'une tendance, celle-ci est la bienvenue parce que, dans le passé, nous avons pu constater que les tirages qui utilisaient ces artifices, pour apporter une distraction artistique à des sujets pauvres étaient surfaits.

Un aspect intéressant des photographies qui nous ont été soumises réside dans le fait que presque toutes celles en noit et blanc étaient d'une haute qualité, de même que celles en couleur, mais de nombreuses collections de diapositives ne nous ont permis d'en reproduire qu'une ou deux, les autres n'étant, le terme est faible, que d'une qualité très médiocre. Il faut en conclure que les photographes sont beaucoup plus sélectifs pour leurs travaux en noir et blanc. Cette conclusion est appuyée par le fait que la plupart des photographies en noir et blanc qui nous ont été envoyées étaient en moyenne en six exemplaires, alors que pour les diapositives en couleur la moyenne était d'une vingtaine, certains auteurs en ayant même envoyé jusqu'à quarante! Il est agréable de noter que les auteurs de photographies en couleur semblent faire un usage plus esthétique de la couleur et se soucier moins de créer l'impact par le recours aux couleurs primaires. Dans l'ensemble, j'ai eu le sentiment qu'il y avait là davantage d'originalité que je n'en ai vue dans de nombreux concours et expositions. Des sujets tels que des enfants malaisants grimaçants, des pêcheurs jetant leur filet sur des lacs embrumés et des nus derrière du verre marbré — qui sont trois sujets que l'on retrouve d'une année sur l'autre — se signalent cette fois par leur absence.

Les lecteurs sont cordialement invités à nous envoyer leurs meilleures images pour l'édition de 1981. A cet effet, nous joignons un dépliant donnant le détail des éléments qui nous sont nécessaires, et nous souhaitons que ces observations contribuent à faire mieux comprendre la politique qui sous-tend la publication de cet album. En dernière analyse, évidemment, la sélection est l'aboutissement d'une décision personnelle du rédacteur en chef, mais nous espérons que la présente édition du Photography Year Book sera une source de réflexions, voire de controverses, tout en apportant au lecteur l'occasion de se délecter de quelques belles images.

Introduccion
por R. H. Mason

Un anuario es, o debería ser, una recopilación de los mejores trabajos fotográficos del año, aunque en este caso con la exclusión de los correspondientes a los campos especializados de la fotografía médica o científica y de las aplicaciones puramente comerciales. Uno experimenta siempre la tentación de incluir en elevada proporción las fotografías periodísticas, especialmente las de guerra o las que recogen algún tipo de violencia, debido a su fuerte impacto. En opinión de algunos críticos sólo estas fotografías y las que poseen un mensaje sociológico presentan un interés real. Pero yo no estoy de acuerdo con esta opinión y me he guiado por un criterio bastante más amplio al seleccionar las fotografías de este año.

La prensa ha reproducido tantas instantáneas violentas e inhumanas que he creído conveniente eliminar este tipo de fotografías, de modo que en el libro se reflejaran, dentro de lo posible, aspectos más agradables y placenteros. Muy pocas veces hemos reproducido más de una fotografía de un mismo autor, lo que espero que aporte al libro una mayor variedad e interés. El lector encontrará además muchos nombres nuevos.

En los anuarios se acostumbra a sacar conclusiones sobre las nuevas tendencias fotográficas que se han puesto de manifiesto durante el año. En mi opinión, sin embargo, estamos ante un período de tiempo demasiado corto para poder identificar algún cambio o algún movimiento nuevo. En los últimos cien años la fotografía ha experimentado una evolución gradual, tanto en lo que respecta a las técnicas como a las tendencias estéticas; y en las dos últimas décadas se han producido enormes avances en el aspecto técnico, especialmente en la automatización de los aparatos. Pero el buen fotógrafo presta mucha menos atención a la mecánica que a la posibilidad de expresar sus ideas y reflejar sus experiencias de manera clara y satisfactoria.

El prestigio de la fotografía aumenta o disminuye, las modas varían y cambian los sujetos preferidos, pero en estos últimos años hemos visto como un rasgo ha permanecido constante: la sinceridad en el tratamiento de los temas. En los primeros tiempos los aficionados a la fotografía tuvieron que habérselas con un proceso difícil y muy poco de fiar, con lo que no debe extrañarnos que intentasen copiar los métodos pictóricos. Así, eligieron normalmente temas pintorescos o románticos y durante varias décadas las paredes de las salas de exposición se cubrieron fundamentalmente con paisajes. Luego siguió una época en que la gente se aficionó, sobre todo, a la obtención de retratos formales, en los que se deleitaron en introducir una atmósfera pseudoclásica. Fue en esta época cuando se produjeron también las imágenes deleznablemente sentimentales, románticas y alegóricas que tanto apreciaron los victorianos, pero que los pintores eran capaces de reproducir con mayor eficacia.

A principios de nuestro siglo algunos aficionados "iluminados" empezaron a explotar las características que la fotografía posee en exclusiva: la capacidad para captar efectos luminosos transitorios, para contar una historia en un instante, para recoger el momento de máxima expresividad y para dar un nuevo contenido a los temas, tomándolos desde un ángulo insólito o con un primer plano deslumbrante. Es mucho lo que debemos a estos pioneros, quienes, a su manera, fueron tan originales y honestos como los impresionistas franceses; pero su influencia duró poco revirtiéndose al primitivo sentimentalismo y a una especie de artificiosidad de nuevo cuño. Esta moda alcanzó su punto álgido en los años anteriores a la segunda guerra mundial, durante los cuales era habitual fotografiar con la luz del estudio a modelos sin afeitar disfrazados de pescadores, mientras que a otros se les hacía posar con vestidos de época sin ambientarlos, con los elementos materiales adecuados para que resultaran auténticos. En cada Salón hacían su aparición las tiritantes chicas desnudas situadas en las orillas de lagos envueltos en niebla, con títulos tan ridículos y repetidos como "Mañana septembrina"! "Marchitándose", de H.P. Robinson nos cuenta al menos una historial!

Es quizá la dura realidad de la vida moderna, junto con el perfeccionamiento experimentado por los objetivos y materiales, lo que ha introducido en las obras actuales una sinceridad de enfoque que resulta muy de agradecer. Un enfoque honesto produce siempre obras originales, debido a que refleja la visión personal del autor. En los retratos se busca la captación del carácter, los paisajes se presentan de forma atrevida e incluso los llamados "estudios" se piensan fundamentalmente como fotografías y no como imitaciones de otras manifestaciones artísticas.

Está claro que me refiero a los trabajos que vemos en las exposiciones frecuentadas y en los buenos libros. Desgraciadamente existen también fotógrafos que se sirven de las tramas y las técnicas de separación en un vano intento de transformar un mal negativo en una copia "de impacto", pero poco a poco van perdiendo esta afición hasta que llega un momento en que sólo usan estos sistemas cuando realmente son capaces de dar énfasis a la imagen.

Entre todas las formas de expresión de la mente humana, la imagen constituye una de las más antiguas y ni tan siquiera los que aseguran no entenderlas puedan permanecer insensibles a su influencia. Se trata de las primeras señales que entienden los niños, fueron una de las primeras formas en que los hombres de las cavernas dieron rienda suelta a su imaginación y constituyen todavía hoy el único lenguaje universal; pero una imagen no es simplemente un conjunto de objetos ingeniosamente ordenados en un espacio dado; debe expresar también algo sobre la naturaleza: una emoción capaz de reproducirse en otras personas, aunque no necesariamente, como creen algunos fotógrafos, de forma violenta. Podemos comparar una imagen al arpa eólica de la mitología que sólo producía música al situarla en un lugar en que el viento pudiera atravesarla. El hombre construyó el arpa pero la música era obra de la naturaleza y existía entre ambas una íntima relación de dependencia. El fotógrafo actúa como el constructor del arpa; la naturaleza, el viento que despierta nuestras emociones, es el artista que la toca y el observador que contempla una fotografía es comparable a la persona que escucha la música y que reacciona frente a la misma en función de su imaginación y nivel cultural. Es esta reacción que se produce en cada observador en relación con su temperamento, inteligencia y humor lo que ningún artista puede llegar a controlar totalmente. De hecho, lo que hace este último es compartir con el observador una experiencia imaginativa.

Sin embargo, la reacción del observador no es siempre favorable y no es probable que todas las fotografías de un anuario satisfagan a todos los lectores. Así, aquéllos a los que les gusta sentir el impacto de sujetos de gran fuerza representados mediante acentuados contrastes en blanco y negro, no apreciarán demasiado la suavidad de los tonos altos, los paisajes fantasiosos o la euforia apastelada de la sobrecubierta del libro; y viceversa, pero lo importante en estos casos es reaccionar con sinceridad.

No hemos dejado de analizar lo que acabamos de decir al efectuar nuestra selección de 227 fotografías de entre los miles que hemos recibido (o, en unas pocas ocasiones, solicitado). Hemos incluido más de 160 fotógrafos, originarios de 32 países diferentes. Inevitablemente el mayor lote procede de Gran Bretaña, a causa del extraordinario número de obras presentadas por los fotógrafos ingleses, pero la cantidad reproducida de otros países se halla en mayor proporción. Esta vez hemos recibido menos fotos con separaciones tonales o con otros efectos de laboratorio que en los años anteriores. Si ello constituye una tendencia, la saludamos con alborozo, puesto que estábamos un poco cansados de ver cómo mediante estos efectos se intentaba a menudo camuflar la debilidad del tema elegido.

Un detalle interesante es que prácticamente todas las fotos en blanco y negró recibidas, han sido de buena calidad y lo mismo cabe decir de las copias en color, pero de los paneles de transparencias a veces sólo dos o tres han resultado reproducibles, con duplicados más bien pobres. La conclusión a que hemos llegado es que los fotógrafos son más exigentes al seleccionar sus trabajos en blanco y negro. Esta conclusión se ve respaldada por el hecho de que la mayor parte de lotes en blanco y negro han estado constituidos por unas seis copias mientras que en los de transparencias en color, la media ha sido de veinte – y algunos fotógrafos industriosos han llegado incluso a las cuarenta! Es agradable observar que a las copias en color se les da un tratamiento estético más completo y que se concede menor importancia al impacto causado por el uso de colores primarios. En general estoy convencido de haber encontrado una mayor originalidad en las obras recibidas que en las que he visto en los concursos y exposiciones que he visitado recientemente. Afortunadamente han desaparecido tres de los temas más repetidos en años anteriores: los grupos de niños malayos sonriendo a la cámara, los conjuntos de pescadores arrojando sus redes en lagos neblinosos y los desnudos captados tras un cristal multicolor.

Volvemos a formular nuestra invitación a los lectores para que envíen sus fotografías para le edición de 1981 de nuestro anuario. Esta vez incluimos un folleto en el que se detallan las condiciones que los trabajos deben reunir. Evidentemente, la selección depende finalmente de la valoración personal del Editor, pero nuestra esperanza es que la edición del Photography Year Book del presente año se convertirá en tema de controversia entre los aficionados, así como en objeto de una agradable y tranquila contemplación.

R. H. MASON

JOHN DAVIDSON

JOSE TORREGROSA

J. J. ABASSIN

GEORGE WEBBER

RAGHU RAI

JOSEPH MARIA RIBAS PROUS

18

DAVID BEARNE

FRANK TRAVERS

JOHN DAVIDSON

LASZLO LAJOS

MONROE S. FREDERICK

25

ROBERT LLEWELLYN

ASKO SALMI

J. M. ORIOLA

28

BRIAN SUTTON

JOZEF VISSEL

ASADOUR GUZELIAN

TOM DODD

RUDOLF AUER

DIETER KRAFT

A. DUNBAR

ROGER ARRANDALE— WILLIAMS

JAMES BILLIMORIA

XABI OTERA

JOHN WALKER

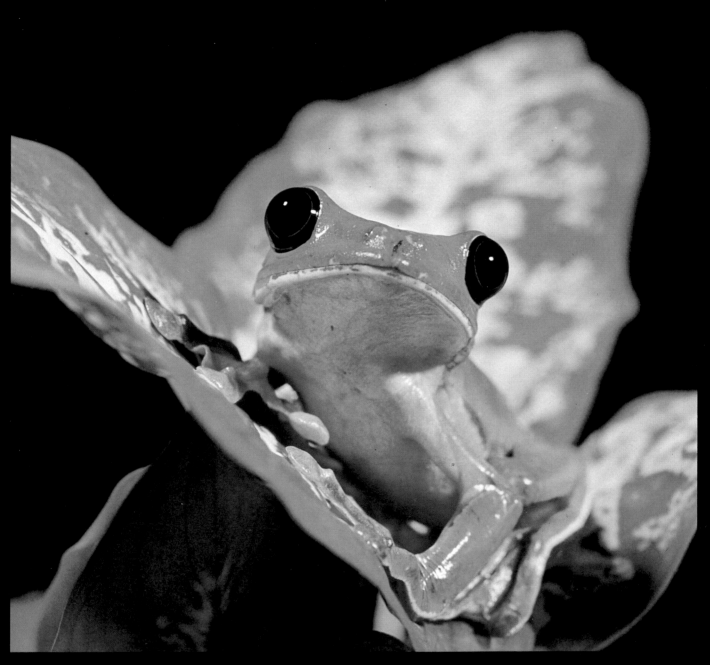

HEATHER ANGEL

BARON BARON

MICHAEL GNADE

43

ROBERT HALLMANN

E. EXTON

LES MANSFIELD

MERVYN REES

FERDINANDO QUARANTA

CHRIS HAIG

IAN TORRANCE

PETER PURTZ

KAZIMIERZ CZAPINSKI

GEORGE WEDDING

J. L. YOUNG

GERI DELLA ROCCA DE CANDAL

JACK RUFUS

ASAD ALI

DONALD A. SMITH

61

FRANK PEETERS

ANDREJ KRYNICKI

MONTSERRAT VIDAL BARRAQUER

RAGHU RAI

65

VLADIMIR FILONOV

VLADIMIR FILONOV

FRANTISEK DOSTAL

68

MIKE HOLLIST

FRANTISEK DOSTAL

VIRENDER MAHAJAN

L. B. FERESOVI

FRANK LOUGHLIN

72

BILL CARDEN

STEPHEN SHAKESHAFT

ROLAND HERPIN

WOLFGANG VOLZ

JOSEP MARIA RIBAS PROUS

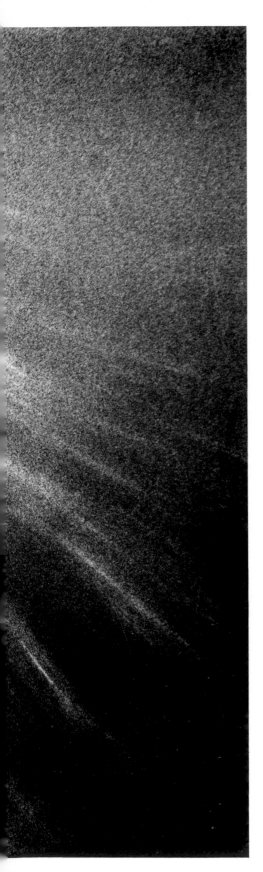

LESLIE E. SPATT

JEAN BERNER

LMARS APKALNS

J. P. DELANEY

V. J. ATTFIELD

FERDINANDO QUARANTA

CLIVE B. HARRISON

85

MIKE HOLLIST

HOWARD WALKER

CLELAND RIMMER

RUDOLF BIERI

ERWIN KNEIDINGER

J. R. RUDIN

VIRENDER MAHAJAN

STANLEY MATCHETT

MARTYN HAYHOW

95

WILHELM MIKHAILOVSKY

MICHAEL BARRINGTON-MARTIN

TONY DUFFY

LARS ODDVAR LOVDAHL

A. FARQUHAR

MARK WOOLSTENCROFT

TREVOR FRY

C. H. J. MARTIN

FRANCIS TOCHER

HEKTOR KROME

A. R. PIPPARD

TERRY FINCHER

FRANCISCO HIDALGO

ALAIN VERDIERE

M. D. CONSTABLE

LUCIANO PESTARINO

ROLF M. AAGAARD

DAVID BAILEY

DAVID BAILEY

WILHELM MICHAILOVSKY

MIKE HOLLIST

ANDREW McGLYNN

E. CHAMBRÉ HARDMAN

VIASTISLAV MACHACEK

121

JOHN DAVIDSON

122

HANS JORGEANDERS

LEON BALODIS

FRANCISCO ASZMANN

BERNHARD HEINZE

MOGENS LERCHE MADSEN

JOSEPH TICHY

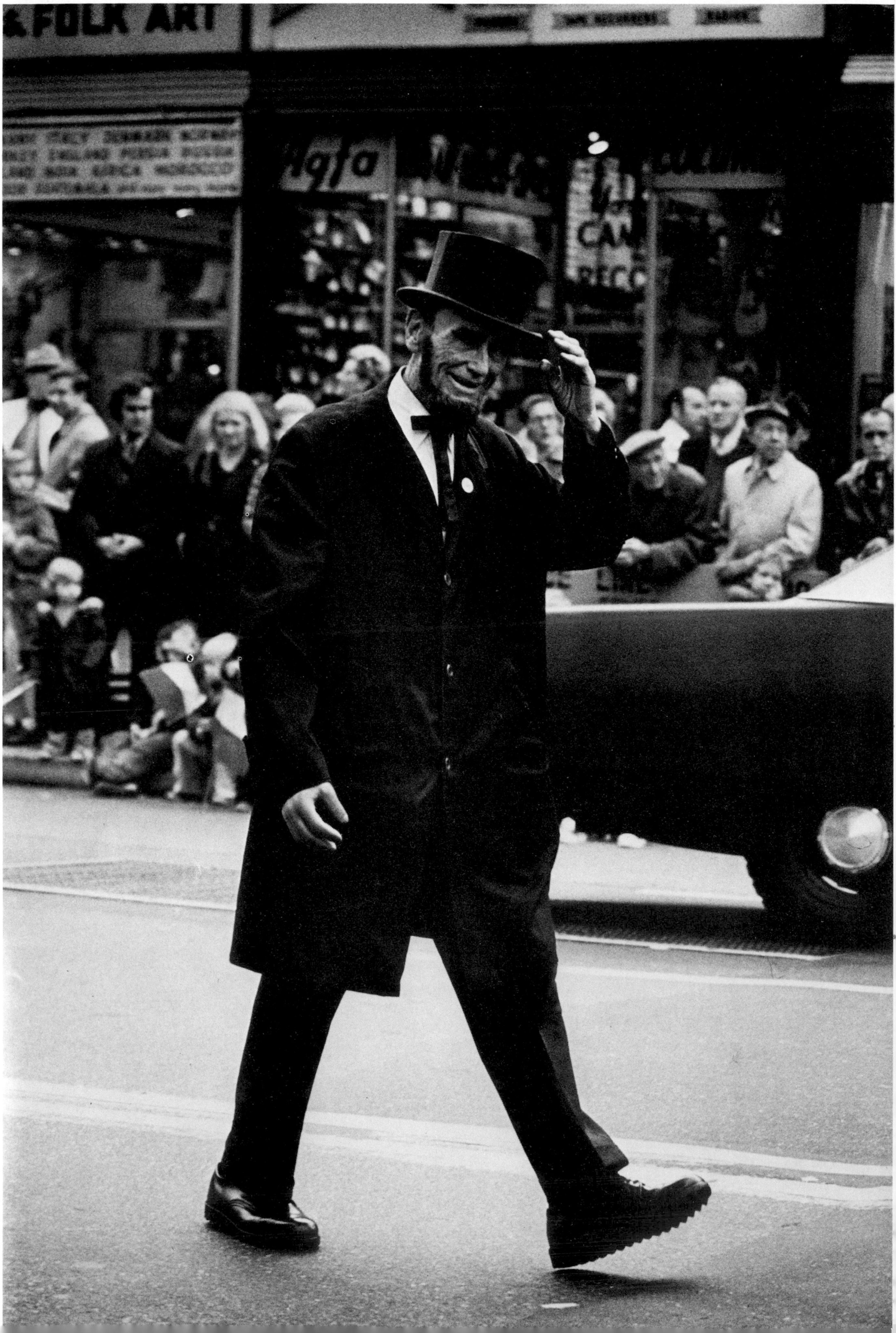

ACHIM SPERBER

MARTIN WOLIN

VLADIMIR FILONOV

133

YAM PAK NIN

CHAN KIN-PONG

K. H. GRATT

ARTHUR PERRY

ILMARS APKALNS

ASKO SALMI

IAN STEWART

GEORGE W. MARTIN

HARM BOTMAN

STEVE HARTLEY

MICHAEL GNADE

147

VLADIMIR BIRGUS

RICARDO GOMEZ PEREZ

149

ALBERTO HERNANDEZ JORDÉ

150

JOHN WILLIAMS

TSANG CHI-YEN

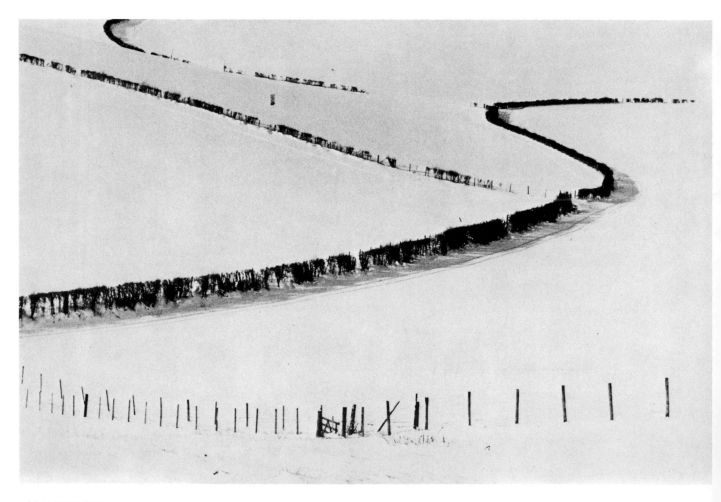

W. BIGGS

VERA WEINERSTROVA

VALDIS BRAUNS

ANDREJ KRYNICKI

JEAN BERNER

P. G. GALE

JIRI HORAK

PETER GANT

G. I. RATCLIFFE

D. R. MACALPINE

TONY HOWARD

J. L. CAWTHRA

WOUT GILHUIS

PATRICK LICHFIELD

JAMES ELLIOTT

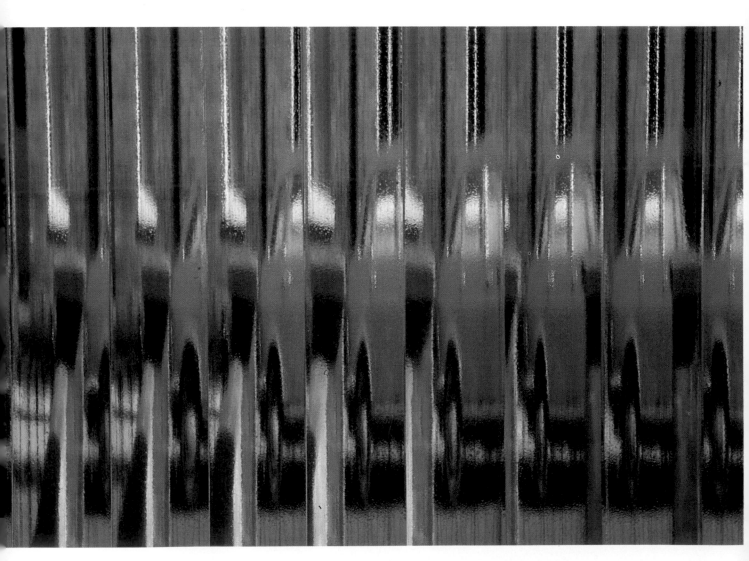

J. F. PERCY

D. J. BELLHAM

RAY WILLIAMSON

ANIL K

C. NUTMAN

JOAN WAKELIN
174

SURENDRA SAHAI
175

MAURICE BRAUN

CARLOS CANOVAS

FRANK PEETERS

HIDEKI FUJII

SIGNE DREVSJO

VERA WEINERSTROVA

MERVYN REES

MERVYN REES

JIRI HORAK

REIJO PORKKA

JIM BARKER

E. CHAMBRÉ HARDMAN

F. RUSSELL

LASZLO LAJOS

HOWARD WALKER

VLADIMIR FILONOV

V. SONTA

DAVID BURROWS

JOHN DAVIDSON

JACK RUFUS

GERI DELLA ROCCA DE CANDAL

197

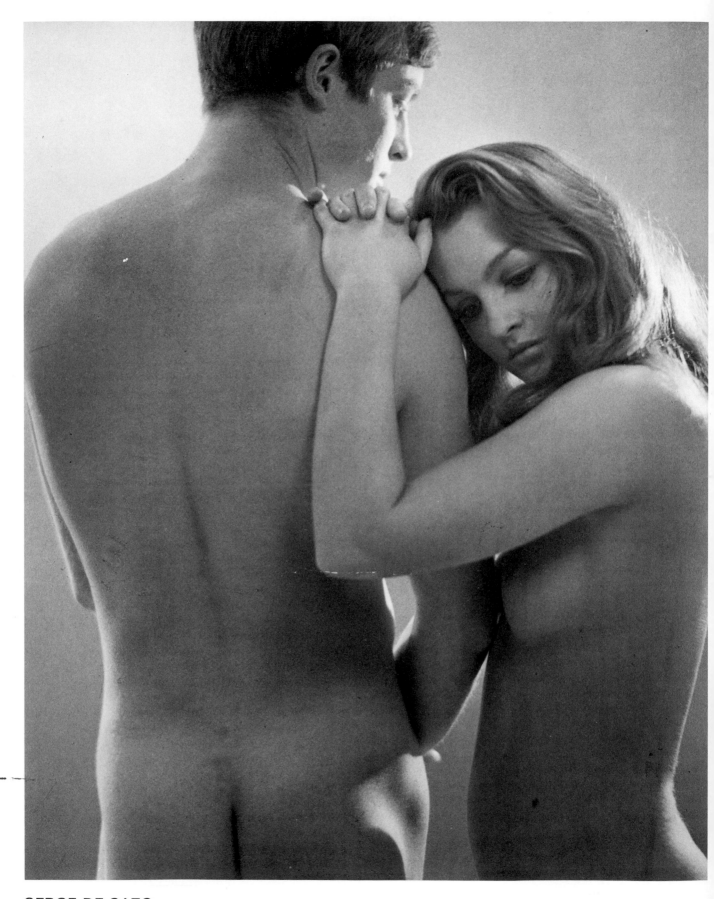

SERGE DE SAZO

KARIN SZEKESSY

GEOFFREY TYRER

LUIS ARTEAGA CERDAN

HENNING CHRISTOPH

VLADO BACA

DAVID DALBY

V. SONTA

JOHN WOODHOUSE

T.G. EDWARDS

CHOI MIN SHIK

DAVID G. WILDING

FRANK PEETERS

JOSEP MARIA RIBAS PROUS

211

SVEN SIMON

MERVYN REES

T. A. COOPER

ACHIM SPERBER

SIGNE DREVSJO

EGONS SPURIS

KARIN SZEKESSY

MICHAEL GNADE

FERRAN ARTIGAS

CHRIS PEET

ROLAND HERPIN

ILMARS APKALNS

MICHAEL SCOTT

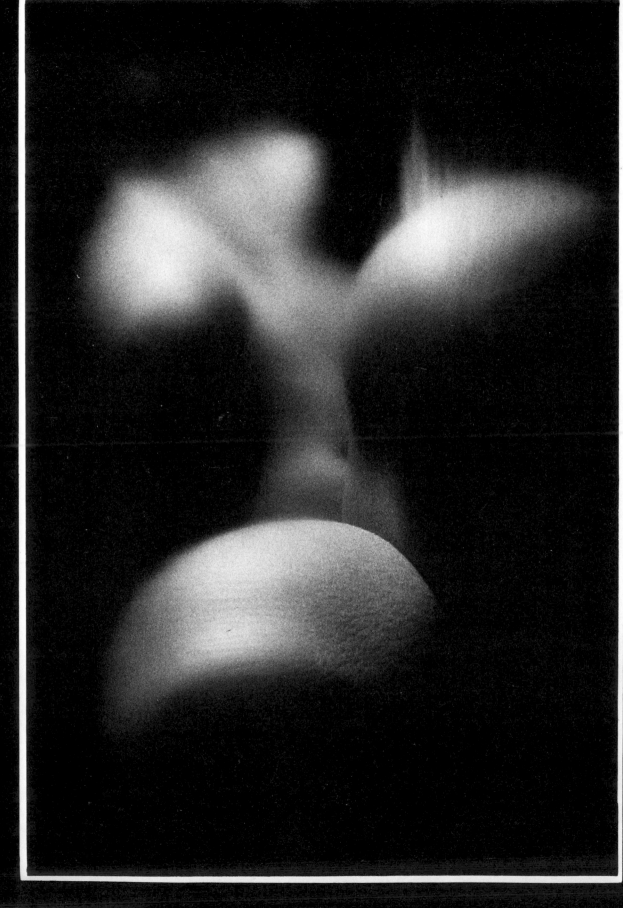

OSE TORREGROSA

Technical Data

Jacket
by Martin Wolin Jr.
A beautiful picture which shows the value of early morning light before the sun appears. It produces delicate pastel tints and a beautiful colour composition. Taken on a Pentax 6 x 7 with a 105mm lens; 1/60th second at f/8 on High Speed Ektachrome. The reproduction is from a Cibachrome print.

Inside Front Cover
AU BEGUINAGE DE BRUGES by Jean Berner
This picture by a well-known French photographer shows a brilliant sense of design in which rhythmic repetition and strong contrasts play a large part. Taken in Belgium on a Nikkormat FT with a 20mm lens on Tri-X film developed in D76.

13
INDUSTRY by John Davidson
This fine shot was taken specifically for use as a cover photograph for an industry supplement in the *Liverpool Daily Post*. A Chromo-filter was used as a neutral density filter to cope with the high contrast. Taken with a Nikon F and 28mm Nikkor lens on Tri-X film developed in D76.

14
SEASCAPE by Jose Torregrosa
Even the most traditional subjects can be given a modern look by defying the guide lines of composition which, in this case, would have demanded that the boat be placed to one side instead of right in the centre. It has added to this picture which is full of evening atmosphere. Taken on a Nikkormat with 24mm lens on Tri-X.

15
VERCORS by J. J. Abassin
A very nice snow scene with an almost Christmas Card effect is dramatized by the very dark sky, usually obtainable in such circumstances with quite a light filter. The inclusion of the diminutive figure gives scale and depth as well as a lead in to the view.

16
INDIANS IN CALGARRY by George Webber
The arrows on the wall give an ironic touch to the message conveyed in this picture by a young Canadian photographer. Taken in open shade with a Canon FT6N and 50 mm lens on Ilford FP4 developed in ID11.

17
IN FATHER'S GARB by Raghu Rai
An amusing picture which catches a happy moment and shows, like others in this book, that there is a place for humour in photography even though it may not have lasting aesthetic value. Taken on Nikon F with 85mm lens on Tri-X film: 1/250th second at f/5.6.

18
CARMEN by Josep Maria Ribas Prous
A most effective use of grain to provide an artistic impact. It was obtained by enlarging a very small part of the negative. Taken by studio tungsten lighting on a Nikon F2 with 105mm lens and Tri-X film developed in Microdol X: 1/60th second at f/5.6. The author is a Spanish tutor of photography.

19
INGRID by F. John Reid
The high key treatment has made the most of a beautiful blonde model. Taken with a Mamiya C330 and 135mm Sekor lens on FP4 film developed in D76. The studio lighting was by two Multilec flash units on the subject, and two more on the background. The enlargement was diffused slightly with silk gauze.

20
HELP by David Bearne
A picture taken during the Hampshire Rugby Cup Final between Basingstoke and Havant. An alert young photographer has captured an incident that has a nice touch of humour. David used a Nikon F2 with 135mm lens and Tri-X film developed in D76. Exposure was 1/250th second at f/5.6.

21
GETTING THE POINT by Frank Travers
Sports photographers have many opportunities to capture significant episodes and gestures but it takes skill and experience to anticipate the right moment, and to be in focus when it occurs. Frank works for the *Sheffield Morning Telegraph* and he used a Canon Ftb with 400mm Novaflex for this shot on Tri-X developed in Qualitol.

22/23
ROLF HARRIS ON LOCATION by John Davidson
A famous entertainer with a group of Liverpool school children during a recording session for a television series. It shows Rolf Harris's infectious enthusiasm for working with youngsters. Taken by available light in a large school hall on a Nikon F with 28mm lens on Tri-X film. developed in D76. Exposure was 1/15 second at f/3.5.

24
S. RICHTER by Laszlo Lajas
A magnificent portrait of this great Russian pianist taken at just the right moment to catch a characteristic expression. The authentic surroundings and applauding audience tell it all. Taken by the available lighting on a Minolta SRT 101 with a 55mm lens on Tri-X developed in Acufine: 1/30th second at f/2.8.

25
JACKIE ROBINSON by Monroe S. Frederick
America's first coloured baseball player photographed with his wife just before his death. The natural expressions and gestures, both unaware of the camera, make this a moving memorial. Taken with a Mamiyaflex 220 and 65mm lens on D76 with electronic flash.

26
INSIGHT by Robert Llewellyn
From a book called "Silver Wings" which the author describes as visual manifestations of his earthly journey towards understanding and the exploration of thought and insight. He has attempted to express this with objects on different planes interacting with each other. Nikon F, 20mm lens.

27
DAWN ON THE LAKE by Asko Salmi
Photographed at 7 a.m. in the UAASA archipelago this picture shows that boats on misty lakes are not the sole prerogative of the Hong Kong school. In fact this treatment is typical of some of the fine work coming from Finland in recent years. Canon AE-1 with 20mm lens, Tri-X film developed in D76.

28
NO TITLE by J. M. Oriola
An amusing picture which shows that back views are sometimes as expressive as frontal viewpoints. This shot is certainly original and it has a very natural look although it could have been posed. The strong contrasts and unusual composition compel a second look.

29
YOGA by Brian Sutton
A picture taken as one of a series to assist a Yoga teacher to check her posture and position, but which inevitably has a touch of humour as well due to the foreshortening. Taken with a 28mm lens on a Pentax SPF loaded with Tri-X film developed in D76.

30
NO TITLE by Jozef Vissel
A picture of contrasts different from the usual kind. It has a nice touch of humour because of its absurdity.

Although obviously posed it is certainly a "stopper". Taken with a Hasselblad on Panatomic X developed in Rodinal.

31
MERLYN REES, MP by Asadour Guzelian
A former Home Secretary caught in a happy moment at a Sikh dinner in Leeds. Apart from telling a lot about the man and the occasion, the composition is original and the picture is more expressive than many more formal portraits of politicians. The camera was a Pentax SP100 with 135mm lens loaded with Tri-X.

32
MOUNTAIN WINTER by Tom Dodd
The use of a 4x orange filter at a height of approximately 2,000 feet in the Moelwyn Mountains of Snowdonia has made a dramatic picture. Taken on a Canon F2 with 28mm lens on FP4 film rated at 164ASA and developed in Aculux. The author used an aperture of f/16 to reduce the flare from the sun.

33
BALLET DANCERS by Rudolf Auer
A superb picture which catches all the movement of a pirouette in a most artistic way. The swirl of the tu-tu's creates rhythm by repetition and the sparkle of sequins makes a fascinating contrast to the blue lighting, while any suggestion of overall coldness is avoided by the warm colours of backs and legs.

34
PORTRAIT by Dieter Kraft
A dramatically executed portrait by a Swiss photographer which was greatly admired among the exhibition of large colour prints shown on the Kodak stand at the last Photokina. The daring use of red on coloured flesh and the off-centre composition give tremendous impact.

35
SUE by Henry Michaels
Reproduced from a superb colour print made from a Vericolour negative taken with a Bronica 6 x 6cm camera. The low key treatment emphasizing the back lighting shows an artistic approach to a conventional subject. Lighting was by two Multilex flash umbrellas, one silver and one gold, with a third flash behind. The print was made on Agfacolor type 4 paper.

36
LANDSCAPE by Dr Alexander Dunbar, FRPS
A typical landscape in the Scottish Highlands taken by a leading member of the Edinburgh Photographic Society who believes that the best pictures are had when there is mist and rain, with a bonus if the sun momentarily breaks through. Taken on a Minolta camera and Kodachrome 64; 1/125th second at f/8.

37
BLUE LANDSCAPE by Erik Steen
This unusual and effective picture was achieved by the use of Ektacolor Slide Duplicating film developed in E4 instead of the recommended C22 process. The first developer was omitted and the time in the colour developer cut by ¼. Taken near the author's home at Drammen in Norway on a Nikon F2 wuth 43-86 zoom lens.

38/39
PRESLEY MOURNERS by Dr. James Billimoria
A picture which typifies the hysteria created in the Western World by the death of a rock and roll star, in which the mourners are dancing rather than weeping. Taken with a Leica and 50mm lens on a Sunday morning in Trafalgar Square. The author has chosen a viewpoint which makes a good composition out of a crowd scene.

The amazing
Yashica FR series

Each member of the FR series is capable of taking a remarkable range of system accessories. Illustrated is the FRI fitted with the infra red remote controller and the West German made 15mm Zeiss Distagon lens, and of course the power winder which provides up to 2fps as well as single frame operation.

What's so amazing about the Yashica FR series? Well it uses modular construction to provide Contax Technology. In fact the shutter, mirror box, pneumatic dampers and electro magnetic controls are all in one module which is identical to that used in the Contax RTS. Thus it is the first SLR system (other than the prestigious Contax itself) to be completely operated by electronics and electro magnetics.

The result? An ultra smooth world of electric pulse firing, on and off the camera.

The FR series accepts sophisticated accessories like the RTF 540 stroboscopic flash system with 5 flashes per second capability, Yashica's revolutionary infra red controller for remote shutter firing without cable connection, an interval timer for time-lapse photography. And even an auto bellows system.

But the FR advantages don't stop there. Optically the FR series has the best and most comprehensive range of lenses of any system SLR. And you can choose from three body types to suit your own approach to photography.

Yashica FR. Manual control of aperture and shutter speed with green and red LEDs to indicate precisely correct TTL metering within the viewfinder.

Yashica FRI. Auto/Manual with full viewfinder information regardless of operational mode.

Yashica FRII. Auto operation with the utmost simplicity and viewfinder information on the shutter speed selected.

All three models have microprism and *diagonal* split-image rangefinder as well as ground glass focusing.

The Yashica FR series offers *you* a better deal – and helps you to make your photography better too.

YASHICA FR SERIES

CONTAX technology

Tough, flexible electronic modules are used to provide unique reliability and ruggedness.

For further information write to:
PHOTAX Eastbourne East Sussex
London Showroom: 59 York Road SE1
Republic of Ireland: 1 George Place
Dublin 1

HOW TO READ IN THE DARK.

The Paterson Digital Thermometer

It's so simple with Paterson's new electronic Digital Thermometer.

The large illuminated display area sees to that. Readings can be made up to 70°C or 150°F and are consistent to better than .03°C/.05°F. The thermometer also registers changes down to 0.1° Centigrade or Fahrenheit.

The stainless steel probe is resistant to all photographic solutions and spare plug-in probes can be obtained to avoid cleaning the probe between one solution and another.

Powered by 4AA batteries it all adds up to yet another idea from Paterson to make life easier in the darkroom.

Further information about Paterson Darkroom products can be obtained by writing to the Paterson Advisory Service, 2-6 Boswell Court, London. WC1N 3PS.

PATERSON®

40 (Upper)

OWL AND PREY by Xabi Otera

A very artistic rendering of a natural history subject. The owl and the lizard in its beak are clearly presented while the background has the atmosphere of night and mystery appropriate to the subject. The whole makes a beautiful colour harmony.

40 (Lower)

MARINE TOAD AND FROG by John Walker

This fine nature study with a double interest was taken by flash on a Nikon EL with a Micro-Nikkor lens on Ektachrome 200 film. The toad, which comes from South America, weighs about 3½ lbs., while the Green Tree Frog from Italy weighs only 3 ounces. The picture was taken in the Welsh Mountain Zoo, Colwyn Bay and several exposures had to be made because the frog kept jumping on the lens!

41

COSTA RICAN FLYING FROG by Heather Angel, FIIP

A very rare frog brought to England for the television series "Life on Earth" and then returned to its rain-forest home in Costa Rica. Author of nearly 30 books on natural history, Heather Angel used a Hasselblad 500C with 80mm lens and Ektachrome E-3 film. The subject was lit by a Braun FZK80 flash with twin heads.

42

CLOWN by Baron Baron

The worm's eye view of this circus character emphasizes the fantasy world which the circus creates for children. The bold and simple design emphasizes it and enough of the circus background has been included to complete the story.

43

NUDE by Michael Gnade

A very natural figure study in which *contre-jour* lighting has played a most important part. The pose is as natural as the surroundings and the overall colour scheme is very pleasing. One of a number of such pictures in the author's book "People in my Camera".

44/45

COMBATITIVE by Wang Yue Lung

A tremendous feeling of action has been imparted by the thrusting arms and striding legs of these gymnasts and it was a really artistic touch to keep the foreground figure so large in relation to the class. Taken with a Canon AE1 and 28m lens on Kodacolour 400 and printed on Ektacolor paper.

46

AFRICAN STEPPE EAGLE by Robert Hallman

A fine picture taken at the Bird of Prey Centre, Chilham Castle, when the bird was uttering a piercing protest at the sight of the camera. Shot with a Kowa Super 66 and 85mm lens plus a 3x close-up attachment. Agfa 50S film at 100 ASA.

47

TAWNY OWL by E. Exton

Britain's largest owl, which is strictly nocturnal and also dangerous because it will attack a photographer with its sharp talons. The author suffered eight claw marks around his left eye when taking this shot with a Pentacon Six and 180mm lens on CPS120 at 9 feet distance. Lighting by flash.

48

NO TITLE by Les Mansfield

An expressive portrait which captures the dignity of an Andelusian flamenco dancer. It is a double exposure, made by photographing the guitar with a standard lens, then changing to a Tamron zoom set to about 135mm for the portrait exposure. Taken with a Nikon Ftn on H.S. Ektachrome, rated at 800ASA for each exposure and developed normally in E6.

49

RUTH KENNEDY by Mervyn Rees

A really dramatic action picture which is full of movement appropriate to this international relay runner. The placing of the figure well to the right, together with the grain, enhances the impression of effort. The camera was a Nikon F2, with 135mm lens and Tri-X film: 1/15th second at f/4.

50

UNDERWATER by Ferdinando Quaranta

A picture of the author's wife taken off Corsica Island in St Florence bay. A well known specialist in underwater photography, usually of fish, Ferdinando uses a Konica Antoreflex in an Ikelite housing with 24 mm lens. The natural lighting is augmented with a Braun F2000 automatic electronic flash. The original was on Kodachrome 64 and it was duplicated on Tri-X film.

51

MUD BATH by John Jones

A picture depicting the happy atmosphere enjoyed during a boys versus girls football match on the mud flats at the annual Old Leigh Regatta. The boys lost! Taken with a Canon Ftb and 100-200 zoom lens on Tri-X film developed in D76.

52

SHERRIL HAGUE by Chris Haig

An excellent candid portrait taken by available light which has caught something of the character of this jolly used car dealer. Taken with a Mamiya C330 on FP4 film developed in Acutol.

53

BOOKED by Ian Torrance

Not many people would have spotted the combination of dog and traffic warden that has made this into a deliciously funny picture which will be appreciated by all who have been "booked". It won a prize for this *Scottish Daily Record* cameraman in the British Press Photographer of the Year Contest.

54

MOURNING IN TEHERAN by Rolf M. Aagaard

Taken in the city's main cemetery during a demonstration against the Ayatollah Khomeini, then still living in Paris. The author developed the film in his hotel room and then wired it to his Norwegian newspaper 'Aftenposten'. The camera was a Nikon F2 with 85 mm lens and the film Tri-X developed in D76.

55

PORTRAIT by Peter Purtz

Typical of the imaginative work coming from Czechoslovakia, in which unconventional and candid poses are used against heavy backgrounds, often industrial in nature. The unusual placing of the subject, together with a lot of grain, makes for compelling impact. Taken with an Exa 500, and 25mm lens on Orwo 27 developed in Formadon R.

56

ANKA by Kazimierz Czapinski

Polish photographers are usually unhampered by any conventional rules of composition and the main action almost on the edge might be criticised by traditionalists but it cannot be denied that it has given force and movement. The nose pushed up by the apple adds to the effect and the grain does no harm either.

57

ADA ROGOVIN by George Wedding

An impressive and candid character study of an 87 year old poker player in Miami Beach, taken for "THE PALM BEACH POST". The author waited for just the right moment to give it action. Taken on a Nikon with 180mm lens on Tri-X film rated at 1600ASA and developed in Acufine.

58 (Upper)

GRAVEYARD by J. L. Young, ARPS

A good example of the intelligent use of infra-red film to dramatise a conventional scene. Wherever there are different varieties of trees, infra-red will build up contrast, especially against a blue sky. Taken in St. Nicholas's Churchyard, Basildon with a Praktica LTL3 with 35mm lens and a deep red filter on Kodak High Speed Infra-Red film rated at 50ASA, developed in Perceptol.

58 (Lower)

TWO SHEDS by Geri Della Rocca

Sheer simplicity and powerful contrasts have given a lot of impact to this picture taken in Nevada by an Italian photographer. The design is powerful and the atmosphere of isolation well portrayed. The camera was a Nikon F with a 20mm lens plus a red filter, and the film was HP5 rated at 600 ASA, developed in IDII.

59

"CHATEAU AT BELCASTEL, DORDOGNE" by Jack Rufus, FRPS

Sadly, the author died shortly after submitting this picture but he leaves a legacy of beautiful landscapes in both traditional and contemporary idiom. This was taken on a Hasselblad with 250mm lens one September evening using Tri-X film developed in Microdol X (see also Page 196).

60

ISOLATION by Asad Ali

A combination print made from the shot of the little bird against a barren sky and a background exposed in the countryside of Lahore. The camera was a Kowa with a 200 mm lens plus a x2 converter and the exposure 1/250th second at f/8 on Agfa Super-Pan 200 developed in D76.

61 (Upper)

HERON FISHING by Donald A. Smith

An excellent bird photograph, full of interest because of the detail rendering and the authentic surroundings to the heron which has been "caught in the act". Taken on a Nikon F2 with 400mm lens on Ilford FP4.

61 (Lower)

BARN OWL WITH COMMON SHREW by Donald A. Smith, ARPS

A superb natural history shot of an owl returning to the nest with its prey. Taken by flash with a Nikon F2 and 35mm lens on Ilford FP4.

62

NUDE by Frank Peeters

A picture by a young Belgian photographer who specializes in figure studies using bold contrasts and graphic interpretation, usually produced by available light. For this picture he used a Nikkormat FT3 with a 28mm lens and Tri-X film rated at 1600ASA, developed in Neutrol S.

63

DANCE by Andrej Krynicki

This very versatile and prolific Polish photographer uses solarisation extensively to fantasize familiar subjects. His ideas are always original and he uses the figure in an artistic and creative way as can be seen in this example. The contrast between the vitality of a nude dancer and the drabness of the house tops is stimulating.

64

THREE NUNS by Montserrat V. Barraquer

Nuns are popular subjects with photographers but it is not easy to get such an excellent arrangement as this. Taken in the Cathedral square at Tarragona, with a Leicaflex SL and 180mm lens on Tri-X film developed in Rodinal.

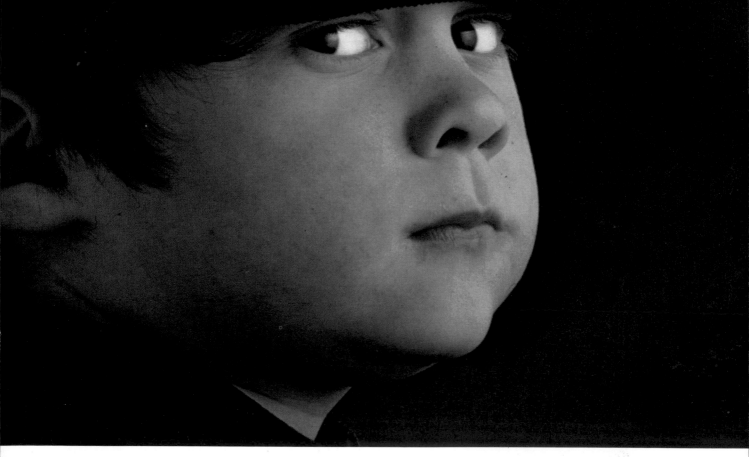

Take your children, seriously.

The Nikon FM and FE Compacts.
Made to perfectionist standards by the world's greatest camera-makers.
For photographers with a serious interest in improving their image.

 One word that's worth a thousand pictures.

 For further details write to: Dept. P.B., Nikon Division, Rank Audio Visual Ltd., P.O. Box 70, Brentford, Middx., TW8 9AR.

Print your colour slides

Some of your best work is in that slide magazine; why keep it hidden?

You can now make your own brilliant colour enlargements using the new 'Photochrome R' chemicals (and Kodak 'Ektachrome' 14RC paper).

'Photochrome R' chemicals are easy to use; no powders to prepare; just concentrates requiring dilution. Colour filtration is simple—the three basic steps take about 12 minutes before your print is ready to dry. 'Photochrome R' chemicals are very economical; up to 60 8 x 10 prints can be processed in one 2-litre kit.

Equipment? Provided your enlarger will accept colour filters you need only your basic black and white equipment. . .

Photochrome® R

Another innovation from

Photo Technology Limited

Potters Bar, Hertfordshire, England.

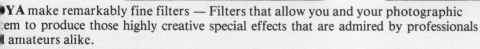
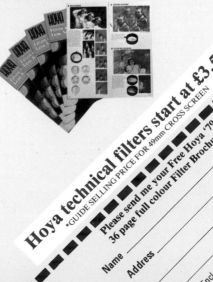

65

MINU by Raghu Rai
A well-posed portrait of a beautiful Indian T.V. announcer, with a picture in the background used to make an interesting but unusual composition. Taken with a Nikkormat and 85mm lens on Tri-X film: 1/60th second at f/5.6 by available light.

66

TWO KISSES by Vladimir Filinov
Taken by one of the leading photographers in the U.S.S.R., who has specialized in line derivation techniques for many years. The emotional moment portrayed in this example avoids over-sentimentality, by the right choice of treatment and the insect on the man's cheek is intriguing.

67

SELF PORTRAIT by Vladimir Filinov
One of the best of an enormous entry from the U.S.S.R., which included a lot of very imaginative and exciting work. The message here is not only clear, but presented with considerable force and originality. One negative was taken on a 6 x 7cm camera and the other on 35mm, with a 2x converter.

68

NO TITLE by Frantisek Dostal
A picture with a nice touch of humour. The author stalked this man around Prague for some time until he was stopped at traffic lights. It shows the value of carrying a camera always. Taken on a Minolta SR-T303 with 50mm lens on Oswo NP20 developed in A49. Exposure 1/250th second at f/11.

69

NO TITLE by Mike Hollist
An amusing picture which looks natural, although it must have been set up. It shows the new puppy on the "Blue Peter" T.V. Show arriving for rehearsals. Taken for "THE DAILY MAIL" on a Nikon with 105mm lens, and Tri-X film developed in D76: 1/250th second at f/5.6.

70

LOVE SPREADING by Virender Mahajan
Two couples seen in the Delhi Zoo gave the author the idea for the message the picture projects. It shows that there are other pictures in a zoo as well as animals if you have a seeing eye. Taken on a Canon FX with 400mm lens on Orwo NP55 film developed in D76; 1/125th second at f/5.6 in dull daylight.

71

LOVE by L. B. Feresovi
One of a series of delightfully expressive pictures portraying human emotion – one of many such pictures from Czechoslovakia. Taken with a Minolta SRT with 80-200mm 200m lens by daylight. The film was Forma 21 developed in metol pyrocatechin.

72/73

PREP SCHOOL by Frank Loughlin
Taken by a photographer on the "LIVERPOOL DAILY POST", this picture epitomises the image of a preparatory school, with the straw "boaters" being almost symbolic of middle class privilege. Shot in a Liverpool school with a Nikon F and 24mm lens on Tri-X film by bounced flash, and developed in D76.

74

HATS OFF TO A LADY by Bill Carden, FRPS
This delightful picture of a lady who carries her life's possessions in carrier bags while roaming the streets of London, was taken in Hyde Park at a Cavalry Annual Parade on a Mamiyaflex C330F with 80mm lens using HP4 film developed in ID11.

75

BIG CYRIL SMITH, M.P. by Stephen Shakeshaft
A very candid picture of a distinguished figure at a political conference which appears to have had its lighter moments. The author has won the "Photographer of the Year" Award twice, and he works for the "LIVERPOOL DAILY POST AND ECHO". Taken by available light with a Nikon F2 and 28mm lens on Tri-X, developed in D76.

76

CONTRASTE by Roland Herpin
It often takes a foreigner to see a picture in our own "backyard" and here is an interesting example of the "seeing eye" of a French photographer visiting Southampton. Taken on a Leica M5 with 90mm lens and Tri-X film. The contrast was built up in the darkroom by shading an Agfa BH111-5 paper

77

WATER COOLING TOWER by Wolfgang Volz
A 590ft high water cooling tower near a nuclear power plant in West Germany has made a dramatic industrial photograph which is also artistic because of the strong contrasts in tone as well as between the tower and the diminutive cottage. Taken with a Nikon F2 and 55mm macro lens on Tri-X film developed in D76.

78

LA ARMISTAD by Josep Maria Ribas Prous
Typical of the fine work being produced by this leading Spanish photographer who is a tutor in a photographic school and an organizer of groups of young photographers for cultural study. He contributes to photo magazines all over the world and he used a Nikon F2 with a 28mm lens for this shot on Tri-X developed in Microdol. Exposure was 1/1000th second at f/2.

79

BALLET by Leslie E. Spatt
Two pictures by an expert in this very specialized field taken during the actual performance. One shows Richard Cragum of the Stuttgart Ballet as Prince Siegfried in *Swan Lake,* and the other features him with Egon Madsen in *Songs of a Wayfarer.* Taken with a Leica M3 and 90mm lens on Tri-X rated at 100ASA and developed in Microdol.

80

OLD TURK, USKUDAR by Jean Berner
A fine and natural character study, with a powerful sense of depth and movement created by the use of a wide angle lens at a distance close enough to give a sharply diminishing perspective. Taken in the old quarter of Istanbul with a Nikkormat FT and 20mm lens on Tri-X film developed in D76.

81

MOTHER by Ilmar Apkalns
Like many pictures from the USSR this example gives a modern and imaginative treatment to an age-old sentiment. The distance between mother and child, emphasized by exaggerated perspective, is expressive of the yearning suggested by the outstretched hands. The artificial halo behind the mother could signify an even deeper meaning.

82

LUMINAIRE by John P. Delaney, FRPS
Taken on Derwentwater in the English Lake District, this picture aptly expresses the prevailing mood of this area through the Winter months. A Rolleiflex f/3.5, plus an X2 yellow filter with Plus X Professional film developed in Microdol was used. Exposure 1/500th second at f/4.5.

83

HUT ON THE SHORE by Victor J. Attfield, FRPS
The stark shape of the fisherman's hut silhouetted when the sun burst through a storm-laden sky has made a dramatic picture, and the seaweed in front of an expanse of beach has given tremendous depth to the composition. Taken on Nikkormat with a 28mm lens and orange filter on Tri-X film developed in D76.

84

FODOMODELLA SUB by Ferdinando Quaranta
Taken off Ventotene island near Naples at about 30ft depth and the model and photographer were part of a scientific research project on local fish. This well known Italian amateur photographer used a Konica Autoreflex in an Ikelite underwater housing equipped with a 55mm lens. Originally shot on Kodachrome 64 and then duplicated on Tri-X.

85

**SKATEBOARD EAGLE
by Clive Harrison, FRPS**
A fine action picture taken at a Paddington skateboard rink built on waste land by a community enterprise for the benefit of local children. Taken with an Olympus OM-1 and 100mm Zuiko lens on HP5 film developed in ID11.

86

THE QUEEN AT THE DERBY by Mike Hollist
Every press photographer tries to show the Queen's enthusiasm for horse racing by catching her expressions of joy, excitement or disappointment according to the success or otherwise of her favourite. This example, while not flattering, has certainly captured a tense moment. Nikon camera with 1000mm lens and Tri-X film developed in D76.

87

HOLY SMOKE by Howard Walker
A picture with a nice touch of humour which was posed by an amateur actor who was playing the part of a vicar. It took three hours to get the smoke ring to the right size and in the right place! Taken on a motor-driven Nikon F2 with 85mm lens, using bounce flash and Tri-X film.

88/89

BANKING ON THE LORD by Cleland Rimmer
A successful attempt to symbolize progress by showing a reflection of earlier architecture in a modern building. The attractive policewomen were persuaded to include the building on the "beat" in order to suggest the safety of the bank for which the picture was commissioned. The author is a Lecturer on photography at the Hull College of Higher Education and he used a 5 x 4in. Speed Graphic with 150mm lens and a yellow filter; the FP4 film was developed in Autophen; 1/60th second at f/8.

90

CHRIS BARBER by Rudolf Bieri
The famous jazz and blues trombonist has been well portrayed in this picture which also captures the atmosphere at the Kursaal, Bern, where it was taken during a performance. Shot with available light with a Leicaflex SL2 and Apo-Telyt 180mm lens on Tri-X film, push-developed in Tetanal Emofin for 2 x 10 min. at 30°C (86°F).

91

**SAMMY DAVIS Jnr.
by Erwin Kneidinger, EFIAP**
A shot which well expresses the vitality of this dynamic character and the atmosphere is emphasized by the available light as well as the grain. Taken with a Nikon F and 105mm lens on Tri-X film developed in Neutol; 1/250th second at f/2.5.

92

NO TITLE by J. R. Rudlin
Coloured people well know the value of contrasts and the white garment against the skin is imaginative as well as being a technical *tour de force*. The composition is original, and even daring, but most successful. The author owns a Caribbean Art Gallery, and he took the picture with a Pentax on Tri-X rated at 1600ASA by the light from a window.

SIGMA MINI-WIDE 28mm f/2.8:
Unprecedented Focusing Range In a New Ultra-Compact Size.

Capture a landscape in all its panoramic impact. Then, move in for a close-up just inches away. Emphasize size or shape. All with the same incredibly compact multi-purpose lens: Sigma tradition, to give you a fascinating new perspective in creative imagery...

Focusing to under five inches. Using advanced computer technology, Sigma engineers have added a new and marvelously exciting dimension to wide-angle photography—ultra-close focusing. Now, you can enjoy frame-filling close-ups of subjects as near as 12.5 cm (4.9˝) to your Sigma 28mm f/2.8 Mini-Wide, without accessories of any kind...and, without sacrificing the expanded perspective and depth-of-field this most popular of all wide-angle focal lengths provides. It's an exceptional advantage—one certain to inspire your photography with a fresh, fascinating new outlook.

Compact design for today's cameras. Because this lens represents a totally new design, close focus capability has been added to an array of their practical advantages— of particular importance, compact size. Only 45.5 mm (1.8˝) short, and about 198g (7oz.) light, it's strikingly easier to hold and handle than conventional slr wide angles. Which makes it the perfect match for today's newer, smaller cameras. And the perfect lightweight, compact companion for all 35mm slrs.

Fast focusing, easy handling. To complement its revolutionary compactness, Sigma's engineers and designers have given this lens smooth and convenient operating characteristics. Move from closest range to infinity with a less than 180° turn of the oversize, rubberized focusing ring. Your f-stop setting is clearly shown in a special window.

Distance, depth-of-field and even reproduction ratio scales are all clearly engraved for quick and easy reference.

Above all, optical quality. The primary function of any lens is to provide sharp, clear pictures; without this, all other characteristics are meaningless. The Sigma 28mm f/2.8 Mini-Wide delivers images of a sharpness, clarity, contrast and color fidelity that must be seen to be believed. This superior performance is the result of rare earth optical glasses, Sigma multi-layer coating and innovative computer design. As a further example of the Sigma commitment to quality, consider the unique lens hood included with each 28mm Mini-Wide. The usual circular design lens hood provides a compromise in coverage between the vertical and horizontal dimensions of the 35mm frame. But the Sigma Perfect Hood is designed for optimum protection with each dimension. Perhaps best of all, you'll find that the compact Sigma 28mm f2.8 Mini-Wide is priced to make it truly an exceptional value... made even more exceptional by the fact that the Sigma Perfect Hood and deluxe carrying case are included with every lens. And our limited warranty covers 3 full years. To experience a unique new perspective in photography, bring your 35mm slr to your Sigma dealer today for an on-camera test. Sole U.K. Distributors: C.Z. Scientific Instruments Limited, P.O. Box 43, 2 Elstree Way, Borehamwood, Herts. WD6 1NH. Telephone: 01-953 1688.

A product of Sigma Corporation, Tokyo 182, Japan.

Technical Data:
Aperture Range: f2.8–f22
Construction:
　7 elements in 6 groups
Coating: Sigma Multi-Layer
Angles of View: 75° Diagonal,
　65° Horizontal,
　46°30´ Vertical
Min. Focus: 12.5 cm (4.9˝) from lens front:
　22 cm (8.7˝) from film plane
Field Size at Min. Focus:
　108 × 162 mm (4.3 × 6.4˝)
Maximum Reproduction Ratio: 1:4.5
Diaphragm: Fully Automatic
Lens Hood: Sigma Perfect Hood Supplied
Filter Size: 52mm Screw-In
Dimensions: 62.5 × 45.5mm (2.5 × 1.8˝)
Weight: 198g (7 oz.)

ΣSIGMA

The Image of Excellence for Canon, Contax RTS/Yashica FR, Fujica, Konica, Minolta MD/MC, Nikon/Nikkormat AI, Olympus, Pentax K/M, Praktica Universal Thread

93

MAGNETIC LOOK by Virender Mahajan
A portrait of a typical old "momden phase" taken on his journey to the Festival City of Garh-Ganga-Mela in India at a low angle to produce a white sky background, accentuated by printing on hard paper. Taken with a Canon FX and 50mm lens on Orwo NP55, developed in D76.

94 (Upper)

NO HAND SIGNALS by Stanley Matchett
A young pony enthusiast, obviously with a sense of humour, makes an amusing picture at a riding school in County Down. The author is with "THE DAILY MIRROR" in Belfast and he used a Nikon F2 with an 80-200mm lens and HP5 film developed in D76; 1/250th second at f/8.

94 (Lower)

LOOK, NO HANDS by Stanley Matchett
Boy Magician Darren Swann (age ten) successfully performs his first levitation illusion, assisted by Hilary Thompson. This is a straight photograph, which shows how well the trick is performed. Taken on a Nikon F2 with an 80-200mm lens on HP5 film, by available light.

95

PIERRE, THE CLOWN by Martyn Hayhow
The author, who is a photographer on the *Evening Post,* has captured the atmosphere surrounding a clown entertaining a holiday crowd with his comedy car, and this gives it an artistic value as well. Taken on a Nikon F2 camera with a 70-210 zoom lens on HP5 film developed in ID11; 1/250th second at f/8.

96

LOVERS by Wilhelm Mikhailovsky
In recent years, photographers from the USSR have shown themselves to be masters at expressing human sentiments in a modern context. The powerful contrast in tones between the man and the girl emphasizes his masculinity against her femininity, and this has also made a good design. See also pages 116 and 117.

NO TITLE by Michael Barrington Martin
This well known London glamour photographer is constantly experimenting with new ideas and uses large sizes of film so that he can experiment with combinations of two or more. The results are usually striking and artistic as can be deduced from the fact that his work is constantly seen on calendars and magazine covers. Here a tone simplified and screened black and white has been effectively sandwiched with an out of focus pattern shot.

98

PIETRO ALBERTELLI by Tony Duffy
A spectacular ski-ing shot by one of Britain's leading sports photographers who has won many prizes in home and international sports photography contests. This example is intensely dramatic because of the low viewpoint and the deep sky tone and it is also a tremendous technical achievement to have rendered the eyes and face behind the mask while still retaining tone in the highlights.

99

TENNIS PLAYER by Leo Mason
A very graphic viewpoint high above the tennis court at Flushing Meadow Stadium, New York has produced an unusual shot of Virginia Wade in action. The Nikon F2 with 200mm lens was left in position on a special mounting for two weeks, and the shutter was operated by remote control. The film was Ektachrome Professional and the exposure was 1/500th second at f/8.

100 (Upper)

STONES by Lars Oddvar Lovdahl
A type of picture that looks much better when projected than when reproduced because the subtle browns of the autumn leaves are emphasized. The placing of the mushrooms show a good sense of design on the part

of this Norwegian freelance. Nikon F2 with 20mm lens on Kodak photomicrography film 2483.

100 (Lower)

CROWD by Nigel Stone
Crowd scenes generally make good patterns in colour when shot from above but they can also be monotonous unless there is a point of interest or contrast. Like the picture above it, this example relies on a high spot of red on one man who is strategically placed in the picture space and also appears to be standing head and shoulders above the rest.

101 (Upper)

MOONLIT LAKE by Dr A. Farquhar
From a sandwich of two slides – one taken of a small yacht after sundown on Lake Okanagan in British Columbia and the other of the moon – both on Kodachrome 64 in a Canon EF camera, the former with a 100mm lens and the latter with a 400mm lens. Exposure was made with the camera on automatic so no data is available. The sandwich was duplicated on Ektachrome 5071.

101 (Lower)

TOMBSTONE by Mark Woolstencroft
Cemeteries seem to be popular subjects with this year's photographers but this is a far more original and imaginative treatment than most of those submitted. The striking colour scheme is complemented by the pattern of spots which lead the eye to the cross giving the whole a somewhat ethereal effect.

102/103

SEPTEMBER EVENING IN MILAN by Trevor Fry, FRPS
This fairy tale impression of the pinnacles of Milan Cathedral was taken from some steps opposite, with Ektachrome 160ASA tungsten film using a Leicaflex SL and 90mm lens. Exposure was approximately one second at f/8 and the reproduction is from a Cibachrome print.

104

KALEIDOSCOPE by C. H. J. Martin LRPS
Reproduced from an original consisting of eight identical prints on Kodak 37RC paper. An imaginative conception which has won a number of prizes for the author. The original Kodacolor negative was shot on a Pentax Spotmatic with a 55mm lens.

105

ST THOMAS, ABOYNE by Francis Tocher Jr.
The atmosphere created by light passing through a stained glass window has been cleverly enhanced by zooming for 25 seconds out of a 30 second exposure. Taken on a Nikkormat FT2 with a Tamron 70-150mm zoom lens at f/11 on Ektachrome 64.

106

SELF PORTRAIT by Hektor Krome
An amusing juxtaposition of actual subjects reflected from a painted van door that provides a puzzle as well as a picture. Taken on an Olympus OM-2 with a 28mm lens and reproduced from an Ektacolor print.

107

MOSAIC 2 by A. R. Pippard, OBE, FRPS
This is from one of a series of experimental prints in which negatives were printed through various coloured screens. The screen used for this was made by spraying dye on to a piece of fixed-out film. The author is the distinguished chemist responsible for Photocolor II and other colour processing chemistry.

108/109

MULTIPLE EXPOSURE
An interesting experiment with overlapping exposures through various filters taken by a Dutch photographer. It is reproduced from a 10 x 8in Polaroid print.

110

H.R.H. PRINCE CHARLES by Terry Fincher FRPS
An unusually candid picture of this popular prince taken on the banks of the River Negro in Manans just before sunset by one of Britain's foremost freelance news photographers. The camera was an Olympus with a 28 mm lens and the exposure 1/15th second at f/5.6 augmented with flash on Ektachrome E6 film.

111 (Upper)

TRANSVESTITES by Alain Verdier
A striking double portrait taken from the author's book "Messieurs, Mesdames" which is a study of gay theatricals from all over the world, some sad and some exhuberant and which the author who is also a musician, says was inspired by the painter Rene Magritte. Taken with a Nikon F and 20mm lens.

111 (Lower)

CUB DREAMS by Dr. M. D. Constable, ARPS
A sandwich of two transparencies made on Agfa CT18 film with a Canon Ftb camera and an 80mm lens. The boy is the author's younger son who was anxious to join his elder brother in the "Cubs" and, seeing him asleep, Dr. Constable thought this might be the subject of his dreams. Taken by flash.

112

NEUROPOLIS by Luciano Pestarino, EFIAP
A picture which has an unquestionable impact of neurosis, characteristic of man in an urban environment. The author used his son as the symbolic figure in the corner of a Plaza in Buenos Aires. Mr. Pestarino is a prolific amateur exhibitor through the world.

113

IAN SMITH by Rolf M. Aagaard
Taken in Salisbury airport as the Rhodesian Prime Minister was about to leave for the United States after a long delay in granting him a visa. Quite by coincidence the author was on the same plane en route for New York from Johannesburg so he snatched this shot. The camera was a Nikon F2 with 180 mm lens and the film, Tri-X developed in D76.

114/115

PICTURES by David Bailey, FRPS
Most photographers will envy the opportunities that this famous photographer has to work for prestige fashion magazines, and with the world's best models. His technique is always impeccable, but when working to a brief or for fun, he is original. He defies conventional poses and composition with great success, as these two pictures show. Framing with a lens hood would scare a more timid worker and few would dare the inclusion of such domestic props or the emphasis given to them.

116/117

PARALLEL by Wilhelm Michaelovsky
A tremendously powerful picture by a Russian master that is enhanced by dramatic perspective, strong contrasts and grain. The expressions on the faces stimulate the viewer's imagination and the very unusual composition breaks all the "rules" with great success. See also page 96.

118

IN WINDSOR SAFARI PARK by Mike Hollist
Animals never fail to appeal and this unusual encounter between a zebra and a young giraffe has a touch of humour as well. Taken with a Nikon and a squeeze-focus 400mm lens which has kept the background nicely out of focus. Tri-X film developed in D76. 1/500th second at f/5.6.

119

SON AND PETS by Andrew McGlynn
Domestic animals have a lot of appeal and this touching moment captured by an Irish photographer has been well captured. The relation between the subjects is obvious and the backlighting has helped the group to stand out from the background. Taken with a Leica M4 and 50mm lens on FP4 developed in Rodinal. 1/125th second at f/5.6.

You're looking at the revolutionary new Durst C35.

It costs about £110. Which is about the price of a good black and white enlarger.

And if you're printing black and white that's exactly how it works, giving you crisp sharp black and white prints with its f 2.8 50mm lens.

But if you want to switch over to colour prints, from negative or slides, you don't have to fiddle around with gelatine filters.

For the C35 includes an advanced Durst easy to use colour head in its price.

And if you've never made a colour print before, we've another special offer for you: the Durst starter kit. This includes every piece of equipment you need to make your own colour or black and white prints for under £40.

As with every Durst enlarger you buy, you get a year's free membership of the Durst Darkroom Club, as well as protection through the special two year Durst Care warranty scheme.

Send us the coupon. And we'll send you full details of our special offer, in colour and black and white.

Free black and white enlarger with every Durst colour enlarger.

120

AN OLD FRENCHMAN
by E. Chambré Hardman, FRPS
A sensitive study by a leading Liverpool professional and distinguished by superb print quality as well. Taken on a quarter plate SLR camera with a 6⅜″ Tessar lens; 1/100th second at f/8 on Super XX film.

121

HAUGHTY GIRL by Vlastislar Machacek
A very unusual pose presumably taken to emphasize her pregnancy although it is not at first obvious. Like a lot of work coming from Czechoslovakia it ignores problems of grain, uprights and traditional poses, concentrating solely on putting lots of "punch" into the message. The backlighting which gives a halo effect is most effective.

122

EDGE HILL FOOTY by John Davidson
Taken by a leading photographer on the *Liverpool Daily Post* this picture typifies the love of football that starts at an early age in this city. A cobbled street in a derelict area, an old ball and a couple of bricks is all they need to start on their way to Wembley! Taken with a Nikon F and 28mm lens on Tri-X film developed in D76. Exposure was 1/60th second at f/3.5.

123/124

WEDDING by Hans-Jorge Anders
Taken on an assignment for *Stern* Magazine, this shows a Memmonite wedding party in Paraguay – one of a series showing this event and the vitality of the participants. The camera used was a Leicaflex SL2 with a 19mm lens together with Tri-X film.

125

TO HOME by Leon Balodis
A simple country wedding in a USSR village has been well documented with the inclusion of guests and spectators running ahead of the bride and creating a lot of movement. The dramatic sky makes the bride, the principal point of interest, stand out well and the picture is full of interest all over, at least to a foreigner.

126

NO TITLE by Francisco Aszmann
A picture which needs no title, because everything in it says "Spring". The backlighting has made a prominent frame of the blossom and given both depth and sparkle, which is very appropriate to the subject. Although taken in Brazil, it could be expressive of Spring anywhere in the world.

127

GOOSE STEP by Bernhard Heinz
A picture shown at Photokina that won a prize in the German Newspaper Readers Contest *"Aperture"* which attracted more than 30,000 entries. It is a striking composition, and notable for a skilful graduation of tones. Taken on PF4 film.

128

NATURE AND BEAUTY
by Mogens Lerche Madsen
A positive on lith film was made from a tree negative, and the model's back was used as a screen when it was projected with the image slightly softened. Taken on a Leica with Summicron lens on HP4 developed in Rodinal.

129

SUSAN by Josef Tichy
Figure studies were not so common this year but this is a very good example in traditional style from Czechoslovakia. Although a lot of its charm comes from the beauty of the subject, the soft window light has helped a lot and the low key treatment is pleasing. Taken on a Pentacon Six with a Biometer lens on Orwo 20 developed in Atomal: 1/15th second at f/8.

130

"MR LINCOLN I PRESUME" by Achim Sperber
A picture by a Hamburg photographer from a series entitled "New York – Up and Down". Taken on a Pentax with an 85-210mm zoom lens on Tri-X film developed in D76. Exposure was 1/500th second at f/4.

131

IN CONFERENCE by Stephen Shakeshaft
Taken at a political conference at a controversial time for the subject, the photographer has caught a pensive expression. The author (see also Page 75) has become one of England's most successful photo-journalists and has broken all records by having a picture in *"Photography Year Book"* for the seventh time. Nikon F2 and 28mm lens; Tri-X film.

132

FAMILY PORTRAIT by Martin Wolin Jr.
Showing the value of background fog to isolate the subject. The three cows almost appear to be posing and the trees and post form a rhythmic echo. Taken with a Minolta XE7 and 50mm lens on Plus X film, developed in Rodinol; 1/60th second at f/8.

133

SKI WALK by Vladimir Filinov
A short focus lens and a tone separation treatment have given this picture a very powerful, almost aggressive, impact. The composition is arresting and the tiny figure in the distance plays a big part in it – somewhat akin to the insect in the picture on Page 66. Taken with a 35mm camera and wide angle lens on 300ASA film.

134

YAWN by Pak Nin Yam
Typical of many powerful photographs of youngsters in the Far East, this one has achieved considerable success and been hung in the London Salon. No doubt the low key treatment and the interesting composition have contributed to it while the superb print quality of the original cannot be discounted.

135

BLOW-UP by Kin-Pong Chan
Like the previous picture from Singapore, this example which comes from Hong Kong, is traditional but so lively and so well presented that it also reached the Salon walls. The hair blowing across the face is an unusual touch and the rich glossy original exudes vitality.

136/137

BATTLE OF WORDS by Don McPhee
An all too familiar sight in these days of industrial strife has been pictured at exactly the right moment by a "Guardian" photographer. Taken at the Chrysler motor works when wives tried to stop a strike. The camera was a Minolta SRT101, with 28mm lens, and the film – FP4 – developed in Microphen.

138

GESICHT EINES HAUSES by W. H. Gratt
A simple design has been well seen by this German photographer and a viewpoint carefully chosen to give a well balanced composition which is attractive because of its clean lines and minimum of detail. Taken on a Bronica 6x6 with 50mm lens on Plus-X developed in HC110: 1/60th second at f/8.

139

ANGELS-ANGELS by Arthur Perry
The simplicity of line and form produced by the strong contrasts and well-chosen viewpoint, have given a lot of impact to this church roof photographed in California. Taken with a Rolleiflex 3.5 on FP4 film plus a yellow-green filter; 1/60th second at f/16.

140

AFTER THE STORM by Ilmars Apkalns
A highly dramatic landscape from the USSR which has a Wagnerian atmosphere. The rocks outlined with light make a fitting foreground to the turmoil beyond and the relief of the sunlight breaking through a menacing sky.

141

STONE LANDSCAPE by Asko Salmi
Photographed on the island of Norrskari on the west coast of Finland, this landscape is typical of the strong attack evident among the younger generation of amateur photographers. A wide angle lens and powerful tones have produced a dramatic picture. Canon AE-1 and 20mm lens plus a red filter with Tri-X film developed in D76.

142

DIANE by Ian Stewart
A photograph by an Australian freelance of Diane Minchin, a professional model, showing a provocative pose in a deserted farmhouse window, so there is subject contrast as well as tonal. Hasselblad 500, 150mm lens, and Tri-X film developed in D76.

143

NO TITLE by George W. Martin Jr.
A striking profile portrait of a professional model by a New York studio photographer, which was notable in the original for sparkling print quality. Taken by tungsten lighting with a Nikon and 105mm lens on Plus X film, developed in D76. The print was on Poly-contrast paper developed in Dektol.

144

KINGS ROAD by Harm Botman
A picture taken by a Dutch photographer when visiting a famous swinging Chelsea street in London where Lord Snowdon had some life-size prints on a wall outside the theatre. Taken with a Rollei 35 on Tri-X rated at 800ASA, and developed in Promicrol.

145

NO TITLE by David Burrows, AIIP
Taken by a young television stills photographer, to publicise a snooker game. The group is very well arranged, and the merging of the less important characters into a dark background is intriguing. Taken with a Hasselblad, and 150mm lens, on Ilford FP4, and lit by a flash unit with a snoot aimed at the figure in the centre.

146

HENLEY ROYAL REGATTA by Steve Hartley
The Reverend Gillen W. Craig, Curate of St. Marks Church in the Old Marylebone Road in London, braves the weather in a typically British way, determined to keep up the traditional Edwardian atmosphere of this annual rowing week. Taken on a Nikkormat with 85mm lens and HP5 developed in ID11; 1/250th second at f/5.6.

147

NO TITLE by Michael Gnade
An appealing child picture which commands attention because of the high viewpoint as well as the cheeky expression and pose. One of a number of excellent candids in this Bavarian teacher's book "People in my Camera".

148

LONDON SPEAKER by Vladimir Birgus
One of a series taken in London by a teacher of fine art photography in Prague. He has captured the climax of a heated dialogue between a religious speaker and an on-looker. It was taken with a Pentax Spotmatic and 28mm lens on Orwo NP27 film developed in Formadon N.

149

TEDDY BOY by Ricardo Gomez Perez
Taken at Crystal Palace by a student at the London College of Printing who is already achieving distinction through exhibiting and publications in several countries. From a portfolio on "teddy boys" taken with a Leica CL, 40mm lens, on Tri-X developed in D76.

BEYOND 35MM, THERE'S A DIFFERENT WORLD TO EXPLORE. MAMIYA M645.

Even the finest 35mm camera systems have one drawback. The image area on 35mm film is simply too small for quality enlargements.

Medium-format cameras solve the problem. But before the M645, medium-format meant 2¼ x 2¼ or larger — cameras that lacked the 35's responsiveness and handling ease.

The dilemma had a revolutionary solution. Mamiya took the best of both formats and built a better all-round camera.

The M645 System handles and performs like the finest 35mm SLR systems and delivers the usable area of 2¼ square negative cropped to the common 4.5 ratio. A 6 x 4.5cm image — 2.7 times larger than 35mm — isn't important for snapshots. But it's vital for quality enlargements.

The system's two bodies, eleven lenses, four viewfinders, five focusing screens and an array of accessories accommodate virtually every photographic challenge. And every element is built with the precision and craftsmanship that helped Mamiya become the World's largest maker of professional medium-format cameras.

Some M645 features are Mamiya exclusives. The electronic focal plane shutter consumes 1/10th the power of a conventional electromagnetic shutter, yet permits accurate exposures from 1/1000 to a full 8 seconds on the M645 1000 S (1 second to 1/500 on the M645J model). Both bodies accept interchangeable 120 and 220 roll film inserts that load in about 15 seconds.

When you've explored the M645 System you'll know how far the limits of photography have expanded.

Mamiya M645

J. Osawa and Co. (UK) Ltd., Exclusive distributors of Mamiya equipment. Stand no. 25

150

NO TITLE by Alberto H. Jordé
High key portraits generally have a glamourous effect because of the delicate tones, but they are rarely successful when grainy. This example from Spain is an exception to the rule and the pose, as well as the sweeping lines below the figure, give mood and meaning. Taken on a Leica with 35mm lens on Tri-X: 1/100th second at f/8.

151

THE GUARD by John Williams
A photograph taken by an Australian photographer when visiting the Louvre in Paris. The author was intrigued by the Guard's apparent indifference to the priceless Mona Lisa painting and to the crowd using forbidden flash all around him. Olympus OM-1 camera and 35mm lens; exposure 1/60th second at f/2 on Tri-X film developed in Acufine.

152/153

HAPPY CHILDREN' TIME
by Tsang-Chi Yen
Judging by the number of pictures submitted Taiwan is emerging as an active centre of amateur photography in the Far East, and this is a good example. The vitality of these attractive children is emphasized by the low viewpoint which produces an unobtrusive background of sky. The inclusion of clapping hands was a master touch. Taken on a Minolta SR101 on PX125 film; 1/125th second at f/11.

154

SNOW SCENE by W. Biggs
The Chiltern Hills provide plenty of opportunities for the artistically-minded landscape photographer and here an interesting pattern of hedgerows against the snow has been well-composed. Taken on a Mamiyaflex with 180mm lens on FP4 film developed in ID11.

155

GLACIER BLANC by Vera Weinerstrova
A picture full of space and depth due to a well chosen low viewpoint which has emphasized the menace of this natural phenomena while the lines of the rifts lead the eye into the distance and the dramatic sky. Taken on a Praktisix with 50mm lens on Orwo NP 20: 1/25th second at f/16.

156

FIGURE STUDY by Valdis Brauns
A nude in traditional, almost dated, style which has been lifted out of the ordinary by the bold tone treatment instead of the high key which was once the rule for studio studies. The lines of the shawl make an interesting juxtaposition with the echoing forms of the arms.

157

IN THE FOREST by Andrej Krynicki
One of a series of outdoor figure studies submitted by this prolific Polish photographer (see also page 157) but, in this case, not solarized or simplified. Like all his pictures it is original in concept and the backlighting (not the light on the back!) has given it a nice luminosity.

158

FROM THE CITY HALL, TORONTO
by Jean Berner
This brilliant young French photographer, who was born in Vietnam and travels widely for ''Le Nouvel Observateur'', shows tremendous versatility and a very perceptive eye. See also Pages 80, 214 and the inside front cover. Taken with a Nikkormat FT with 105mm lens on Tri-X developed in D76.

159

POWER STATION, NEW ZEALAND by P. G. Gale
A fine industrial picture in which the towering chimneys have been given an appearance of great height by a low

viewpoint and a vertical format, a considerable achievement without a rising front. The bold contrasts and the smoke provide an authentic atmosphere. Exa 11 with 50mm lens on Adox KB21 developed in Microphen.

160

DIREKTOR by Jiri Horak
A stimulating picture which is presumably intended to portray the aggressive executive against an industrial background. Whatever way the viewer interprets the combination and the clenched fist it cannot fail to arrest attention and the composition is artistic. Petri FT with 28mm lens on Orwo 27 developed in Atomal.

161

WHEELIE by Peter Gant, ARPS
A dramatic picture of movement enhanced by a slow shutter speed, that was one of a set which won the AP ''Sports Photographer of the Year'' panel. It was taken at Skate City, London with a 200mm lens on an Olympus OM-1 at 1/15 second on Kodachrome 64.

162 (Upper)

GLIDER by Gordon Ratcliffe
An excellent hang-glider picture taken in the Pennines, in which there is a good impression of space and a dramatic sky. The glider is a ''Sunspot'' piloted by Len Gabriels. Taken with a Pentax Spotmatic and 200mm lens, plus a crystal filter on Kodachrome 64; 1/125th second at f/11.

162 (Lower)

NO TITLE by David R. MacAlpine
A landscape which amply demonstates that dramatic lighting conditions are just as effective in colour as in black and white and can overlay an ordinary landscape with a powerful mood. Pentax SIA, with 55mm lens on Kodachrome II: 1/125th second at f/5.6.

163 (Upper)

TURBULANCE by John L. Cawthra
This picture was taken with the specific intention of giving an impression of future space travel. It is a sandwich of a transparency on Agfa CT21 taken through the bottom of a milk bottle, together with a shot of a hang glider on Fuji 100 taken with a 135mm lens on a Canon AT1.

163 (Lower)

REMEMBERED by Tony Howard
Taken late on a midsummer evening in an English churchyard when the sun was reflecting from the marble finish of the cross. The camera was a Nikkormat FTN with 50mm lens and the exposure was 1/30th second at f/5.6 on Ektachrome-X film, trade processed.

164/165

MOTOR CROSS by Woot Gilhuis
A dynamic action shot by the author of ''Between sharp and unsharp'' published by Argus Books Ltd. Woot is freelance photographer and a leading member of the Dutch Association of Professional Photographers. Taken on a Canon F1 with a 400mm lens and Kodachrome 64 film. The movement was obtained by planning at 1/8th second.

166

NO TITLE by Patrick Lichfield
This portrait of the Duchess of Roxburghe and the Countess of Lichfield was taken for ''Vogue'', and is reproduced by kind permission of Condé Nast. It shows a pleasing and original pose which is, nevertheless, appropriate for two sisters, and the sensitive handling of colour in high key is most artistic. Taken with an Olympus OM-2 and Ektachrome film.

167

CARON by James Elliott
A portrait which achieves glamour and artistry with a beautiful combination of pastel colours in perfect harmony, while the high placing of the head retains dignity. Photographed with a 70-210mm zoom lens on a

35mm camera with Ektachrome film and lit by electronic flash.

168

CAR THROUGH FLUTED GLASS
by John F. Percy
One of a set which explored the world through a fluted glass panel 9''wide in the author's front door. The car was on the other side of the road, so the Olympus OM-1 with a 50mm lens and a 2x Komura converter was stopped down to f/16. Taken on Kodachrome 64.

169

NO TITLE by D. J. Bellham
An unusual picture obtained by double exposing, on the same frame, a landscape shot at sunset and the pattern on a black corrugated surface by evening light. The result is somewhat reminiscent of a Japanese fan. Taken with a Canon EF camera and 50mm lens, on Kodachrome 25.

170

PORTRAIT by Ray Williamson
A deliberate use of the distorted perspective created by getting close to the subject with a standard lens in order to emphasize a sultry and perhaps enigmatic mood which the author describes as a ''painter's eye view''. Taken by bounced umbrella flash on Kodachrome 25 film in a Contax RTS camera with 50mm lens at f/5.6.

171

PORTRAIT by K. Amil
A picture in which the colour design dominates, and the author has shown artistic perception in concentrating on the turban rather than takng a straight portrait. The rest of the colour provides harmony without being obtrusive.

172/173

TRISUL by Frank Martin, FIIP
This picture of the 23,406 ft. high peak in the Himalayas shows a moraine formed by a retreating glacier, and it was taken by a professional photographer who went mountaineering for a holiday. He used a Petri TTL camera with a 70-230mm zoom lens and Kodachrome 64 film.

174 (Upper)

PORTRAIT by C. Nutman
It has become acceptable to use colour filters for certain types of colour photographs provided their use adds something to the atmosphere. In this case, the warmth, plus the sunset effect obtained by zooming the background separately during exposure, has made an artistic portrait.

174 (Lower)

NO TITLE by Joan Wakelin, FRPS
The author, who has travelled widely in Zambia and Sri Lanka making photographic essays on the peoples, has here found a subject in a Sheffield back garden. Taken with a Pentax SV and 28mm lens on Agfa CT18. Reproduced from a Cibachrome print.

175

VISION by Dr. Surendra Sahai
An exciting sandwich of two slides, one of fireworks and one of sun worshippers on the Konorak beach in India. The combination makes a picture which stimulates the imagination. A Pentax SPII camera and Kodachrome 64 film was used for both shots, and a duplicate was made on Kodak Special film.

176

PORTRAIT by Maurice Braun
A very appealing child portrait which has something of the quality of a painting because of the subdued colour scheme and the dark background. This was one of the superb collection of large portrait prints shown on the Kodak stand at Photokina. See also page 34.

A butterfly photographed with an ordinary macro zoom lens.

The elusive butterfly disappeared a second or so before this shot was taken.

Hardly surprising when the front of the lens was as close as six inches.

Had the butterfly been approached by our new 'SP' 70–210mm f3.5–4 Tele-Macro zoom lens, it would have been a different picture.

At a macro magnification of 1:2, the front element keeps the remarkable distance of 20.5 ins from the subject.

But we went a lot further than that. For our new 'SP' Range is the result of a totally new approach to optical and mechanical design concepts.

For example, with a constant f-number from infinity through macro, automatic flash is much easier. So even if your subject does take to the wing, you can freeze it in mid-flight.

The traditional, often time wasting macro switch has been eliminated.

Instead, you simply rotate the quick focusing ring, and you're there. So you can zoom in macro and frame your shot just how you want.

Of course, there's much more to our new 'SP' lenses than we can tell you about here. So much, in fact, that we have a leaflet on each of them. Send us the coupon and we'll send you details.

Or maybe you'd rather go out and buy an ordinary lens.

PRAKTICA

Many of the more traditional photographers still prefer a separate light meter; but in every other respect, they require the most advanced techniques of the modern miniature camera… accuracy, compactness, ease of handling and quality of lens…which is why the PRAKTICA L2 must be the obvious choice.

The beautifully styled, light-weight body houses a Swedish-steel, vertical, focal-plane shutter of unsurpassed accuracy, allowing flash synchronisation up to 1/125th sec. Loading the PRAKTICA L2 is simplicity itself, thanks to the PL automatic film-loading system. The shutter speed dial is speeded from 1/1000th sec. and B, and there is an angled shutter release and a sure-grip rapid wind-on lever. Flash synchronisation is made possible by the central hot-shoe contact. *All this adds up to a camera with everything the 'separate meter' photographer requires in an SLR — add the convenience of the 42mm screw thread lens mount and you have the ultimate in a low-cost system SLR.*

SPECIFICATION:
• *Swedish steel bladed vertical focal plane shutter speeded from 1 sec. to 1/1000th sec. and B, synchronising up to 1/125th sec. with electronic flash • Built-in accessory shoe with hot-shoe connection • Fresnel focusing screen with micro-diaprism centre spot and matt surround • Pentacon PL quick-loading system • Sure-grip rapid wind-on lever • Angled shutter release • Eye-level prism viewfinder with readiness indicator • Automatic exposure counter • Hinged camera back • Return mirror • Available with 50mm f2.8 Domiplan FAD • Dimensions: (with 50mm f2.8 Domiplan) 5½" x 3½" x 3¾" • Weight: (with 50mm f2.8 Domiplan) 23½ozs.*

See the PRAKTICA L2 at your local photographic dealer today.

PENTACON
QUALITY PRODUCTS
FROM THE GDR

Sole U.K. Distributors
C. Z. Scientific Instruments Ltd.,
P.O. Box 43, 2 Elstree Way,
Borehamwood, Herts. WD6 1NH.
Tel: 01-953 1688

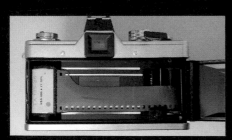

PL Easy-load system

Angled shutter release

Hot-shoe

177

MANIKIN by Carlos Canovas
A lifelike rendering of a plastic face in which a natural flesh texture has been rendered by grain. The bold design and close up treatment adds to the realism and gives a powerful three-dimensional effect. Taken with a Nikon F2 and 135mm lens on Tri-X film developed in HC100.

178

NUDE STUDY by Frank Peeters
An expressive study which shows an artistic interpretation of the human form used as the basis of a powerful design. Taken on a Nikkormat FTN with 28mm lens on Tri-X film rated at 1600ASA and developed in Neutrol S.

179

NUDE by Hideki Fujii
A study which retains the characteristic individuality which is found in all Japanese art. This is partly due to the very unusual pose with the figure almost suspended in space, and partly due to the mask.

180

LANDSCAPES by Signe Drevsjo
Two pleasing landscapes from Norway – the upper taken in Gimsoy in the Lofoten Islands. The particularly happy cloud formation leads the eye into the distance and gives a strong impression of depth. The lower makes a very good design. Both taken with a Canon F1 and red filter on Tri-X developed in D76. A 17mm lens was used for the open view and a 50mm macro for the grass picture below.

181

MYSTERIOUS CASTLE by Vera Weinerstrova
The use of a wide angle lens for landscapes together with the inclusion of a bold object in the foreground has become very fashionable. Coupled with a strong and contrasty tone treatment plus plenty of grain and rich black, it is undoubtedly impressive as in this example. Praktisix camera and Orwo NP20 film.

182

DIVER by Mervyn Rees, FRPS
This wonderful action shot was taken at Crystal Palace, London, during a training session for the Commonwealth Games. It was taken on a Nikon F2 with a 50mm lens on Tri-X film developed in D76. Exposure 1/250th second at f/3.5.

183

KARIN FITZNER by Mervyn Rees
A dramatic photograph of an East German shot putter at the point of releasing the shot. The grain which is inevitable when forcing fast film actually adds to the mood of strength and effort while the strong diagonal suggests movement. Nikon F2 with 500mm lens. 1/1000th second at f/8 on Tri-X film.

184

WINGS TOWN by Jiri Horak
Typical of the imaginative work coming from Czechoslovakia. There is a similarity of idea between this and the picture on page 160 by the same author but both have a most creative treatment. The camera was a Petri FT with 28mm lens and the exposure was 1/125th second on Orwo NP27 developed in Atomal.

185

EDDY BOYD by Reijo Porkka
The author has seen the interesting outline formed by the backlighting and wisely emphasized it by a tone simplification treatment to give an intense impression of a night club atmosphere. Taken on a Nikon with 50mm lens on Tri-X rated at 1600 ASA.

186

NO TITLE by Jim Barker
Many people would have passed by this amusing situation created by the contrast between the girl in the poster and the lady on the seat. It shows the value of keeping one's eyes open and carrying a camera always. Taken with a Hasselblad on FP4 developed in Unitol.

187

UNEMPLOYED by E. Chambré Hardman, FRPS
A fine industrial study showing a derelict boiler at a Welsh colliery. Taken with a Rolleiflex on HP3 film; the negative was enlarged on to Ilford Fine Grain Ordinary film to give a transparency which was then printed on hard bromide paper.

188

HYDE PARK by F. Russell, FIIP, FRPS
Taken from one of a series depicting the parks and the peoples of London, by a young industrial photographer who is achieving distinction in that field. The series was a purely leisure project he set himself. His camera was a Nikkormat with a 43-86 zoom lens, and the film was HP5 rated at 800ASA.

189

AUTUMN by Laszlo Lajas
The placing of leaves on the sleeping girl has a slightly macabre effect but she certainly augments the atmosphere of autumn and makes a stimulating picture out of a rather dull landscape. The treatment underlines the similarity of approach between Hungarian and Czech photographers.

190

HEAD IN HANDS by Howard Walker
This well-known *Sunday Mirror* photographer was having a bit of fun when he photographed his Father-in-Law in a concave shaving mirror in the bathroom, but it has produced a strange abstract dimension as well. Taken with a Nikon F2, and 50mm lens by the available light on Tri-X film developed in D76.

191

JANUARY by Vladimir Filinov
Another intriguing picture from the U.S.S.R., which gives an unusual treatment to a common enough subject by isolating one figure from a group. The boy sets the mood and the others set the scene. Taken on a 35mm camera with standard lens and a 3x converter, then copied on to a 6 x 9cm line negative film.

192

UNCLE JOHN by V. Sonta
Chosen from a whole series on Lithuanian country people, the author wisely chose a profile treatment in this case and the pose adds stability and strength. Taken with a Konica A3 and 50mm lens on Tri-X developed in Microphen.

193

NO TITLE by David Burrows, AIIP
Taken at a piano recital in Manchester, there is no need to name the subject, even though his face is partly concealed. Mr. Heath's association with music is well known and the viewpoint chosen has produced an unusual and intriguing composition. Taken with a Nikon F2, and 135mm lens, on Tri-X film developed in D76.

194/195

PETER BONETTI by Mike Hollist
The famous Chelsea goalkeeper, nicknamed "Cat", Is joined by his nine year old son in training. He hopes to succeed his father! Mike, who is with "THE DAILY MAIL", used a Nikon F2 with 180mm lens and Tri-X film developed in D76. Exposure was 1/500th second at f/5.6.

196

WINDOW ON LONDON by Jack Rufus, FRPS
When not on an East African Safari, the late Jack Rufus loved to roam around London with his camera, and he usually managed to find an artistic interpretation of both modern and ancient architecture, like this one taken in the Barbican. Hasselblad, with 80mm lens, on Tri-X, developed in Microdol. See also Page 59.

197

TOWER by Geri Della Rocca
A very unusual view of the World Trade Centre in New York which shows that when circumstances make it impossible to keep verticals upright it is a positive advantage to shoot from close up to exaggerate the feeling of height and produce a strong design. Taken on a Nikon F with 20mm lens on HP5 rated at 600 ASA.

198

TENDRESSE by Serge de Sazo
The emotion of love can be projected in many ways but it takes an artist to employ nudes of both sexes without giving a lascivious overtone to the picture. The French have been masters of this in sculpture and painting and this shows that they can do it in photography as well. It makes an interesting comparison with the pictures on pages 71 and 211.

199

KALHAMA AND GUTTA by K. Szebessy
A photograph which captures the atmosphere of an artist's studio because of the background paper and the props, but it is lifted out of the ordinary by the figure walking towards the camera, giving movement and a perfect balance to the composition.

200

BRIAN BECK by Geoffrey Tyrer
A well timed shot of this Olympic gymnast executing a flying somersault. Not only has the action been caught at its dramatic peak but the whole story has been told. Taken for the *Sheffield Star* on a Canon FT with 50mm lens by bounce flash at f/5.6 on Tri-X.

201

GYMNAST by Luis Arteaga Cerdan
Like the facing page this photograph also shows very precise timing to get the action at its height. It also completes the story by showing an authentic background, and the rear view is an unusual touch. Taken with a Nikon F2A and 105mm lens on Tri-X developed in Rodinal.

202

CAST OFF IN RIO by Henning Christoff
One of a series documenting the homeless children of Ipanema who sleep in the streets after forced evacuation from their homes. Taken with a Leica M4 and 35mm Summilux by flash on Tri-X film, developed in D76.

203

VISIONS by Vlado Bacă
One of a series by this young Slovak freelance photographer taken for the Magazine "Slovensko". The prints were made from reflections in chromium-plated sheets using a Pentacon Six with 50mm lens, on Orwo NP27 developed in D76.

204

GLENEVE by David Dalby
The menacing atmosphere of a storm in the Highlands has been well caught and well presented by the use of heavy blacks. The different layers, plus a highlight in the distance, give a good sense of depth. Pictured with a Hasselblad and 80mm lens on Tri-X developed in D76: 1/250th second at f/16.

205

MY FRIEND by V. Sonta
A photograph which would please those who fight what they call the "motor cycle menace". Dramatic lighting and the unusual placing of the figure give an impression of speed threatening the viewer. A red filter was used on a Pentacon Six with 80mm lens. Photo 65 film developed in D76: 1/60th second at f/5.6.

206

ON CURBAR EDGE by John Woodhouse
A self portrait taken in the Peak District National Park by a well-known, award-winning climber/mountaineer, with the help of a tripod and delayed-action release. The camera was an Olympus OM-1 with 35mm lens plus an orange filter. The FP4 film was developed in Aculux.

207

HANG GLIDER by T. G. Edwards
A picture which makes an interesting comparison with the hang glider picture on Page 162 and raises the argument which takes place in many Clubs as to whether colour or black and white gives more atmosphere or drama. Taken at Devils Dyke on a Nikon F2, with 85mm lens and a polarizing filter on FP4 film.

208

PIGGY BACK by Min Shik Choi
The theme of a child's love of a domestic pet is appealing and well tried, but it is unusual to see a fox as tame as this one in Korea. The determined walk and expression adds piquancy and movement. A 200mm lens was employed on a Leica M3 loaded with Tri-X developed in Microdol X: 1/120th second at f/4.

209

PIGGY BACK by David Wilding
A candid shot taken at the Edinburgh Tattoo when the subject was looking for a seat. Another picture which shows the benefit of carrying a camera always. Taken with a Pentax Spotmatic and 135mm lens on Tri-X film rated at 650ASA.

210

SCULPTOR'S MODEL by Frank Peeters
Taken in a Belgian art school by available tube lighting this picture has retained the atmosphere of an art class – something that would have been lost by the use of flash. The camera was a Nikkormat FT3 with 105mm lens and the film was Tri-X rated at 1600 ASA, developed in Neutrol S.

211

**RETRATO DE DOS ENAMORADOS
by Josep Maria Ribas Prous**
The picture of a male and female nude in the same photograph has been handled with taste and the treatment is right for such a difficult subject. The result is artistic and expressive. Taken on a Nikon F2 with 105mm lens by available light on Tri-X film developed in Microdol X. Exposure was 1/30th second at f/2.

212

MITSUO TSAKAHARA by Sven Simon
Sports pictures provide a strong challenge to photographers because of the very precise timing required if the action is to be caught at its height. The result always looks easy but it takes a lot of experience. The inclusion of the horizontal bars completes the story.

213 (Upper)

FIONA ROGERS by Mervyn Rees, FRPS
This picture of a leading hurdler was taken at Crystal Palace, London when she was training. The dramatic effect was obtained by using a Sigma fish-eye lens on a Nikon F2 camera. Exposed at 1/1000th second on Tri-X and developed in D76.

213 (Lower)

LADY BOWLER by Terry Cooper
A typically English scene taken as part of a "Community and Environment" project, which won an Award from the South Eastern Arts Association. Taken in Preston Park, Brighton, with an Olympus OM-1 and 50mm lens on FP4 film developed in ID11.

214

IN A MUSEUM IN ATHENS by Jean Berner
An amusing picture of the author's daughter protesting her reluctance to take in more culture! Originally shot on Fujichrome 100 with a Nikkormat camera and 20mm lens. A reversal print was then made and copied onto Tri-X film to obtain the enlargement and to isolate the subject by shading.

215

SUBWAY by Achim Sperber
Taken in New York's subway for a series entitled "New York – Up and Down" it has caught the atmosphere of this much reviled transport system. Taken on a Leica camera with 35mm lens on Tri-X film developed in D76. Exposure was 1/125th second at f/2.8.

216

NO TITLE by Signe Drevsjo
A candid double portrait which expresses a moment of happiness in a way that only photography can. The contrast of youth and age carries its own message and both heads are well placed to give a composition of great vitality. Taken with a Canon F1 and 50mm lens on Tri-X developed in D76.

217

DOUBLE PORTRAIT by Egons Spuris
A portrait which defies all the text books which say that there should always be a physical or suggested connection between two people in a portrait and, furthermore, "that one should be more prominent than the other". However, this very unusual composition has come off and the intense expressions stimulate the imagination.

218

NO TITLE by Karin Szekessy
A remarkable arrangement of figures by a photographer who obvious goes all out to present an idea and is not worried by the technical considerations of balancing the lighting. In fact, the flare from the window seems to add authenticity. See also page 199.

219

NO TITLE by Michael Gnade
A picture which makes an interesting comparison with the one opposite. The delicate feminine touch is replaced by strong contrasts, not only in subject matter but in tones, and the composition is remarkably cohesive in spite of so many elements.

220

CALELLA by Ferran Artigas
A low angle and strong contrasts have enabled the author to dramatise the impression that the apartments appear to be in danger of slipping down during the next storm, because of the erosion beneath. Taken with a Minolta SRT and 28mm lens on Tri-X film.

221

SKYE LANDSCAPE by Chris Peet, FRPS
Taken by an exhibitor who has given up colour work in favour of black and white. The original print was a deep sepia tone, obtained by two developments in a strong sulphide solution. It was shown in the London Salon and was taken with a Praktica, and 20mm lens plus an orange filter on FP4 film.

222 (Upper)

THE DOMES by Roland Herpin
An interesting design picture which also has atmosphere, due to the use of a screen and the shading used on the sky in printing. Taken in Tunisia with a Minolta SRT 101 and 135mm lens on Tri-X, and printed on a hard Agfa paper.

222 (Lower)

COMPOSITION by Ilmar Apkalns
This is almost a text book exercise which does not appear to have any hidden meaning or message, but it shows a remarkable eye for an interesting composition. The original showed immaculate print quality.

223

BEACH ARCHITECTURE by Michael Scott
Taken by an art teacher as one of a series, this picture illustrates how the "seeing eye" will seek out the interesting interplay of pattern, texture and tone in the most commonplace of subjects. Taken on a Praktica LTL, with 50mm lens on HP5 film. The print was sepia-toned to emphasize the character and age of the structure.

224

NUDE by Jose Torregrossa
The use of the female figure for abstract or semi-abstract design is not unusual but the powerful effect of simple shapes and bold modelling makes this a better example than most. Taken with a Nikon F and 24mm lens on Tri-X developed in HC110.

Inside Back Cover

APRES LA COURSE by Raymonde Jarry
A very interesting pattern picture. High angle shots of crowds are not easy because the components rarely form a balanced composition, or else they are too repetitious. In this case the empty chairs obviate monotony and the rear view gives an unusual touch.

Technische Daten

SCHUTZUMSCHLAG von Martin Wolin Jr.
Ein schones Bild, das erweist, welch zarte Pastelltöne und schonen Farbzusammenstellungen im Licht des frühen Morgens, bevor die Sonne aufsteigt, erz ielt werden konnen. Aufgenommen mit einer Pentax 6 x 7 mit 105mm Objektiv auf High Speed Ektachrome; 1/60 Sekunde bei Blende 8. Die Reproduktion beruht auf einer Cibachrome-Kopie.

Vorderdeckel innen

AU BEGUINAGE DE BRUGES von Jean Berner
In diesem Bild eines bekannten französischen Fotografen gelangt ein brillantes Gefühl der Komposition zum Ausdruck, wofür rhythmische Wiederholung und kräftige Kontraste weitgehend verantwortlich sind. In Belgien mit einer Nikkormat FT mit 20 mm Objektiv aufgenommen. Der Tri-X-Film wurde in D76 entwickelt.

13

INDUSTRIE von John Davidson
Diese schöne Aufnahme wurde eigens als Titelbild für eine Industrieanlage der *Liverpool Daily Post* gemacht. Um dem hohen Kontrast zu entsprechen, bediente sich der Künstler eines Chromfilters als Graufilter. Aufgenommen mit einer Nikon F mit 28 mm Nikkor-Objektiv auf in D76 entwickeltem Tri-X-Film.

14

AM MEERE von José Torregrosa
Selbst die traditionellsten Themen können modern behandelt werden, indem man den Regeln der Komposition zuwiderhandelt. Diesen Regeln zufolge hätte das Boot ein wenig rechts oder links im Bilde sein sollen, und nicht unmittelbar in der Mitte. Es erhöht jedoch die Wirkung dieser Aufnahme, dass der abendlichen Stimmung so guten Ausdruck verleiht. Aufgenommen mit einer Nikkormat mit 24 mm Objektiv auf Tri-X-Film.

15

VERCORS von J. J. Abassin
Eine sehr hübsche Schneescene, die nahezu weihnachtskartenmäßig wirkt, ist durch den sehr dunklen Himmel, der sich normalerweise unter solchen Bedingungen mit einem ganz hellen Filter erzielen läßt, dramatisiert. Die Einbeziehung der winzigen Gestalt verleiht Maßstab und Tiefe und lenkt den Blick in das Innere des Bildes.

For the best in Black & White

Call on the ILFORD Partnership

16

INDIANER IN CALGARRY von George Webber
Die Pfeile an der Wand verleihen der in dieser Aufnahme eines jungen kanadischen Fotografen enthaltenen Botschaft eine ironische Note. In offenem Schatten mit einer Canon FT6N mit 50 mm Objektiv auf in ID11 entwickeltem Ilford FP4-Film aufgenommen.

17

IN VATERS KLEIDUNG von Raghu Rai
Ein amüsantes Bild, das einen glücklichen Augenblick erhascht und wie andere Aufnahmen in diesem Buch erweist, daß es in der Fotografie Raum für Humor gibt, obgleich damit nicht unbedingt ein bleibender ästhetischer Effekt erzielt wird. Die Kamera war eine Nikon F mit 85 mm Objektiv und der Film Tri-X. 1/250 Sekunde bei Blende 5,6.

18

CARMEN von Josep Maria Ribas Prous
Die außerordentlich effektvolle Körnung bedingt künstlerische Wirkung. Das Bild wurde durch Vergrößern eines sehr kleinen Teils des Negativs erzielt. Aufgenommen bei Wolframlicht mit einer Nikon F2 mit 105 mm Objektiv. Der Tri-X-Film wurde in Microdol X entwickelt. 1/60 Sekunde bei Blende 5,6. Der Verfasser ist ein spanischer Lehrer der Fotografie.

19

INGRID von F. John Reid
Dank der stilvollen Behandlung ist dies ein besonders geglücktes Bild des schönen blonden Modells. Aufgenommen mit einer Mamiya C330 mit 135 mm Sekor-Objektiv auf FP4-Film und in D76 entwickelt. Die Atelierbeleuchtung bestand in zwei Multilec-Blitzlichtern, die auf das Modell und zwei Männer im Hintergrund gerichtet waren. Die Anwendung von Seidengaze bewirkte einen leichten Weichzeichnereffekt bei der Vergrößerung.

20

HILFE von David Bearne
Eine während des Endspiels für den Hampshire Rugby-Pokal zwischen Basingstoke und Havant gemachte Aufnahme. Der geistesgegenwärtige junge Fotograf hat einen Vorfall erhascht, der recht humoristisch wirkt. Er bediente sich einer Nikon F2 mit 135 mm Objektiv, und der Tri-X-Film wurde in D76 entwickelt. 1/200 Sekunde bei Blende 5,6.

21

BEGRIFFEN von Frank Travers
Sportfotografen haben viele Möglichkeiten der Verewigung bedeutender Vorgänge und Gesten, doch ist Geschick und Erfahrung erforderlich, um den richtigen Augenblick zu erfassen. Auch muß die Schärfeneinstellung der Kamera stimmen. Frank fotografiert im Dienste des SHEFFIELD MORNING TELEGRAPH und hat diese Aufnahme mit einer Canon Ftb mit 400 mm Novaflex-Objektiv aufgenommen. Der Tri-X-Film wurde in Qualitol entwickelt.

22/23

ROLF HARRIS IN AKTION von John Davidson
Ein bekannter Star mit einer Gruppe von Schulkindern in Liverpool, als sie für eine Fernseh-Reihe gefilmt wurden. Man sieht wie enthusiastisch Rolf Harris mit den Kindern zusammenarbeitet. Aufgenommen bei verfügbarem Licht in einem große Schulsaal. Die Kamera war eine Nikon F mit 28 mm Objektiv und der Tri-X-Film wurde in D76 entwickelt. 1/15 Sekunde bei Blende 3,5.

24

S. RICHTER von Laszlo Lajas
Ein hervorragendes Porträt dieses großen russischen Klavierspielers, das gerade im richtigen Augenblick aufgenommen wurde, um einen charakteristischen Ausdruck festzuhalten. Die authentische Umgebung und das applaudierende Publikum sagen alles. Aufgenommen bei verfügbarem Licht mit einer Minolta SRT 101 mit 55 mm Objektiv auf Acufine entwickeltem Tri-X. 1/30 Sekunde bei Blende 2,8.

25

JACKIE ROBINSON von Monroe S. Frederick
Amerikas erster farbiger Baseball-Spieler ist hier mit seiner Frau kurz vor seinem Tode abgebildet. Die natürlichen Gesichtsausdrücke und Gesten der beiden – sie bemerkten die Kamera nicht – machen dies zu einer rührenden Erinnerung. Aufgenommen bei elektronischem Blitzlicht mit einer Mamiyaflex 220 mit 65 mm Objektiv auf D76.

26

EINBLICK von Robert Llewellyn
Aus einem Buch mit dem Titel "Silver Wings", von dem der Verfasser erklärt hat, daß es visuelle Manifestationen seiner irdischen Reise zur Einsicht und Erkundung der geistigen Welt bilde. Er hat versucht, dies durch miteinander in Wechselbeziehung stehende Gegenstände in verschiedenen Ebenen auszudrücken. Nikon F mit 20 mm Objektiv.

27

MORGENGRAUEN AM SEE von Asko Salmi
Dieses Bild, das um 7 Uhr morgens im UAASA-Archipel aufgenommen wurde, zeigt, daß nicht nur die Mitglieder der Hongkong-Schule Boote auf nebelverschleierten Seen fotografieren. In der Tat ist diese Behandlung für einige der besten finnischen Arbeiten der letzten Jahre typisch. Die Kamera war eine Canon AE-1 mit 20 mm Objektiv und der Tri-X-Film wurde in D76 entwickelt.

28

KEIN TITEL von J. M. Oriola
Dieses amüsante Bild zeigt, daß eine Ansicht von hinten ebenso ausdrucksvoll sein kann wie eine Aufnahme von vorn. Dieses Bild ist gewiß originell und wirkt sehr natürlich, obgleich es auch gestellt sein könnte. Die kräftigen Kontraste und die ungewöhnliche Komposition regen zu genauerer Betrachtung an.

29

YOGA von Brian Sutton
Eines von einer Reihe von Bildern, die einer Yoga-Lehrerin die Kontrolle ihrer Körperhaltung erleichtern soll. Infolge der Verkürzung legt das Bild aber einen gewissen Humor an den Tag. Mit einer Pentax SPF mit 28 mm Objektiv auf Tri-X-Film aufgenommen. Zur Entwicklung diente D76.

30

KEIN TITEL von Jozef Vissel
Ein Bild ungewöhnlicher Kontraste. Es ist absurd und daher recht humorvoll. Obgleich es sich offensichtlich um eine künstlich arrangierte Szene handelt, kann man dieses Bild bestimmt nicht übersehen. Mit einer Hasselblad auf Panatomix X aufgenommen und in Rodinal entwickelt.

31

MERLYN REES, M.P. von Asadour Guzelian
Ein früherer britischer Innenminister in einer glücklichen Stimmung während eines in Leeds abgehaltenen Banketts der Sikhs. Abgesehen davon, daß das Bild viel über den Mann und den Anlaß aussagt, ist die Komposition origineller und die Wirkung größer als bei vielen mehr förmlichen Porträts von Politikern. Die Kamera war eine Pentax SP100 mit 135 mm Objektiv. Der Film war Tri-X.

32

WINTER IN DEN BERGEN von Tom Dodd
Ein dramatisches Bild, das mit Hilfe eines 4x-Orangefilters in den Moelwyn-Bergen von Snowdonia – Höhe rund 600 m – aufgenommen wurde. Die Kamera war eine Canon F2 mit 28 mm Objektiv, und der 164 ASA FP4-Film wurde in Aculux entwickelt. Der Fotograf benutzte Blende 16, um Sonnenreflexion einzuschränken.

33

IM BALLETT von Rudolf Auer
Eine hervorragende Aufnahme, die eine Pirouette auf außerordentlich kunstlerische Weise zur Geltung bringt. Der Schwung der Tu-Tus wirkt durch Wiederholung rhythmisch, und der Glanz der Sequine bildet einen faszinierenden Kontrast zu der blauen Beleuchtung. Die warmen Farben an Rücken und Beinen vermeiden jeden Eindruck allgemeiner Kälte.

34

PORTRÄT von Dieter Kraft
Dieses dramatische Porträt eines Schweizer Fotografen wurde auf der letzten Photokina sehr bewundert. Es wurde im Rahmen einer Ausstellung großer Farbkopien auf dem Kodak-Stande zur Schau gestellt. Das kühne Rot auf farbigem Fleisch und die exzentrische Komposition verleihen dem Bild eine enorme Wirkung.

35

SUE von Henry Michaels
Aufgrund einer hervorragenden Farbkopie eines mit einer Bronica 6 x 6 cm Kamera aufgenommenen Kodak Vericolour-Negativs reproduziert. Die künstlerische Behandlung eines herkömmlichen Gegenstands wird durch die überwiegend dunklen Bildtöne erwiesen, die die Hintergrundbeleuchtung betonen. Beleuchtung durch zwei Multilex- "Flash Umbrellas", einem in Silber und einem in Gold, mit einem dritten Blitzlicht im Hintergrund. Die Kopie wurde auf Agfacolor Typ 4 Papier hergestellt.

36

LANDSCHAFT von Roger Arrandale-Williams
Dieses Bild gehört einer Reihe an, die "maskierte Modelle in Weiß" in eine natürliche Umgebung einfügt. Diese Kombination ergibt fantastische und manchmal unangenehme Nebeneinanderstellungen. Aufgrund eines mit einer Minolta XE7 aufgenommenen Kodachrome 64 Dias.

37

LANDSCHAFT IN BLAU von Erik Steen
Dieses ungewöhnliche, wirksame Bild wurde durch Anwendung von Ektacolor Slide Duplicating Film erzielt, der in E4 und nicht, wie empfohlen, nach dem C22-Verfahren entwickelt wurde. Der erste Entwickler wurde ausgelassen und die Zeit im Farbentwicklungsgerät um 1/4 reduziert. Nahe dem Heim des Künstlers in Drammen, Norwegen, mit einer Nikon F2 mit 43-86 Zoom-Objektiv aufgenommen.

38/39

PRESLEY-TRAUERNDE von Dr. James Billimoria
Ein Bild, das die in der westlichen Welt durch den Tod eines Rock and Roll-Stars erzeugte Hysterie veranschaulicht und in der Trauernden nicht weinen sondern tanzen. Aufgenommen mit einer Leica mit 50 mm Objektiv an einem Sonntagmorgen auf dem Trafalgar Square. Der Künstler hat den Aufnahmepunkt so gewählt, daß die Massenszene eine gute Komposition ergibt.

40 (oben)

EULE UND OPFER von Xabi Otera
Eine sehr künstlerische Behandlung eines naturgeschichtlichen Themas. Die Eule und die Eidechse sind deutlich hervorgehoben, während der Hintergrund dem Thema gemäß nächtlich und mysteriös wirkt. Der Gesamteindruck ist der einer sehr schönen Farbkomposition.

40 (unten)

MEERESKRÖTE UND FROSCH von John Walker
Diese schöne Naturstudie von zwei Tieren wurde bei Blitzlicht auf Ektachrome 200 Film aufgenommen. Die Kamera war eine Nikon EL mit Micro-Nikkor-Objektiv. Die südamerikanische Kröte wiegt etwa 1½ kg, während der grüne Baumfrosch aus Italien nur 85 Gramm schwer ist. Das Bild wurde in dem Welsh Mountain Zoo, Colwyn Bay, aufgenommen, und es waren mehrere Belichtungen nötig, da der Frosch immer wieder auf das Objektiv hüpfte!

41

FLIEGENDER FROSCH AUS COSTA RICA
von Heather Angel, FIIP, FRPS

Ein sehr seltener Frosch, der für die Fernsehserie "Life On Earth" nach England gebracht und dann in seine Heimat, den Regenwald von Costa Rica, zurücktransportiert wurde. Heather Angel, die nahezu dreißig naturgeschichtliche Bücher veröffentlicht hat, fotografierte mit einer Hasselblad 500C mit 80 mm Objektiv auf Ektrachrome E-3 Film. Der Frosch wurde mit Hilfe eines Braun FZK80 Zweikopf-Blitzgeräts beleuchtet.

42

CLOWN von Baron Baron

Diese Aufnahme aus der Froschperspektive betont die Fantasiewelt, die der Zirkus vom Standpunkt der Kinder bildet. Die kühne, einfache Gestaltung unterstreicht diesen Effekt, und es wurde genug von der Zirkusumgebung einbezogen, um die Story abzurunden.

43

AKTSTUDIE von Michael Gnade

Eine sehr natürliche Studie, in der Gegenlicht eine außerordentlich wichtige Rolle spielt. Die Pose ist ebenso natürlich wie die Umgebung, und der allgemeine Farbeffekt ist sehr ansprechend. Dies ist eines von mehreren ähnlichen Bildern in dem von dem Verfasser veröffentlichten Buch.

44/45

KÄMPFERISCH von Wang Yue Lung

Die Arme und Beine dieser Turner geben ein enormes Aktionsgefühl. Daß die Gestalt im Vordergrund im Verhältnis zur Klasse zu groß ist, verleiht dem Bild eine wirklich künstlerische Note. Aufgenommen mit einer Canon AE1 mit 28 mm Objektiv auf Kodacolor 400 und auf Ektacolor-Papier kopiert.

46

AFRIKANISCHE STEPPENADLER
von Robert Hallman

Ein schönes Bild, das am Bird of Prey Centre in Chilham Castle aufgenommen wurde, als der Vogel kreischend gegen die Kamera protestierte. Aufgenommen mit einer Kowa Super 66 mit 85 mm Objektiv und 3 x Naheinstellansatz. 100 ASA Agfa 50S-Film.

47

WALDKAUZ von E. Exton

Die größte britische Eule ist ein Nachtvogel, der gefährlich ist, da er Fotografen mit seinen scharfen Krallen angreift. Der Künstler erlitt acht Kratzwunden rings um sein linkes Auge, als er diese Aufnahme aus einer Entfernung von 3 m mit einer Pentacon Six mit 180 mm Objektiv auf CPS120 aufnahm. Blitzlichtbeleuchtung.

48

KEIN TITEL von Les Mansfield

Ein ausdrucksvolles Porträt, das die Würde einer Flamenco-Tänzerin aus Andalusien gut zur Geltung bringt. Es handelt sich dabei um eine doppelte Belichtung, und zwar wurde zuerst die Gitarre mit einem Normalobjektiv fotografiert, und dann die Tänzerin mit Hilfe eines auf rund 135 mm eingestellten Tamron-Zoom-Objektivs. Aufgenommen mit einer Nikon Ftn auf 800 ASA H.S.-Ektachrome (beide Belichtungen) und auf übliche Weise in E6 entwickelt.

49

RUTH KENNEDY von Mervyn Rees

Eine wirklich dramatische Aktionsaufnahme, in voller Bewegung, wie dies bei dieser internationalen Staffelläuferin angebracht ist. Der große Kraftaufwand wird durch die Körnung und dadurch zum Ausdruck gebracht, daß die Läuferin ziemlich rechts im Bilde erscheint. Die Kamera war eine Nikon F2 mit 135 mm Objektiv und Tri-X-Film: 1/15 Sekunde bei Blende 4.

50

UNTER WASSER von Ferdinando Quaranta

Ein Bild der Frau des Künstlers in der St. Florenz-Bucht,

Korsika. Ferdinando, ein bekannter Spezialist der Unterwasser-Fotografie – gewöhnlich nimmt er Fische auf – hat sich einer Konica Autoreflex in einem Ikelite-Gehäuse mit 24 mm Objektiv bedient. Das natürliche Licht wurde durch eine elektronische Braun F2000-Blitzautomatik verstärkt. Die Vorlage war auf Kodachrome 64 und wurde auf Tri-X-Film kopiert.

51

SCHLAMMBAD von John Jones

Ein Bild, das die glückliche Stimmung während eines Fußballkampfes zwischen Jungen und Mädchen zum Ausdruck bringt, der während der jährlichen Old Leigh Regatta auf schwammigem Gelände ausgetragen wurde. Die Jungen verloren! Mit einer Canon Ftb mit 100-200 Zoom-Objektiv auf Tri-X-Film aufgenommen und in D76 entwickelt.

52

SHERRIL HAGUE von Chris Haig

Ein ausgezeichneter unerwarteter Schnappschuß bei normalem Licht, der etwas von der Persönlichkeit dieses lustigen Altwagenhändlers wiedergibt. Aufgenommen mit einer Mamiya C330 auf FP4-Film und in Acutol entwickelt.

53

AUFGESCHRIEBEN von Ian Torrance

Nicht viele hätten die Kombination von Hund und Verkehrshilfspolizist bemerkt, die diesem entzückend komischen Bild zugrundeliegt. Jeder, der einmal "aufgeschrieben" wurde, wird die Aufnahme, die diesem Fotografen des *Scottish Daily Record* im "British Press Photographer of the Year" – Wettbewerb einen Preis eintrug, zu schätzen wissen.

54

TRAUER IN TEHERAN von Rolf M. Aagaard

Aufgenommen am Hauptfriedhof der Stadt während einer Demonstration gegen den Ayatollah Khomeini, der damals noch in Paris lebte. Der Fotograf entwickelte den Film in seinem Hotelzimmer und übermittelte das Bild dann telegrafisch an die norwegische Zeitung "Aftenposten". Die Kamera war eine Nikon F2 mit 85 mm Objektiv, und der Tri-X-Film wurde in D76 entwickelt.

55

PORTRÄT von Peter Purtz

Typisch für die fantasiereichen Arbeiten aus der Tschechoslowakei, in denen ungewöhnliche, natürliche Posen mit seltsamen, oft industriellen, Hintergründen kombiniert sind. Die ungewöhnliche Position der Person ergibt in Verbindung mit starker Körnung eine eindringliche Wirkung. Mit einer Exa 500 mit 25 mm Objektiv auf Orwo 27 aufgenommen und in Formadon R entwickelt.

56

ANKA von Kazimierz Czapinski

Polnische Fotografen lassen sich in der Regel durch konventionelle Regeln der Komposition nicht beeinflussen. Der Umstand, daß sich die Hauptaktion nahezu am Rande abwickelt, mag von Traditionalisten abgelehnt werden, doch läßt sich nicht verleugnen, daß das Bild dadurch an Energie und Bewegung gewonnen hat. Der Apfel, der die Nase hochdrückt, trägt zu der Allgemeinwirkung noch bei, und auch die Körnung schadet nicht.

57

ADA ROGOVIN von George Wedding

Eine eindrucksvolle, unbemerkte Charakterstudie einer 87-jährigen Pokerspielerin in Miami Beach, die im Auftrag von THE PALM BEACH POST aufgenommen wurde. Der Fotograf wartete genau den richtigen Augenblick ab, um ein Aktionsbild zu erzielen. Mit einer Nikon mit 180 mm Objektiv auf 1600 ASA Tri-X-Film aufgenommen und in Acufine entwickelt.

58 (oben)

FRIEDHOF von J. L. Young, ARPS

Ein gutes Beispiel für die intelligente Verwendung von Infrarot-Film zur Dramatisierung einer herkömmlichen Szene. Wo immer es verschiedene Baumarten gibt, unterstreicht Infrarot die Kontraste, besonders bei

blauem Himmel. Aufgenommen in St. Nicholas's Churchyard, Basildon, mit einer Praktica LTL3 mit 35 mm Objektiv und tiefrotem Filter auf Kodak High Speed Infra-Red Film (50 ASA). Der Film wurde in Perceptol entwickelt.

58 (unten)

ZWEI SCHUPPEN von Geri Della Rocca

Größte Einfachheit und starke Kontraste haben dieser von einem italienischen Fotografen in Nevada gemachten Aufnahme große Wirkung verliehen. Die Komposition ist eindrucksvoll, und das Gefühl der Entlegenheit ist gut zum Ausdruck gebracht. Die Kamera war eine Nikon F mit 20 mm Objektiv und Rotfilter. Aufgenommen auf 600 ASA HP5-Film, der in IDII entwickelt wurde.

59

CHÂTEAU IN BELCASTEL, DORDOGNE
von Jack Rufus, FRPS

Leider starb der Künstler, kurz nachdem er dieses Bild einreichte. Er hat jedoch ein Erbe schöner Landschaftsaufnahmen traditioneller und zeitgenössischer Art hinterlassen. Dieses Bild wurde an einem Septemberabend mit einer Hasselblad mit 250 mm Objektiv auf Tri-X-Film aufgenommen. Zur Entwicklung diente Microdol X (siehe auch Seite 196).

60

GANZ ALLEIN von Asad Ali

Eine aufgrund der Aufnahme des kleinen Vogels gegen einen leeren Himmel und einen in der Landschaft von Lahore fotografierten Hintergrund angefertigte kombinierte Kopie. Die Kamera war eine Kowa mit 200 mm Objektiv und einem x2-Konverter. 1/250 Sekunde bei Blende 8. In D76 entwickelter Agfa Super-Pan 200.

61 (oben)

REIHER BEIM FISCHFANG von Donald A. Smith

Ein ausgezeichnetes Vogelbild, das dank der detaillierten Wiedergabe und der authentischen Umgebung des "auf frischer Tat" beobachteten Reihers sehr interessant wirkt. Aufgenommen mit einer Nikon F2 mit 400 mm Objektiv auf Ilford FP4.

61 (unten)

SCHLEIEREULE MIT SPITZMAUS
von Donald A. Smith, ARPS

Eine hervorragende naturgeschichtliche Aufnahme einer Eule, die mit ihrer Beute in das Nest zurückkehrt. Aufgenommen bei Blitzlicht mit einer Nikon F2 mit 35 mm Objektiv auf Ilford FP4.

62

AKTSTUDIE von Frank Peeters

Ein Bild eines jungen belgischen Fotografen, der sich auf Aktstudien mit kühnen Kontrasten und graphischer Interpretation spezialisiert. Er macht in der Regel von dem verfügbaren Licht Gebrauch. Für diese Aufnahme verwendete er eine Nikkormat FT3 mit 28 mm Objektiv und 1600 ASA Tri-X-Film, der in Neutol S entwickelt wurde.

63

TANZ von Andrej Krynicki

Dieser sehr vielseitige, produktive polnische Fotograf macht oft von Solarisation Gebrauch, um vertrauten Gegenständen eine fantastische Wirkung zu verleihen. Seine Ideen sind stets originell, und er verwertet die Figur auf künstlerische, schöpferische Weise, wie dies aus diesem Beispiel hervorgeht. Der Kontrast zwischen der Vitalität einer nackten Tänzerin und der Alltäglichkeit der Dächer ist anregend.

64

DREI NONNEN von Montserrat V. Barraquer

Fotografen nehmen gern Nonnen auf, doch ist es nicht leicht, eine so hervorragende Komposition wie diese zu erzielen. Mit einer Leicaflex SL mit 180 mm Objektiv auf dem Domplatz von Tarragona auf Tri-X-Film fotografiert und in Rodinal entwickelt.

65

MINU von Raghu Rai

Ein gut aufgebautes Porträt einer schönen indischen Fernseh-Ansagerin. Das Bild im Hintergrund ergibt eine interessante und gleichzeitig ungewöhnliche Komposition. Mit einer Nikkormat mit 85 mm Objektiv auf Tri-X-Film aufgenommen: 1/60 Sekunde bei Blende 5,6 und normalem Licht.

66

ZWEI KÜSSE von Vladimir Filinov

Diese Aufnahme stammt von einem der führenden Fotografen der Sowjetunion, der sich bereits seit vielen Jahren auf Linienfotografie spezialisiert. Der Hier dargestellte emotionale Augenblick wurde nicht zu sentimental behandelt, und das Insekt an der Wange des Mannes wirkt mysteriös.

67

SELBSTPORTRÄT von Vladimir Filinov

Aus der Sowjetunion erreichte uns eine riesige Anzahl von Fotografien, die zum Teil sehr fantasiereich und interessant waren. Eine der besten davon war dieses Porträt. Nicht nur ist der Grundgedanke hier klar, sondern er wurde mit erheblicher Kraft und Originalität zum Ausdruck gebracht. Ein Negativ wurde mit einer 6 x 7 cm Kamera und das andere mit einer 35 mm mit 2x-Unformer aufgenommen.

68

KEIN TITEL von Frantisek Dostal

Ein recht humorvolles Bild. Der Fotograf ging diesem Mann einige Zeit nach, bis er durch das Verkehrssignal aufgehalten wurde. Man sieht, wie nützlich es ist, wenn man stets eine Kamera mitführt. Aufgenommen mit einer Minolta SR-T303 mit 50 mm Objektiv auf Orwo NP20 und in A49 entwickelt. 1/250 Sekunde bei Blende 11.

69

KEIN TITEL von Mike Hollist

Eine amüsante Aufnahme, die natürlich wirkt, obgleich sie bestimmt geplant wurde. Sie zeigt, die Ankunft des neuen Hündchens der Fernseh-Schau "Blue Peter" bei der Ankunft zur Probe. Im Auftrag des DAILY MAIL mit einer Nikon mit 105 mm Objektiv auf Tri-X-Film aufgenommen und in D76 entwickelt. 1/250 Sekunde bei Blende 5,6.

70

LIEBE GREIFT UM SICH von Virender Mahajan

Zwei Pärchen im Tiergarten von Delhi gaben dem Künstler die Idee für die Botschaft, die das Bild zum Ausdruck bringt. Es zeigt, daß für den scharfen Beobachter in einem Tiergarten nicht nur die Tiere von Interesse sind. Mit einer Canon FX mit 400 mm Objektiv auf Orwo NP55 Film aufgenommen und in D76 entwickelt; 1/125 Sekunde bei Blende 5,6 in trübem Tageslicht.

71

LIEBE von L. B. Feresovi

Eines von einer Reihe wunderbar ausdrucksvoller Bilder, die menschliche Gefühle zum Ausdruck bringen. Viele Bilder dieser Art erreichten uns aus der Tschechoslowakei. Aufgenommen mit einer Minolta SRT mit 80-200 mm Zoom-Objektiv bei Tageslicht. Forma 21-Film, der in Metolpyrocatechin entwickelt wurde.

72/73

PREP SCHOOL von Frank Loughlin

Dieses Bild, das von einem Fotografen der LIVERPOOL DAILY POST aufgenommen wurde, gibt ein Begriff von einer "Preparatory School", wobei die Strohhüte für die privilegierte Mittelklasse nahezu symbolisch sind. Aufgenommen in einer Schule in Liverpool mit einer Nikon F mit 24 mm Objektiv auf Tri-X-Film unter Anwendung von reflektiertem Blitzlicht. Zur Entwicklung diente D76.

74

HÜTE AB VOR EINER DAME von Bill Carden, FRPS

Dieses entzückende Bild einer Dame, die alles, was sie auf Erden besitzt, in Einkaufstaschen mit sich führt, während sie die Straßen von London durchstreift, wurde während einer Jahresparade der Kavallerie im Hyde Park mit einer Mamiyaflex C330F mit 80 mm Objektiv auf HP4-Film aufgenommen. Zur Entwicklung diente ID11.

75

CYRIL SMITH, DAS GROSSE PARLAMENTSMITGLIED von Stephen Shakeshaft

Eine sehr natürliche Aufnahme eines prominenten Politikers während einer Konferenz, die ihre leichteren Augenblicke gehabt zu haben scheint. Der Künstler wurde zweimal mit der Auszeichnung "Photographer of the Year" bedacht und arbeitet im Dienste der Zeitung "LIVERPOOL DAILY POST AND ECHO". Bei normalen Licht mit einer Nikon F2 mit 28 mm Objektiv auf Tri-X-Film und in D76 entwickelt.

76

KONTRAST von Roland Herpin

Oft sieht nur ein Fremder, was es in unserem eigenen "Hinterhof" an Interessantem gibt. Hier haben wir ein gutes Beispiel für das "sehende Auge" eines französischen Fotografen, der Southampton besuchte. Mit einer Leica M5 mit 90 mm Objektiv auf Tri-X-Film aufgenommen. Der Kontrast wurde in der Dunkelkammer durch Abschatten auf Agfa BH111-5 Papier erzeugt.

77

WASSERKÜHLTURM von Wolfgang Volz

Ein 180 m hoher Wasserkühlturm in der Nähe eines Kernkraftwerks in der BRD hat diese dramatische industrielle Aufnahme ergeben, die dank den kräftigen Kontrasten im Ton und zwischen dem Turm und der winzigen Hütte auch künstlerisch wirkt. Aufgenommen mit einer Nikon F2 mit 55 mm Makro-Objektiv auf Tri-X-Film und in D76 entwickelt.

78

LA ARMISTAD von Josep Maria Ribas Prous

Typisch für die schönen Werke dieses führenden spanischen Fotografen, der in einer Schule für Fotografie als Lehrer tätig ist und das kulturelle Studium junger Fotografen organisiert. Seine Aufnahmen erscheinen in Fotomagazinen der ganzen Welt. Für dieses Bild machte er von einer Nikon F2 mit 28 mm Objektiv Gebrauch, und er entwickelte den Tri-X-Film in Microdol. Belichtungszeit 1/1000 Sekunde bei Blende 2.

79

BALLETT von Leslie E. Spatt

Zwei während der Vorführung selbst von einem Experten auf diesem sich spezialisierten Sektor aufgenommene Bilder. Das eine zeigt Richard Cragum vom Stuttgarter Ballett als Prinz Siegfried in *Schwanensee*, während ihn das andere mit Egon Madsen in *Lieder eines fahrenden Gesellen* darstellt. Aufgenommen mit einer Leica M3 und einem 90 mm Objektiv auf 100 ASA Tri-X und in Microdol entwickelt.

80

ALTER TÜRKE IN USKÜDAR von Jean Berner

Eine schöne, natürliche Charakterstudie mit einem starken Gefühl für Tiefe und Bewegung. Sie wurde mit Hilfe eines Weitwinkelobjektivs aus genügender Nähe aufgenommen, um eine stark verkürzte Perspektive zu erzielen. Aufgenommen im alten Viertel von Istanbul mit einer Nikkormat FT mit 20 mm Objektiv auf Tri-X-Film und in D76 entwickelt.

81

MUTTER von Ilmar Apkalns

Wie so viele Bilder aus der Sowjetunion behandelt diese Aufnahme ein uraltes Thema auf moderne, fantasiereiche Weise. Der Abstand zwischen Mutter und Kind, der durch die übertriebene Perspektive noch hervorgehoben wird, bringt die durch die ausgestreckten Hände angedeutete Sehnsucht zum Ausdruck. Der Lichtschein hinter der Mutter könnte eine noch tiefere Bedeutung haben.

82

LICHTEFFEKT von John P. Delaney, FRPS

Auf Derwentwater im englischen Seendistrikt aufgenommen bringt dieses Bild die während der Wintermonate in dieser Gegend vorherrschende Stimmung gut zum Ausdruck. Der Künstler bediente sich einer Rolleiflex f/3.5 und eines X2-Gelbfilters. Der Plus X Professional Film wurde in Microdol entwickelt. Belichtung 1/500 Sekunde bei Blende 4,5.

83

HÜTTE AM STRAND von Victor J. Attfield, FRPS

Die schlichte Form der Fischerhütte, die sich bei Durchbruch der Sonne durch den stürmischen Himmel vom Horizont abhebt, hat dieses dramatische Bild ergeben. Seetang im Vordergrund des Strandes verleiht der Komposition enorme Tiefe. Aufgenommen mit einer Nikkormat mit 28 mm Objektiv und Orangefilter auf Tri-X-Film. Zur Entwicklung diente D76.

84

FODOMODELLA SUB von Ferdinando Quaranta

Aufgenommen im Bereiche der Insel Ventotene bei Neapel in einer Tiefe von rund 10 m. Das Modell und der Fotograf wirkten an einem wissenschaftlichen Forschungsvorhaben über örtliche Fische mit. Dieser bekannte italienische Amateurfotograf verwendete eine Konica Autoreflex in einem Ikelite-Unterwassergehäuse mit einem 55 mm Objektiv. Ursprünglich auf Kodachrome 64 aufgenommen und dann auf Tri-X-Film kopiert.

85

HELD DES SKATEBOARD von Clive Harrison, FRPS

Eine schöne Aktionsaufnahme einer in Paddington befindlichen Skateboard-Arena, die von der Gemeinschaft für ortsansässige Kinder auf brachliegendem Gelände gebaut wurde. Olympus OM-1 mit 100 mm Zuiko-Objektiv und in ID11 entwickelter HP5-Film.

86

DIE KÖNIGIN AUF DEM DERBY von Mike Hollist

Jeder Pressefotograf versucht die Freude der Königin am Rennsport wiederzugeben, indem er ihre Gefühlsäußerungen - Vergnügen, Spannung oder Enttäuschung je nach dem Erfolg ihres Favoriten - erhascht. In diesem Bilde, das ihr zwar nicht schmeichelt, ist ohne Zweifel ein spannender Moment festgehalten. Eine Nikon-Kamera mit 1000 mm Objektiv und in D76 entwickelter Tri-X-Film.

87

RAUCHRING ALS HEILIGENSCHEIN? von Howard Walker

Ein recht humoristisches Bild, bei dem ein Amateurschauspieler die Rolle eines Priesters spielte. Es dauerte drei Stunden, bis der Rauchring die richtige Größe hatte und sich am richtigen Punkt befand! Aufgenommen mit einer Nikon F2 mit 85 mm Objektiv und Motorantrieb unter Anwendung von reflektiertem Blitz und Tri-X-Film.

88/89

BANK UND GOTTESHAUS von Cleland Rimmer

Der Fortschritt wird hier erfolgreich durch die Spiegelung älterer Architektur an einem modernen Gebäude symbolisiert. Die hübschen Polizistinnen wurden überredet, an dem Gebäude vorbeizugehen, um die Sicherheit der Bank, für die das Bild bestellt wurde, zu unterstreichen. Der Künstler ist Dozent für Fotografie des Hull College of Higher Education und er bediente sich einer 5 x 4 in. Speed Graphic mit 150 mm Objektiv und Gelbfilter. Der FP4-Film wurde in Autophen entwickelt; 1/60 Sekunde bei Blende 8.

WHEN YOU DEMAND THE VERY BEST
YOUR CHOICE IS SOMEWHAT LIMITED

LEICA R3
Single Lens Reflex Camera

In 35mm. cameras this is especially true. The best made 35mm. camera in the world is, and always has been, the legendary LEITZ Indisputably. And understandably. Because when LEITZ built their first LEICA (and in so doing introduced the technique of 35mm. photography) they had already been making some of the world's finest microscopes for close on a hundred years. Today, as well as LEICA cameras LEITZ also make projectors, enlargers, binoculars and of course microscopes and other advanced optical instruments. Each is the best of its kind the world has to offer.

LEICA R3-MOT
Single Lens Reflex
with Motor Winder.

LEITZ Pradovit C
Slide Projector.

LEICA M4–2
Rangefinder Camera
with Motor Winder.

LEITZ
Trinovid
Binoculars

LEITZ Focomat V35
Autofocus Enlarger

LEITZ
Trinovid
Compact
Binoculars

Available from specialist dealers throughout the U.K.
For literature and dealer address list please contact
E. Leitz (Instruments) Ltd., 48 Park Street, Luton, Beds. Tel: Luton 413811.

 Leitz means precision worldwide

90

CHRIS BARBER von Rudolf Bieri
Dieses Bild vermittelt einen guten Eindruck von dem berühmten Jazz- und Blues-Posaunisten und gibt auch die Stimmung gut zum Ausdruck, die in dem Kursaal Bern, wo es während einer Vorführung aufgenommen wurde, herrschte. Mit einer Leicaflex SL2 und einem Apo-Telyt 180 mm Objektiv auf Tri-X-Film bei verfügbarem Licht aufgenommen und 2 x 10 Min. bei 30°C in Tetanal Emofin entwickelt.

91

SAMMY DAVIS JNR.
von Erwin Kneidinger, EFIAP
Eine Aufnahme, die die Vitalität dieser dynamischen Persönlichkeit gut zum Ausdruck bringt. Die Stimmung wird durch das verfügbare Licht sowie die Körnung hervorgehoben. Aufgenommen mit einer Nikon F mit 105 mm Objektiv auf Tri-X-Film und in Neutrol entwickelt; 1/250 Sekunde bei Blende 2,5.

92

KEIN TITEL von J. R. Rudin
Farbige Menschen wissen gut, wie wertvoll Kontraste sind, und die Art und Weise, wie sich das weiße Kleidungsstück von der Haut abhebt, ist fantasiereich und gleichzeitig eine technische Tour de Force. Die Komposition ist originell – ja sogar kühn – aber außerordentlich geglückt. Der Künstler ist Besitzer einer westindischen Kunstgalerie und nahm das Bild mit einer Pentax auf 1600 ASA Tri-X bei Fensterlicht auf.

93

MAGNETISCHER BLICK von Virender Mahajan
Ein Porträt eines typischen alten "Momden Phase", das der Künstler auf seiner Reise in die indische Feststadt Garh-Ganga-Mela aufnahm. Er fotografierte von einem tiefgelegenen Punkte, um einen Hintergrund von weißem Himmel zu erzielen, der durch Kopieren auf hartem Papier noch hervorgehoben wurde. Die Kamera war eine Canon FX mit 50mm Objektiv, und er verwendete Orwo NP55-Film, den er in D76 entwickelte.

94 (oben)

KEINE HANDSIGNALE von Stanley Matchett
Ein jugendlicher Pony-Enthusiast, dem es offensichtlich nicht an Humor fehlt, hat dieses amüsante, in einer Reitschule in County Down aufgenommene Bild ermöglicht. Der Künstler ist im Auftrag von THE DAILY MIRROR in Belfast tätig. Aufgenommen mit einer Nikon F2 mit 80-200mm Objektiv auf in D76 entwickeltem HP5-Film; 1/250 Sekunde bei Blende 8.

94 (unten)

SCHAU, GANZ OHNE HÄNDE
von Stanley Matchett
Der junge Zauberkünstler Darren Swann (Alter zehn Jahre) führt unterstützt von Hilary Thompson mit Erfolg seinen ersten Levitationstrick aus. Dies ist eine unbearbeitete Aufnahme, die zeigt, wie gut der Trick ausgeführt wurde. Mit einer Nikon F2 mit 80-200 mm Objektiv bei Tageslicht auf HP5-Film aufgenommen.

95

PIERRE, DER CLOWN von Martyn Hayhow
Der Künstler, ein Mitarbeiter der Evening Post, hat die diesen Clown umgebende Stimmung eingefangen, der gerade Urlauber mit seinem "Wagen" unterhielt. Der künstlerische Wert dieses Bildes liegt auf der Hand. Aufgenommen mit einer Nikon F2 mit 70-210 Zoom-Objektiv auf HP5-Film, der in ID11 entwickelt wurde; 1/250 Sekunde bei Blende 8.

96

LIEBESPAAR von Wilhelm Mikhailovsky
In den letzten Jahren haben Fotografen aus der Sowjetunion erwiesen, daß sie sich meisterhaft darauf verstehen, menschliche Gefühle in modernem Zusammenhang zum Ausdruck zu bringen. Der kräftige Kontrast in der Tönung des Mannes bzw. des Mädchens betont seine Männlichkeit ihrer Weiblichkeit gegenüber. Diese Methode hat auch eine gute Komposition ergeben. Siehe auch Seiten 116 und 117.

97

KEIN TITEL von Michael Barrington Martin
Dieser bekannte Londoner Modefotograf experimentiert laufend mit neuen Ideen und benutzt großt Filmformate, die ihm die Verbindung von zwei oder mehr Bildern gestatten. Die Ergebnisse sind in der Regel überzeugend und künstlerisch, was schon daraus hervorgeht, daß seine Aufnahmen immer wieder in Kalendern und als Titelbilder von Zeitschriften zu sehen sind. Hier wurde eine gerasterte Schwarzweiß-Aufnahme vereinfachter Tönung wirksam mit einer unscharfen Schablonenaufnahme überlagert.

98

PIETRO ALBERTELLI von Tony Duffy
Eine spektakuläre Skiaufnahme von einem der führenden britischen Sportfotografen, der in einschlägigen britischen und internationalen Wettbewerben viele Preise gewonnen hat. Dieses Bild ist infolge des niedrigen Aufnahmepunkts und der tiefen Tönung des Himmels außerordentlich dramatisch. Es ist auch eine enorme technische Leistung, daß die Augen und das Gesicht hinter der Maske zu sehen sind und der Ton in den Glanzlichtern doch gewahrt wurde.

99

TENNISSPIELERIN von Leo Mason
Dieses ungewöhnliche Bild, das Virginia Wade in Aktion zeigt, wurde von einem sehr hochgelegenen Punkt oberhalb eines Tennisplatzes im Flushing Meadow Stadium in New York aufgenommen. Die Nikon F2 mit 200 mm Objektiv wurde zwei Wochen lang auf einem Spezialgestell in Position belassen, und die Blende wurde ferngesteuert. Der Film war Ektachrome Professional und die Belichtungszeit bei Blende 8 1/500 Sekunde.

100 (oben)

STEINE von Lars Oddvar Lovdahl
Bilder dieser Art sehen bei Projektion viel besser aus als bei Reproduktion, da die subtilen Brauntöne der herbstlichen Blätter betont werden. Die Verteilung der Pilze läßt erkennen, daß dieser als freiberuflicher Fotograf tätige Norweger ein gutes Gefühl für Komposition hat. Aufgenommen mit einer Nikon F2 mit 20 mm Objektiv auf Kodak Photomikrographiefilm 2483.

100 (unten)

MENSCHENMENGE von Nigel Stone
Von oben aufgenommene Menschenmengen ergeben in der Regel gute Farbmuster, können aber auch monoton wirken, wenn kein Brennpunkt des Interesses oder Kontrastes vorhanden ist. Ebenso wie bei dem darüber befindlichen Bild dient diesem Zwecke ein kräftiger roter Fleck an einem Manne, der eine strategische Position in der Bildfläche einnimmt und die anderen Menschen hoch zu überragen scheint.

101 (oben)

SEE IM MONDLICHT von Dr. A. Farquhar
Das Ergebnis der Überlagerung von zwei Diapositiven, von denen das eine eine kleine Jacht nach dem Sonnenuntergang auf Lake Okanagan, Britisch-Kolumbien, und das andere den Mond zeigt. Beide wurden mit einer Canon EF-Kamera auf Kodachrome 64 aufgenommen, das erste mit einem 100 mm und das zweite mit einem 400 mm Objektiv. Die Kamera war auf Automatik geschaltet, so daß keine Belichtungsdaten verfügbar sind. Endkopie auf Ektachrome 5071.

101 (unten)

GRABSTEIN von Mark Woolstencroft
Friedhöfe scheinen bei den Fotografen, die uns ihre Bilder dieses Jahr zustellten, beliebt zu sein. Diese Aufnahme ist aber bedeutend origineller und fantasiereicher als die meisten anderen eingereichten Fotografien. Das interessante Farbschema wird durch ein Muster von Punkten ergänzt, die das Auge zu dem Kreuz führen, so daß eine etwas ätherische Gesamtwirkung erzielt wird.

102/103

SEPTEMBERABEND IN MAILAND
von Trevor Fry, FRPS
Diese märchenhafte Aufnahme der Türme des Mailänder Doms wurde mit einer Leicaflex SL mit 90 mm Objektiv auf 160 ASA Ektachrome-Wolframfilm von einer gegenüberliegenden Treppe aus gemacht. Belichtungszeit etwa 1 Sekunde bei Blende 8. Die Reproduktion beruht auf einer Cibachrome-Kopie.

104

KALEIDOSKOP von C. H. J. Martin, LRPS
Reproduktion eines Originals, das sich aus acht identischen Kopien auf Kodak 37RC-Papier zusammensetzt. Ein fantasiereiches Konzept, das dem Künstler mehrere Preise eingetragen hat. Das ursprüngliche Kodacolor-Negativ wurde mit einer Pentax Spotmatic mit 55 mm Objektiv aufgenommen.

105

ST. THOMAS, ABOYNE von Francis Tocher Jr.
Die Stimmung, die das durch eine Scheibe aus buntem Glas strömende Licht erzeugt, wurde geschickt dadurch verstärkt, daß die Brennweite des Objektivs während einer Belichtungszeit von 30 Sekunden 25 Sekunden lang verändert wurde. Mit einer Nikkormat FT2 mit Tamron 70-150 mm Zoom-Objektiv bei Blende 11 auf Ektachrome 64 aufgenommen.

106

SELBSTPORTRÄT von Hektor Krome
Eine amüsante Nebeneinanderstellung von Gegenständen, die von einer gemalten Lieferwagentür widergespiegelt werden. Nicht nur ein Bild sondern auch ein Rätsel. Aufgenommen mit einer Olympus OM-2 mit 28 mm Objektiv und aufgrund einer Ektacolor-Kopie reproduziert.

107

MOSAIK 2 von A. R. Pippard, O.B.E., FRPS
Dies ist eine von mehreren versuchsweisen Kopien, bei denen Negative durch verschiedene farbige Siebe hindurch gedruckt wurden. Das Sieb für dieses Bild wurde durch Besprühen eines Stückes ausfixierten Films mit Farbstoff erzeugt. Der Künstler ist der prominente Chemiker, der Photocolour II und andere Farbverarbeitungsverfahren entwickelt hat.

108/109

MEHRFACHBELICHTUNG
Ein interessanter Versuch, bei dem ein holländischer Fotograf von einander überdeckenden Belichtungen und verschiedenen Filtern Gebrauch gemacht hat. Reproduziert aufgrund einer 10 x 8 Zoll Polaroid-Kopie.

110

SEINE KÖNIGLICHE HOHEIT PRINZ CHARLES
von Terry Fincher, FRPS
Eine ungewöhnlich spontane Aufnahme dieses beliebten Prinzen, die von einem der führenden britischen freiberuflichen Pressefotografen knapp vor Sonnenuntergang am Ufer des Negro in Manans erzielt wurde. Die Kamera war eine Olympus mit 28 mm Objektiv. 1/15 Sekunde bei Blende 5,6. Unter Anwendung von Blitzlicht auf Ektrachrome E6-film aufgenommen.

111 (oben)

TRANSVESTITEN von Alain Verdier
Ein augenfälliges Doppelporträt aus dem Buch "Messieurs, Mesdames", in dem sich der Künstler mit homosexuellen Persönlichkeiten der Bühnenwelt in allen Teilen der Welt befaßt. Manche sind traurig und manche lustig. Wie Alain Verdier, Der übrigens auch Musiker ist, berichtet, inspirierte ihn der Maler René Magritte bei diesem Werk. Aufgenommen mit einer Nikon F mit 20 mm Objektiv.

111 (unten)

WÖLFLINGTRÄUME
von Dr. M. D. Constable, ARPS
Eine Überlagerung von zwei mit einer Canon Ftb mit 80 mm Objektiv auf Agfa CT 18-Film aufgenommenen Dias. Das Bild zeigt den jüngeren Sohn des Fotografen, der ebenso wie sein älterer Bruder ein Mitglied der Wölflinge werden wollte. Dr. Constable meinte, dies könne der Gegenstand seiner Träume sein. Aufnahme bei Blitzlicht.

112

NEUROPOLIS von Luciano Pestarino, EFIAP
Ein Bild, bei dem alles von der für den Menschen in städtischer Umgebung kennzeichnenden Neurose spricht. Die symbolische Gestalt ist der Sohn des Künstlers, der während der Aufnahme in der Ecke eines Platzes in Buenos Aires stand. Mr. Pestarino ist ein Amateur, der zahlreiche Bilder in allen Teilen der Welt zur Schau stellt.

113

IAN SMITH von Rolf M. Aagaard
Aufgenommen auf dem Flughafen von Salisbury, als der rhodesische Ministerpräsident, nachdem er lange auf ein Visum gewartet hatte, im Begriffe war in die Vereinigten Staaten abzureisen. Ganz zufällig befand sich der Fotograf in dem gleichen Flugzeug, das von Johannesburg nach New York flog. Die Kamera war eine Nikon F2 mit 180 mm Objektiv und der Tri-X-Film wurde in D76 entwickelt.

114/115

BILDER von David Bailey, FRPS
Dieser weltbekannte Fotograf ist oft im Dienste führender Modezeitschriften tätig und arbeitet mit den besten Mannequins der Welt zusammen – etwas, worum ihn die meisten anderen Fotografen bestimmt beneiden. An seinen Techniken ist niemals das geringste auszusetzen, und er ist stets originell, ganz gleich ob er nach Kundenvorschrift oder nach eigenen Ideen arbeitet. Er lehnt herkömmliche Posen und Kompositionen mit großem Erfolg ab, wie diese beiden Aufnahmen zeigen. Begrenzung des Bildfeldes durch eine Gegenlichtblende würde weniger kühnen Fotografen als zu riskant erscheinen, und die wenigsten würden es wagen, solche häuslichen Gegenstände in ihre Aufnahmen einzubeziehen bzw. auf diese Weise zu behandeln.

116/117

PARALLEL von Wilhelm Michaelovsky
Eine außerordentlich wirksame Aufnahme eines russischen Meisters, deren Wirkung durch dramatische Perspektive, kräftige Kontraste und Körnung noch erhöht wurde. Die Ausdrücke auf den Gesichtern regen die Fantasie der Betrachter an, und die ganz ungewöhnliche Komposition bricht alle "Regeln" mit großem Erfolg. Siehe auch Seite 96.

118

IM SAFARIPARK WINDSOR von Mike Hollist
Tiere sind immer interessant, und dieses ungewöhnliche Treffen eines Zebras mit einer jungen Giraffe hat auch einen gewissen Humor. Aufgenommen mit einer Nikon und einem "Squeeze-Focus" 400 mm Objektiv, das den Hintergrund gewollt unscharf bietet. Tri-X-Film in D76 entwickelt. 1/500 Sekunde bei Blende 5,6.

119

SOHN UND TIERE von Andrew McGlynn
Haustiere sind sehr ansprechend und dieser rührende Augenblick wurde von dem irischen Fotografen gut wiedergegeben. Die Beziehung zwischen den einzelnen Mitgliedern der Gruppe ist offensichtlich, und infolge des Gegenlichts hebt sie sich gut vom Hintergrund ab. Aufgenommen mit einer Leica M4 mit 50 mm Objektiv auf in Rodinal entwickeltem FP4. 1/125 Sekunde bei Blende 5,6.

120

EIN ALTER FRANZOSE
von E. Chambre Hardman
Eine gefühlvolle Studie eines führenden Liverpooler Berufsfotografen, die sich übrigens durch hervorragende Güte der Kopie auszeichnet. Aufgenommen mit einer "Quarter Plate"-SLR-Kamera mit 6 " Tessar-Objektiv auf Super XX Film; 1/100 Sekunde bei Blende 8.

121

HOCHMÜTIGES MÄDCHEN
von Vlastislav Machacek
Eine recht ungewöhnliche Pose, die wohl die Schwangerschaft des Mädchens betonen soll, obgleich diese zunächst nicht ins Auge fällt. Wie so viele Aufnahmen aus der Tschechoslowakei liegt die ganze Betonung auf der "Durchschlagkraft" der Botschaft, während Probleme der Körnung, Linienführung und traditionellen Darstellung außer acht gelassen sind. Das Gegenlicht hat einen außerordentlich wirksamen Lichtscheineffekt zur Folge.

122/123

FUSSBALL IN EDGE HILL von John Davidson
Dieses von einem führenden Fotografen der *Liverpool Daily Post* aufgenommene Bild gibt einen Begriff davon wie selbst die Kinder bereits den Fußballsport lieben. Eine gepflasterte Straße in einem verfallenen Bereich, ein alter Ball und ein paar Ziegel – das ist alles, was sie am Anfang ihres Weges nach Wembley brauchen! Aufgenommen mit einer Nikon F mit 28 mm Objektiv auf in D76 entwickeltem Tri-X-Film. Belichtungszeit 1/60 Sekunde bei Blende 3,5.

124

HOCHZEIT von Hans-Jorge Anders
Dieses für die Zeitschrift *Stern* aufgenommene Bild zeigt die Teilnehmer an einer mennonitischen Hochzeit in Paraguay. Es gehört einer Reihe von Bildern an, die diesen Gegenstand behandeln, und bringt die Vitalität der verschiedenen Personen gut zum Ausdruck. Die Kamera war eine Leicaflex SL2 mit 19 mm Objektiv, und es wurde Tri-X-Film verwendet.

125

NACH HAUSE von Leon Balodis
Eine einfache ländliche Hochzeit in einem sowjetischen Dorf wurde hier gut erfaßt. Die der Braut vorauseilenden Gäste und Zuschauer erzeugen viel Bewegung. Die Braut, der Brennpunkt des Interesses, hebt sich von dem dramatischen Himmel ab. Dieses Bild ist ganz allgemein interessant, besonders vom Standpunkt ausländischer Betrachter.

126

KEIN TITEL von Francisco Aszmann
Ein Bild, das keinen Titel erfordert, da alles darin vom "Frühling" zeugt. Dank dem Gegenlicht bilden die Blüten einen prominenten Rahmen, und gleichzeitig wurden die dem Thema gemäße Tiefe und Leuchtkraft erzielt. Obgleich die Aufnahme in Brasilien gemacht wurde, könnte sie ebenso gut aus anderen Teilen der Welt stammen.

127

GÄNSEMARSCH von Bernhard Heinz
Ein auf der Photokina gezeigtes Bild, das in dem für deutsche Zeitungsleser veranstalteten Wettbewerb "Blende", in dessen Rahmen mehr als 30 000 Bilder eingereicht wurden, einen Preis erhielt. Es ist dies eine hervorragende Komposition, die sich durch kunstvolle Abstufung der Töne auszeichnet. Aufgenommen auf FP4-Film.

128

NATUR UND SCHÖNHEIT
von Mogens Lerche Madsen
Von dem Negativ eines Baumes wurde auf lithographischem Film ein Positiv hergestellt, das unter leichter Abschwächung der Bildkonturen auf die Rückansicht des Modells projiziert wurde. Aufgenommen mit einer Leica mit Summicron-Objektiv auf HP4 und in Rodinal entwickelt.

129

SUSANNE von Jozef Tichy
Aktstudien waren dieses Jahr nicht so stark vertreten, doch dies ist ein sehr gutes Beispiel im traditionellen Stil aus der Tschechoslowakei. Obgleich der Reiz dieser Aufnahme weitgehend durch die Schönheit des Modells bedingt ist, hat auch das sanfte Licht vom Fenster viel beigetragen, und die zurückhaltende Behandlung wirkt angenehm. Aufgenommen mit einer Pentacon Sechs mit Biometer-Objektiv auf in Atomal entwickeltem Orwo 20-Film. 1/15 Sekunde bei Blende 8.

130

MR. LINCOLN, NEHME ICH AN
von Achim Sperber
Ein Bild eines Hamburger Fotografen, das der Reihe "New York – Up and Down" angehört. Aufgenommen mit einer Pentax mit 85-210 mm Zoom-Objektiv auf in D76 entwickeltem Tri-X-Film. 1/500 Sekunde bei Blende 4.

131

WÄHREND DER KONFERENZ
von Stephen Shakeshaft
Dieses während einer Konferenz aufgenommene Bild zeigt einen Politiker in nachdenklicher Stimmung. Der Fotograf (siehe auch Seite 75) ist heute einer der erfolgreichsten britischen Foto-Journalisten und hat alle Rekorde gebrochen, denn dies ist das siebente "Photography Year Book", in dem seine Aufnahmen erscheinen. Nikon F2 mit 28 mm Objektiv; Tri-X-Film.

132

FAMILIENPORTRÄT von Martin Wolin Jr.
Das Bild zeigt, wie sich der Aufnahmegegenstand durch Hintergrundnebel herausstellen läßt. Die drei Kühe scheinen fast Modell zu stehen, während die Bäume und der Pfosten ein rhythmisches Echo bilden. Aufgenommen mit einer Minolta XE7 mit 50 mm Objektiv auf Plus X Film und in Rodinol entwickelt; 1/60 Sekunde bei Blende 8.

133

AUF SKIERN von Vladimir Filinov
Ein Objektiv mit kurzer Brennweite und Tontrennung haben diesem Bild eine sehr starke, nahezu aggressive Wirkung verliehen. Die Komposition ist interessant, und die kleine Figur im Hintergrund spielt darin eine große Rolle – etwa wie das Insekt in dem Bild auf Seite 66. Mit einer 35 mm Kamera mit Weitwinkelobjektiv auf 300 ASA Film aufgenommen.

134

GÄHNEN von Pak Nin Yam
Diese Aufnahme, die für viele aus dem Fernen Osten zugesandte eindrucksvolle Fotografien von Kindern typisch ist, hatte erheblichen Erfolg und wurde im Londoner Salon zur Schau gestellt. Ohne Zweifel haben die zurückhaltende Behandlung und die interessante Komposition einen Beitrag geleistet, doch darf auch die hervorragende Güte der Kopie des Originals nicht übersehen werden.

135

BLOW-UP von Kin-Pong Chan
Ebenso wie das vorhergehende Bild aus Singapur ist diese Aufnahme aus Hongkong traditionell aber so lebhaft und gut ausgeführt, daß sie ebenfalls im Salon zur Ausstellung gelangte. Das über das Gesicht gewehte Haar verleiht eine ungewöhnliche Note, und das Original in kräftiger Glanzausführung vermittelt einen Eindruck großer Vitalität.

136/137

WORTGEFECHT von Don McPhee
In unseren Tagen industrieller Zwietracht ist dies ein nur zu vertrauter Anblick. Der für die Zeitung "Guardian" tätige Fotograf hat genau den richtigen Augenblick erfaßt. Diese Szene spielte sich vor der Autofabrik Chrysler ab, als Frauen versuchten, einen Streik zu beenden. Die Kamera war eine Minolta SRT 101 mit 28 mm Objektiv und der FP4-Film wurde in Microphen entwickelt.

138

GESICHT EINES HAUSES von W. H. Gratt

Eine einfache, gut geglückte Aufnahme dieses deutschen Künstlers. Der Aufnahmepunkt wurde sorgfältig gewählt, um eine gut ausgeglichene Komposition zu erzielen, die dank ihrer schlichten Linienführung und einem Mindestmaß an Detail anspricht. Aufgenommen mit einer Bronica 6x6 mit 50 mm Objektiv auf in HC110 entwickeltem Plus-X-Film. 1/60 Sekunde bei Blende 8.

139

KIRCHENDACH von Arthur Perry

Die Einfachheit der Linienführung und Form, die durch die kräftigen Kontraste und den gut gewählten Aufnahmepunkt bedingt ist, hat diesem in Kalifornien aufgenommenen Kirchendach eine künstlerisch starke Wirkung verliehen. Aufgenommen mit einer Rolleiflex 3,5 mit gelbgrünem Filter auf FP4-Film; 1/60 Sekunde bei Blende 16.

140

NACH DEM GEWITTER von Ilmars Apkalns

Eine außerordentlich dramatische Landschaftsaufnahme aus der Sowjetunion, die sich durch wagnerische Stimmung auszeichnet. Die durch das Licht hervorgehobenen Felsbrocken bilden einen passenden Vordergrund für den stürmischen, von Sonnenlicht durchbrochenen Himmel.

141

FELSIGE LANDSCHAFT von Asko Salmi

Diese Landschaftsaufnahme, die auf der Insel Norrskär an der Westküste von Finnland gemacht wurde, ist für die robuste Einstellung der jüngeren Generation von Amateurfotografen typisch. Diese dramatische Aufnahme mit ihren kräftigen Tönen wurde unter Anwendung eines Weitwinkelobjektivs erzielt. Canon AE-1 mit 20 mm Objektiv und Rotfilter. Der Tri-X-Film wurde in D76 entwickelt.

142

DIANE von Ian Stewart

Eine Aufnahme von Diane Minchin, einem professionellen Modell, die von einem freiberuflichen australischen Fotografen gemacht wurde. Eine herausfordernde Pose im Fenster eines verlassenen Bauernhofs, was zusätzlich zu dem tonalen einen thematischen Kontrast bedingt. Hasselblad 500 mit 150 mm Objektiv; Tri-X Film in D76 entwickelt.

143

KEIN TITEL von George W. Martin Jr.

Ein augenfälliges Profilporträt eines professionellen Modells von einem New Yorker Atelierfotografen, das sich im Original durch besondere Leuchtkraft auszeichnete. Mit einer Nikon mit 105 mm Objektiv bei Wolframlicht auf Plus X Film aufgenommen und in D76 entwickelt. Die Kopie war auf Poly-Contrast-Papier und wurde in Dektol entwickelt.

144

KINGS ROAD von Harm Botam

Der holländische Fotograf nahm dieses Bild auf, als er die berühmte Straße in Chelsea, London, besuchte, wo Lord Snowdon einige lebensgroße Anschläge an einer Mauer außerhalb eines Theaters hatte. Aufgenommen mit einer Rollei 35 auf 800 ASA Tri-X-Film, der in Promicrol entwickelt wurde.

145

KEIN TITEL von David Burrows, AIIP

Diese Aufnahme, deren Thema eine Snooker-Partie ist, stammt von einem jungen Fernseh-Standfotografen. Die Komposition ist sehr gut, und das Einblenden der weniger prominenten Personen in einen dunklen Hintergrund ist interessant. Mit einer Hasselblad und 150 mm Objektiv auf Ilford FP4 aufgenommen. Beleuchtung durch ein auf die Person in der Mitte gerichtetes Blitzlicht.

146

HENLEY ROYAL REGATTA von Steve Hartley

Der Reverend Gillen W. Craig, Hilfspfarrer der St. Marks Church in der Old Marylebone Road in London, bietet dem Wetter auf typisch britische Art die Stirn, denn er ist entschlossen, die traditionell eduardische Stimmung dieser dem Rudersport alljährlich geweihten Woche aufrechtzuerhalten. Aufgenommen mit einer Nikkormat mit 85 mm Objektiv auf HP5-Film. Dieser wurde in ID11 entwickelt; 1/250 Sekunde bei Blende 5,6.

147

KEIN TITEL von Michael Gnade

Ein hübsches Kinderbild, das wegen des hohen Aufnahmepunktes und der übermütigen Art und Weise, wie das Kind blickt und steht, von Interesse ist. Es gehört einer Reihe ausgezeichneter unerwarteter Schnappschüsse an, die dieser bayerische Lehrer in einem Buche veröffentlicht hat.

148

LONDON SPEAKER von Vladimir Birgus

Aus einer in London aufgenommenen Bildreportage eines Lehrers für Kunstfotografie in Prag. Er hat den Höhepunkt eines hitzigen Zwiegesprächs zwischen einem religiösen Sprecher und einem Zuhörer erhascht. Aufgenommen mit einer Pentax Spotmatic mit 28 mm Objektiv auf in Formadon N entwickeltem Orwo NP27 Film.

149

TEDDY BOY von Ricardo Gomez Perez

Dieses Bild wurde in Crystal Palace von einem Studenten des London College of Printing aufgenommen, der durch Ausstellung seiner Werke und verschiedene Veröffentlichungen bereits in mehreren Ländern bekannt ist. Es gehört der Sammlung "Teddy Boys" an. Die Kamera war eine Leica CL mit 40 mm Objektiv, und der Tri-X-Film wurde in D76 entwickelt.

150

KEIN TITEL von Alberto H. Jordé

Porträts in hellen Bildtönen erzielen in der Regel eine auf der zarten Tönung beruhende reizvolle Wirkung. Bei grober Körnung sind sie jedoch selten erfolgreich. Dieses Beispiel aus Spanien bildet eine Ausnahme, und die Pose sowie die Streifen am unteren Ende des Bildes verleihen diesem Stimmung und Bedeutung. Aufgenommen mit einer Leica mit 35 mm Objektiv auf Tri-X-Film. 1/100 Sekunde bei Blende 8.

151

DER WÄCHTER von John Williams

Diese Aufnahme wurde von einem australischen Fotografen während eines Besuches des Louvre in Paris gemacht. Was den Künstler besonders interessierte, war die anscheinende Gleichgültigkeit des Wächters dem unbezahlbaren Gemälde der Mona Lisa und den Zuschauern gegenüber, die rings um ihn von verbotenen Blitzlichtern Gebrauch machten. Olympus OM-1 mit 35 mm Objektiv; Belichtungszeit 1/60 Sekunde bei Blende 2 auf Tri-X-Film; Entwicklung in Acufine.

152/153

FRÖHLICHE KINDERZEIT von Tsang-Chi Yen

Die grosse Anzahl eingesandter Bilder beweisen, dass Taiwan sich als aktives Zentrum für Amateurfotografen im Fernen Osten entwickelt und diese Aufnahme ist ein gutes Beispiel. Die Vitalität dieser reizenden Kinder wird durch die Tiefe der Blickpunkte betont und der Himmel wirkt dadurch als schlichter Hintergrund. Das Festhalten des Händeklatschens ist ein Meisterstück. Aufgenommen mit einer Minolta SR 101 auf TX 125 Film 1/125 Sekunde auf F-11.

154

SZENE IM SCHNEE von W. Biggs

Die Chiltern Hills bieten dem künstlerischen Landschaftsfotografen manche Möglichkeit. Hier haben wir eine schöne Komposition, die die Hecken als die Schneelandschaft kontrastiert. Mit einer Mamiyaflex mit 180 mm Objektiv auf FP4-Film aufgenommen und in ID11 entwickelt.

155

BLANC-GLETSCHER von Vera Weinerstrova

Ein Bild, das sich dank der Wahl eines tiefgelegenen Aufnahmepunkts durch große Räumlichkeit und Tiefe auszeichnet. Die der Szene eigene Drohung ist hervorgehoben, und die dunklen Konturen des Gletschers führen das Auge in die Ferne dem dramatischen Himmel zu. Aufgenommen mit einer Praktisix mit 50 mm Objektiv auf Orwo NO 20-Film. 1/125 Sekunde bei Blende 16.

156

AKTSTUDIE von Valdis Brauns

Eine Aktstudie im traditionellen, nahezu veralteten Stil, die insofern ungewöhnlich ist, als anstelle der hellen Bildtöne, die einst für Atelierstudien kennzeichnend waren, von kühnen Tönen Gebrauch gemacht wurde. Die Linien des Schals kontrastieren auf interessante Weise mit den Konturen der Arme.

157

IM WALDE von Andrej Krynicki

Diese Aktstudie gehört einer Reihe von Freiluft-Studien an, die dieser produktive polnische Künstler eingereicht hat (siehe auch Seite 157). Im vorliegenden Falle hat jedoch keine Solarisation oder Vereinfachung stattgefunden. Wie alle seine Bilder ist auch dieses originell, und das Gegenlicht (nicht des Licht am Rücken) bedingt eine ansprechend leuchtende Wirkung.

158

RATHAUS TORONTO von Jean Bernier

Eine recht ungewöhnliche Behandlung einer architektonischen Studie — sie erinnert an eine gewisse Schule der Malerei bei der die schlichte Linienführung betont ist. Die Kontraste des Alten und des Neuen sind interessant, und das Kind verleiht dem Bild Maßstab und Tiefe. Mit einer Nikkormat FT mit 105 mm Objektiv auf Tri-X-Film aufgenommen. Der Film wurde in D76 entwickelt.

159

KRAFTWERK NEUSEELAND von P. G. Gale

Eine schöne industrielle Aufnahme, bei der den mächtigen Schornsteinen durch Wahl eines niedrigen Aufnahmepunktes und eines senkrechten Formats ein Effekt großer Höhe verliehen wurde. Dies ist eine beachtliche Leistung, wenn man bedenkt, daß der Künstler ohne Höhenverstellung gearbeitet hat. Die kühnen Kontraste und der Rauch schaffen eine authentische Stimmung. Aufgenommen mit einer Exa 11 mit 50 mm Objektiv auf in Microphen entwickeltem Adox KB21-Film.

160

DIREKTOR von Jiri Horak

Ein anregendes Bild, das den aggressiven "Direktor" mit einem industriellen Hintergrund kontrastiert. Wie auch immer der Betrachter die Kombination sowie die geballte Faust interpretiert, — er kann die Aufnahme, deren Komposition so künstlerisch ist, nicht übersehen. Petri Ft mit 28 mm Objektiv auf in Atomal entwickeltem Orwo 27-Film.

PHILIPS

No, we didn't have outside help in designing our new enlarger.

All our own work.

The revolutionary electronic Tri-One colour enlarger system from Philips. The sophisticated result of combining our expertise in two separate fields – those of electronics and lighting. First, there's the PCS130 enlarger. A rugged, all metal enlarger which handles everything from 6×7cm to 110 negatives. There's a universal negative carrier and lens mount for 80mm and 50mm lenses with M39 thread (lens not supplied). Also, there is a special condenser set for 6×7cm negatives and a replaceable lower condenser for formats below 35mm amongst the optional extras.

Now you simply add the PCS150 Tri-One Colour System to build an enlarger unit which is so far ahead of its rivals that it's almost out in space. The Tri-One is a unique colour source which replaces the standard enlarger lamp in the PCS130, operated by an electronic console on your workbench. Because it's electronic, there are no moving parts. Neither is there heat instability in the enlarger head, nor a need for filter adjusting.

Colour balance is obtained by the remote control of three lamps with narrow-cut dichroic primary filters, which means there are no unwanted absorptions. The Tri-One system is voltage stabilised, has a low operating voltage and even includes a built in exposure timer. In short, the Philips Tri-One is way ahead of its time.

And although the results are almost out of this world, the price isn't. The PCS130 enlarger is £168, and the PCS150 colour system is £182 – a down-to-earth total of £350 for the complete system.

Photomakers

Bring new precision
to your photo performance.

For full details and the address of your nearest dealer, write to: Philips Lighting, FREEPOST, City House, 420–430 London Road, Croydon CR9 ET

161

WHEELIE von Peter Gant, ARPS

Eine dramatische Aktionsstudie, die durch eine geringe Verschlußgeschwindigkeit besonders betont wurde. Diese Aufnahme gehört einer Reihe an, mit der der Künstler die AP-Auszeichnung "Sports Photographer of the Year" gewann. In Skate City, London, mit einer Olympus OM-1 mit 200 mm Objektiv aufgenommen; 1/15 Sekunde, Kodachrome 64.

162 (oben)

**IN BESCHWINGTEM FLUGE
von Gordon Ratcliffe**

Eine ausgezeichnete Aufnahme eines Drachenfliegers, die im Penninischen Gebirge gemacht wurde. Der Drachen ist ein "Sunspot" und der Flieger Len Gabriels. Mit einer Pentax Spotmatic mit 200 mm Objektiv und Kristallfilter auf Kodachrome 64 aufgenommen; 1/125 Sekunde bei Blende 11.

162 (unten)

KEIN TITEL von David R. MacAlpine

Eine Landschaft, die deutlich erweist, daß dramatische Beleuchtung in Farbe ebenso wirksam ist wie in Schwarz/Weiß und einer gewöhnlichen Landschaft eine dramatische Stimmung verleihen kann. Pentax SIA mit 55 mm Objektiv auf Kodachrome II: 1/125 Sekunde bei Blende 5,6.

163 (oben)

TURBULENZ von John L. Cawthra

Dieses Bild soll einen Eindruck von der Raumfahrt der Zukunft vermitteln. Es beruht auf der Überlagerung eines durch den Boden einer Milchflasche auf Agfa CT21 fotografierten Dias mit dem Bild eines Drachenfliegers, das mit einer Canon AT1 mit 135 mm Objektiv auf Fuji 100 aufgenommen wurde.

163 (unten)

IM ANDENKEN BEWAHRT von Tony Howard

Spät an einem Mittsommerabend auf einem englischen Friedhof aufgenommen, als sich die Sonne in dem Marmor des Kreuzes spiegelte. Die Kamera war eine Nikkormat FTN mit 50 mm Objektiv und der Ektachrome X Film wurde 1/30 Sekunde bei Blende 5,6 belichtet. Entwicklung durch eine fotografische Firma.

164/165

MOTOR CROSS von Woot Gilhuis

Eine dynamische Aktionsaufnahme des Verfassers von *"Between sharp and unsharp"*, das von Argus Books Ltd. veröffentlicht wurde. Woot ist freiberuflicher Fotograf und ein führendes Mitglied des Holländischen Verbandes der Berufsfotografen. Aufgenommen mit einer Canon F1 mit 400 mm Objektiv auf Kodachrome 64-Film. Die Bewegung wurde durch Schwenken der Kamera während 1/8 Sekunde angedeutet.

166

KEIN TITEL von Patrick Lichfield

Dieses Porträt der Herzogin von Roxburghe und der Gräfin von Lichfield wurde für "Vogue" aufgenommen und wird mit freundlicher Genehmigung von Condé Nast wiedergegeben. Die angenehme originelle Haltung ist für zwei Schwestern geeignet, und der sensitive Gebrauch der Farbe in hohem Ton ist außerordentlich künstlerisch. Aufgenommen mit einer Olympus OM-2 und Ektachrome-Film.

167

CARON von James Elliott

Ein Porträt, das durch eine schöne Kombination von perfekt abgestimmten Pastellfarben Liebreiz und künstlerische Wirkung erzielt. Der hochgehaltene Kopf stellt die Würde des Modells heraus. Aufgenommen mit einer 35 mm Kamera mit 70-210 mm Zoom-Objektiv auf Ektachrome-Film und mit einem elektronischen Blitzgerät beleuchtet.

168

**WAGEN DURCH GERILLTES GLAS
von John F. Percy**

Ein Bild aus einer Reihe, die die Welt zeigt, wie sie durch eine 22 cm breite Scheibe aus gerilltem Glas in der Straßentür des Künstlers wirkt. Der Wagen befand sich auf der anderen Straßenseite, und die Olympus OM-1 mit 50 mm Objektiv und 2x Komura-Umformer wurde daher auf Blende 16 eingestellt. Der Film war Kodachrome 64.

169

KEIN TITEL von D. J. Bellham

Eine ungewöhnliche Aufnahme, die durch Doppelbelichtung des gleichen Bildes einer Landschaft bei Sonnenuntergang und einer gewellten schwarzen Fläche im Abendlicht erzielt wurde. Das Ergebnis erinnert ein wenig an einen japanischen Fächer. Aufgenommen mit einer Canon EF mit 50 mm Objektiv auf Kodachrome 25.

170

PORTRÄT von Rey Williamson

Die planmäßig verzerrte Perspektive wurde dadurch erzielt, daß der Fotograf, dessen Kamera mit einem normalen Objektiv ausgestattet war, ganz nahe an das Modell herantrat. Dadurch wird eine drückende, ja vielleicht enigmatische Stimmung herausgestellt, die der Künstler als "Sicht durch das Auge eines Malers" beschreibt. Aufgenommen bei reflektiertem Blitzlicht und Blende 5,6 auf Kodachrome 25 Film. Die Kamera war eine Contax RTS mit 50 mm Objektiv.

171

PORTRÄT von K. Amil

Ein Bild, in dem die Komposition der Farben vorherrscht und der Künstler durch Konzentration auf den Turban und nicht ein einfaches Porträt künstlerische Einsicht an den Tag legt. Die übrigen Farben schaffen Harmonie ohne störend zu wirken.

172/173

TRISUL von Frank Martin, FIIP

Dieses Bild des 7 134 m hohen Berges im Himalaja-Gebirge zeigt eine durch einen rückläufigen Gletscher gebildete Moräne. Es wurde von einem Berufsfotografen aufgenommen, der seinen Urlaub in den Bergen verbrachte. Er benutzte eine Petri TTL Kamera mit 70-230 mm Zoom-Objektiv und Kodachrome 64 Film.

174 (oben)

PORTRÄT von C. Nutman

Es ist heute annehmbar, gewisse Farbaufnahmen mit Hilfe von Farbfiltern auszufärben, vorausgesetzt daß ihr Gebrauch etwas zu der Stimmung beiträgt. In diesem Falle hat die Wärme in Verbindung mit dem Effekt eines Sonnenuntergangs, der durch – differenziertes Ändern der Hintergrund-Brennweite während der Belichtung erzielt wurde, ein künstlerisches Porträt ergeben.

174 (unten)

KEIN TITEL von Joan Wakelin, FRPS

Die Künstlerin die in Sambia und Sri-Lanka weit gereist ist, um Fotoreportagen über die ortsansässige Bevölkerungen zu machen, hat hier ein Thema in einem Hintergarten in Sheffield gefunden. Aufgenommen mit einer Pentax SV mit 28 mm Objektiv auf Agfa CT18. Reproduktion einer Cibachrome-Kopie.

175

VISI N von Dr. Surendra Sahai

Ein interessantes "Sandwich" von zwei Dias, von denen das eine Feuerwerke und das andere Sonnenanbeter am Konorak-Strande in Indien darstellt. Die Kombination ergibt ein Bild, das die Fantasie anregt. Es wurde bei beiden Aufnahmen von einer Pentax SPII-Kamera und Kodachrome 64 Film Gebrauch gemacht. Eine Kopie wurde auch auf Kodak Special-Film gemacht.

176

PORTRÄT von Maurice Braun

Ein sehr ansprechendes Kinderporträt, das infolge des zurückhaltenden Farbschemas und des dunklen Hintergrunds ein wenig wie ein Gemälde wirkt. Dieses Bild gehörte einer hervorragenden Sammlung großer Porträt-Aufnahmen an, die auf dem Kodak-Stand auf der Photokina gezeigt wurde. Siehe auch Seite 34.

177

MODELLPUPPE von Carlos Canovas

Eine lebensnahe Wiedergabe eines Kunststoffgesichts, bei der die Körnung ein Gefühl von Fleisch und Blut vermittelt. Der Realismus und die kräftige dreidimensionale Wirkung sind durch die kühne Komposition und die Nahaufnahme hervorgehoben. Aufgenommen mit einer Nikon F2 mit 135 mm Objektiv auf Tri-X-Film, der in HC100 entwickelt wurde.

178

Eine ausdrucksvolle Studie, bei der eine künstlerische Interpretation der menschlichen Form die Grundlage eines wirksamen Designs bildet. Aufgenommen mit einer Nikkormat FTN mit 28 mm Objektiv auf 1600 ASA Tri-X-Film und in Neutol S entwickelt.

179

AKTSTUDIE von Hideki Fujii

Eine Studie, die die für alle japanische Kunst charakteristische Individualität bietet. Diese beruht zum Teil auf der sehr ungewöhnlichen Pose – das Modell scheint im Raume zu schweben – und teilweise auf der Maske.

180

LANDSCHAFT von Signe Drevsjo

Zwei hübsche Landschaftsaufnahmen aus Norwegen, von denen die obere in Gimsoy in den Lofoten Inseln aufgenommen wurde. Die besonders interessante Wolkenformation weist in die Ferne und verleiht dem Bild eine starke Tiefenwirkung. Die untere Aufnahme ergibt eine sehr gute Komposition. In beiden Fällen wurde von einer Canon F1 mit Rotfilter Gebrauch gemacht. Der Tri-X-Film wurde in D76 entwickelt. Für die obere Ansicht bediente sich der Künstler eines 17 mm Objektivs, während das entere Bild mit einem 50 mm Makro-Objektiv aufgenommen wurde.

181

**GEHEIMNISVOLLE BURG von
Vera Weinerstrova**

Heute ist die Anwendung eines Weitwinkelobjektivs für Landschaftsaufnahmen in Verbindung mit einem kühnen Objekt im Vordergrund sehr modern. In Verbindung mit einer kräftigen und kontrastreichen Behandlung der Töne sowie reichlicher Körnung und sattem Schwarz ist diese Methode ohne Zweifel eindrucksvoll, wie dies auch aus diesem Bilde hervorgeht. Die Kamera war eine Praktisix und der Film Orwo NP20.

182

TAUCHER von Mervyn Rees, FRPS

Dieses wunderbare Aktionsbild wurde während einer Trainingssitzung für die Commonwealth-Spiele im Crystal Palace, London, aufgenommen. Die Kamera war eine Nikon F2 mit 50 mm Objektiv und der Tri-X-Film wurde in D76 entwickelt. Belichtungszeit 1/250 Sekunde bei Blende 3,5.

183

KARIN FITZNER von Mervyn Rees

Eine dramatische Aufnahme einer Athletin in der DDR beim Kugelstoßen. Die Körnung, die beim "Quälen" von hochempfindlichem Film unvermeidlich ist, trägt zu dem Gefühl von Kraft und Kraftaufwand bei, während die ausgeprägte Diagonale auf Bewegung hindeutet. Nikon F2 mit 500 mm Objektiv. 1/1000 Sekunde bei Blende 8 auf Tri-X-Film.

184

FLÜGELSTADT von Jiri Horak

Eine für die fantasiereichen Bilder aus der Tschechoslowakei typische Aufnahme. Was die Grundidee anbelangt, besteht eine gewisse Ähnlichkeit mit der auf Seite 160 wiedergegebenen Fotografie des gleichen Künstlers. In beiden Fällen ist die Behandlung sehr orignell. Die Kamera war eine Petri FT mit 28 mm Objektiv und das Bild wurde auf Orwo NP27 aufgenommen und in Atomal entwickelt. Belichtungszeit 1/125 Sekunde.

185

EDDY BOYD von Reijo Porkka

Den Künstler sprach die durch das Gegenlicht bedingte interessante Kontur an. Er unterstrich sie mit Erfolg durch Tonvereinfachung und erzielte eine intensive Wiedergabe der Nachtklubatmosphäre. Aufgenommen mit einer Nikon mit 50 mm Objektiv auf 1600 ASA Tri-X-Film.

186

KEIN TITEL von Jim Barker

Viele hätten diese amüsante Situation übersehen, die durch den Kontrast zwischen dem Mädchen auf dem Plakat und der Dame auf dem Sitz erzielt war. Man sieht, wie wichtig es ist, stets bewußt zu schauen und nie ohne Kamera auszugehen. Aufgenommen mit einer Hasselblad auf FP4-Film, der in Unitol entwickelt wurde.

187

ARBEITSLOS von E. Chambré Hardman

Eine schöne Industriestudie, die einen alten Dampfkessel in einer Zeche in Wales zeigt. Aufgenommen mit einer Rolleiflex auf HP3-Film. Das Negativ wurde auf Ilford Fine Grain Ordinary Film vergrößert, um ein Diapositiv zu erzielen, das dann auf hartem Bromsilberpapier kopiert wurde.

188

HYDE PARK von F. Russell, FIIP, FRPS

Aus einer Bildreportage eines jungen Industriefotografen, deren Gegenstand die Parkanlagen und die Bevölkerung von London bilden. Der Künstler, der diese Aufnahmen aus reinem Interesse gemacht hat, hat auf diesem Sektor bereits einen erheblichen Ruf gewonnen. Seine Kamera war eine Nikkormat mit 43-86 Zoom-Objectiv, und er bediente sich eines 800 ASA HP5-Films.

189

HERBST von Laszlo Lajas

Die Blätter auf dem schlafenden Mädchen ergeben eine etwas makabre Wirkung, doch trägt sie ohne Zweifel zu der herbstlichen Stimmung bei und verwandelt die etwas langweilige Landschaft in ein anregendes Bild. Die Behandlung läßt erkennen, wie ähnlich die ungarischen und tschechischen Künstler in ihrer Auffassung der Fotografie sind.

190

KOPF IN DEN HÄNDEN von Howard Walker

Dieser bekannte Fotograf des *Sunday Mirror* machte sich den Spaß seinen Schwiegervater in einem konkaven Rasierspiegel im Badezimmer zu fotografieren, hat dabei aber auch eine merkwürdige abstrakte Wirkung erzielt. Aufgenommen mit einer Nikon F2 mit 50 mm Objektiv bei verfügbarem Licht; in D76 entwickelter Tri-X-Film.

191

JANUAR von Vladimir Filinov

Ein weiteres interessantes Bild aus der Sowjetunion, in dem ein recht alltägliches Thema durch Absonderneiner Person aus der Gruppe auf ungewöhnliche Weise behandelt wurde. Der Junge schafft die Stimmung, während die anderen Kinder den Hintergrund schaffen. Aufgenommen mit einer 35 mm Kamera mit Normalobjektiv und 3x-Umformer und dann auf einen 6 x 9 cm Strichnegativfilm kopiert.

192

ONKEL JOHN von V. Sonta

Der Künstler, der die litauische Landbevölkerung in einer ganzen Reihe von Aufnahmen verewigt hat, entschied sich in diesem Falle mit Recht für eine Profilaufnahme. Die Pose bedingt zusätzliche Stabilität und Stärke. Aufgenommen mit einer Konica A3 mit 50 mm Objektiv auf Tri-X-Film, der in Microphen entwickelt wurde.

193

KEIN TITEL von David Burrows, AIIP

Trotzdem sein Gesicht teilweise verborgen ist, erkennt man ihn sofort. Es ist allgemein bekannt, daß sich Mr. Heath musikalisch betätigt, und diese Aufnahme wurde während einer Klavierdarbietung in Manchester aufgenommen. Der Winkel wurde so gewählt, daß eine ungewöhnliche, interessante Komposition entstanden ist. Mit einer Nikon F2 und einem 135 mm Objektiv auf Tri-X-Film aufgenommen und in D76 entwickelt.

194/195

PETER BONETTI von Mike Hollist

Der berühmte Torwart der Mannschaft Chelsea – er ist unter dem Spitznamen "Cat" bekannt – trainiert hier gemeinsam mit seinem neunjährigen Sohn, der hofft, in die Fußstapfen seines Vaters zu treten! Mike, ein Fotograf des DAILY MAIL, verwendete eine Nikon F2 mit 180 mm Objektiv und entwickelte den Tri-X-Film in D76. Belichtungzeit 1/500 Sekunde bei Blende 5,6.

196

AUSBLICK AUF LONDON von Jack Rufus, FRPS

Wenn er nicht in Ostafrika auf Safari war, liebte es der verstorbene Jack Rufus London mit seiner Kamera zu durchkreuzen, und es gelang ihm meistens eine künstlerische Interpretation moderner und alter Architektur zu bieten, wie bei diesem Bilde, das er im Barbican aufnahm. Hasselblad mit 80 mm Objektiv auf Microdol entwickeltem Tri-X-Film. Siehe auch Seite 59.

197

TURM von Geri Della Rocca

Eine recht ungewöhnliche Ansicht des World Trade Centre in New York. Wenn es nicht möglich ist, senkrechte Linien senkrecht darzustellen, ist es, wie das Bild zeigt, ein positiver Vorteil, aus großer Nähe zu fotografieren, um das Gefühl der Höhe zu verstärken und eine kräftige Komposition zu erzielen. Die Kamera war eine Nikon F mit 20 mm Objektiv und der Film 600 ASA HP5.

198

TENDRESSE von Serge de Sazo

Das Gefühl der Liebe läßt sich auf viele Weisen darstellen, doch kann nur ein Künstler von nackten Gestalten beider Geschlechter Gebrauch machen, ohne dem Bild eine lüsterne Note zu verleihen. Die Franzosen haben das in ihren Skulpturen und Gemälden meisterhaft getroffen, und wie das Bild zeigt, gelingt es ihnen auch in der Fotografie. Ein Vergleich mit den Aufnahmen auf den Seite 71 und 211 ist recht interessant.

199

KALHAMA UND GUTTA von K. Szebessy

Eine Aufnahme, in der der Hintergrundvorhang und die verschiedenen Requisiten die Stimmung eines Künstlerateliers hervorrufen, die aber insofern ungewöhnlich ist, als die auf die Kamera zugehende Gestalt der Komposition Bewegung und ein perfektes Gleichgewicht verleiht.

200

BRIAN BECK von Geoffrey Tyrer

Eine gelungene Aufnahme dieses olympischen Turners, der einen fliegenden Salto ausführt. Der Vorgang wurde an seinem dramatischen Höhepunkt erfaßt und in jeder Hinsicht verdeutlicht. Bei reflektiertem Blitzlicht im Auftrag des SHEFFIELD STAR mit einer Canon FT mit 50 mm Objektiv auf Tri-X aufgenommen. Blende 5,6.

201

TURNERIN von Luis Arteaga Cerdain

Ebenso wie das Bild auf der gegenüberliegenden Seite zeichnet sich diese Aufnahme durch sehr genaue Zeitkontrolle aus. Die Aktion ist im interessantesten Moment wiedergegeben, und die Story wird durch den authentischen Hintergrund vervollständigt. Die Rückenansicht verleiht der Aufnahme eine ungewöhnliche Note. Die Kamera war eine Nikon F2A mit 105 mm Objektiv, und der Tri-X-Film wurde in Rodinal entwickelt.

202

VERLASSEN IN RIO von Henning Christoff

Ein Bild aus einer Reportage über die Kinder von Ipanema, die nach zwangsweiser Evakuierung aus ihren Heimen auf den Straßen schlafen. Mit einer Leica M4 mit 35 mm Summilux unter Anwendung von Blitzlicht auf Tri-X-Film aufgenommen und in D76 entwickelt.

203

VISIONEN von Vlado Baca

Diese Aufnahme des jungen freiberuflich tätigen slowakischen Fotografen gehört einer für die Zeitschrift "Slovensko" angefertigten Bilderreihe an. Es handelt sich um Spiegelungen auf verchromten Blechen und der Künstler hat von einer Pentacon Six mit 50 mm Objektiv und in D76 entwickeltem Orwo NP27-Film Gebrauch gemacht.

204

GLENEVE von David Dalby

Die bedrohliche Stimmung eines Gewitters in den Highlands ist durch die massiven Schwarzflecken gut wiedergegeben. Die verschiedenen Schichten und ein Glanzlicht in der Ferne vermitteln erfolgreich ein Gefühl der Tiefe. Aufgenommen mit einer Hasselblad mit 80 mm Objektiv auf in D76 entwickeltem Tri-X-Film. 1/250 Sekunde bei Blende 16.

205

MEIN FREUND von V. Sonta

Eine Aufnahme, die Gegnern der "Motorradgefahr" bestimmt gefallen wird. Dramatische Beleuchtung und die ungewöhnliche Position der Figur im Vordergrund vermitteln einen Eindruck von für den Betrachter bedrohlicher Geschwindigkeit. Die Aufnahme wurde mit einer Pentacon Sechs mit 80 mm Objektiv und Rotfilter aufgenommen. Photo 65-Film in D76 entwickelt. 1/60 Sekunde bei Blende 5,6.

206

AM RANDE DES CURBAR von John Woodhouse

Ein Selbstporträt, das von einem bekannten, preisgekrönten Bergsteiger mit Hilfe eines Stativs und eines Selbstauslösers im Peak District National Park aufgenommen wurde. Die Kamera war eine Olympus OM-1 mit 35 mm Objektiv und Orangefilter. Der FP4-Film wurde in Aculux entwickelt.

207

DRACHENFLIEGER von T. G. Edwards

Eine Aufnahme, die auf interessante Weite mit dem Bild auf Seite 162 kontrastiert. Man fragt sich, wie dies heute in vielen Klubs der Fall ist, ob Farbe oder Schwarz/Weiß mehr Interesse bzw. Drama ergibt. In Devils Dyke mit einer Nikon F2 mit 85 mm Objektiv und einem Polarisierfilter auf FP4-Film aufgenommen.

208

HUCKEPACK von Min Shik Choi

Die Liebe eines Kindes für ein Haustier bildet ein ansprechendes, bewährtes Thema, doch ist es ungewöhnlich, einen Fuchs zu sehen, der so zahm ist wie dieser hier in Korea. Die Entschlossenheit in Gang und Ausdruck verleiht der Aufnahme zusätzliches Interesse und Lebhaftigkeit. Aufgenornen mit einer Leica M3 mit 200 mm Objektiv auf in Microdol X entwickeltem Tri-X-Film. 1/120 Sekunde bei Blende 4.

209

HUCKEPACK von David Wilding

Eine unbemerkte Aufnahme während der Militärparade in Edinburgh, als dieser Herr einen Sitz suchte. Auch dieses Bild erweist, daß es sich lohnt, stets eine Kamera mitzunehmen. Mit einer Pentax Spotmatic mit 135 mm Objektiv auf 650 ASA Tri-X-Film aufgenommen.

210

BILDHAUERMODELL von Frank Peeters

Dieses Bild, das in einer belgischen Kunstschule bei verfügbarer Leuchtröhren- Beleuchtung ausgeführt wurde, gibt die Stimmung in einer Kunstklasse wieder – was bei Anwendung von Blitzlicht nicht möglich gewesen wäre. Die Kamera war eine Nikkormat FT3 mit 105 mm Objektiv, und der 1600 ASA Tri-X-Film wurde in Neutol S entwickelt.

211

RETRATO DE DOS ENAMORADOS von Josep Maria Ribas Prous

Diese doppelte Aktstudie wurde mit Geschmack und auf die für ein so schwieriges Thema richtige Weise behandelt. Das Ergebnis ist künstlerisch und ausdrucksvoll. Aufgenommen mit einer Nikon F2 mit 105 mm Objektiv bei verfügbarem Licht auf Microdol X entwickeltem Tri-X-Film. 1/30 Sekunde bei Blende 2.

212

MITSUO TSAKAHARA von Sven Simon

Sportbilder stellen hohe Ansprüche an Fotografen, da sehr genaue Zeitkontrolle nötig ist, um den richtigen Augenblick nicht zu verfehlen. Das Ergebnis sieht stets einfach aus, erfordert aber viel Erfahrung. Die Einbeziehung des Barrens vollendet die Wirkung.

213 (oben)

FIONA ROGERS von Mervyn Rees, FRPS

Dieses Bild einer führenden Hürdenläuferin wurde während des Trainings in Crystal Palace, London, aufgenommen. Die dramatische Wirkung wurde mit Hilfe eines Sigma-Fischaugenobjektivs an einer Nikon F2 erzielt. Belichtung 1/1000 Sekunde auf in D76 entwickeltem Tri-X-Film.

213 (unten)

BOWLSPIELERIN von Terry Cooper

Eine typisch englische Szene, die im Rahmen eines "Community and Environment"-Projekts aufgenommen und mit einem Preis der South Eastern Arts Association ausgezeichnet wurde. Mit einer Olympus OM-1 mit 50 mm Objektiv im Preston Park, Brighton, fotografiert. Der FP4-Film wurde in ID11 entwickelt.

214

IN EINEM MUSEUM IN ATHEN von Jean Berner

Ein humorvolles Bild der Tochter des Fotografen, die sich weigert, mehr Kultur über sich ergehen zu lassen! Ursprünglich mit einer Nikkormat mit 20 mm Objektiv auf Fujichrome 100 aufgenommen. Es wurde dann eine Umkehrkopie angefertigt und auf Tri-X-Film übertragen, um die Vergrößerung zu erzielen und das Kind durch Abschatten zu isolieren.

215

SUBWAY von Achim Sperber

Aufgenommen in New York für "New York – Up and Down". Die Atmosphäre dieses viel beanstandeten Transportsystems ist gut eingefangen. Aufgenommen mit einer Leica mit 35 mm Objektiv auf in D76 entwickeltem Tri-X-Film. 1/125 Sekunde bei Blende 2,8.

216

KEIN TITEL von Signe Drevsjo

Ein Doppelporträt, das einen glücklichen Augenblick auf eine Weise widerspiegelt, wie dies nur die Fotografie kann. Der Kontrast zwischen Jugend und Alter ist an und für sich bedeutungsvoll, und die beiden Köpfe sind gut plaziert, um eine Komposition mit großer Vitalität zu ergeben. Aufgenommen mit einer Canon F1 mit 50 mm Objektiv auf Tri-X-Film. In D76 entwickelt.

217

DOPPELPORTRÄT von Egons Spuris

Ein Porträt, das alle Regeln bricht, denenzufolge stets eine körperliche oder angedeutete Verbindung zwischen zwei Personen in einem Porträt bestehen sollte und "eine Person prominenter darzustellen sei als die andere". Diese recht ungewöhnliche Komposition ist jedoch erfolgreich, und die intensiven Gesichtsausdrücke regen die Fantasie an.

218

KEIN TITEL von Karin Szekessy

Eine beachtliche Gruppe von Figuren von einer Fotografin, die offensichtlich alles daran setzt, eine Idee zum Ausdruck zu bringen. Technische Überlegungen des Beleuchtungsausgleichs bereiteten ihr offensichtlich kein Kopfzerbrechen. In der Tat scheint das Licht vom Fenster zu der authentischen Wirkung beizutragen. Siehe auch Seite 199.

219

KEIN TITEL von Michael Gnade

Ein Bild, das einen interessanten Kontrast zu der gegenüberliegenden Aufnahme bildet. Anstelle der zarten femininen Note bestehen kräftige Kontraste, nicht nur in thematischer Hinsicht, sondern auch was die Töne anbelangt, und die Komposition ist, trotzdem sie so viele Elemente enthält, erstaunlich kohäsiv.

220

CALELLA von Ferran Artigas

Durch Aufnahme von einem tiefgelegenen Punkt und kräftige Kontraste ist es dem Künstler gelungen, den dramatischen Eindruck zu erwecken, daß das Gebäude in Gefahr sei, wegen Bodenerosion während des nächsten Gewitters abzurutschen. Aufgenommen mit einer Minolta SRT mit 28 mm Objektiv auf Tri-X-Film.

221

LANDSCHAFT IN SKYE von Chris Peet, FRPS

Dieses Bild stammt von einem Künstler, der von Farbe auf Schwarz/Weiß umgeschaltet hat. Die ursprüngliche Kopie war in einem tiefen Sepiaton, der durch doppelte Entwicklung in einer starken Sulfidlösung erzielt wurde. In dem London Salon ausgestellt, wurde die Aufnahme mit einer Praktica mit 20 mm Objektiv und einem Orangefilter auf FP4-Film gemacht.

222 (oben)

DIE KUPPELN von Roland Herpin

Eine interessante Design-Aufnahme, die dank der Rasterung und des Abschattens des Himmels beim Kopieren auch recht stimmungsvoll ist. In Tunisien mit einer Minolta SRT 101 mit 135 mm Linse auf Tri-X aufgenommen und auf hartem Agfa-Papier kopiert.

222 (unten)

KOMPOSITION von Ilmar Apkalns

Dies ist nahezu eine Schulübung, die keine verborgene Bedeutung oder Botschaft zu besitzen scheint. Gewiß besitzt der Künstler aber ein erstaunliches Auge für Komposition. Die Kopie war absolut einwandfrei.

223

STRANDARCHITEKTUR von Michael Scott

Dieses Bild, das einer Reihe von Aufnahmen eines kunstgewerblichen Lehrers angehört, veranschaulicht, wie das "sehende Auge" auch bei den alltäglichsten Themen interessante Wechselwirkungen von Formen, Gefügen und Tönen entdeckt. Mit einer Praktica LTL mit 50 mm Objektiv auf HP5-Film aufgenommen. Der Sepiaton der Kopie unterstreicht die Beschaffenheit und das Alter des Aufnahmegegenstands.

224

AKTSTUDIE von José Torregrossa

Weibliche Gestalten in ganz oder teilweise abstrakten Kompositionen sind nicht ungewöhnlich, doch ist diese Aufnahme den meisten ähnlichen Bildern durch die kräftige Wirkung der einfachen Formen und die kühne Darstellung überlegen. Die Kamera war eine Nikon F mit 24 mm Objektiv, und der Tri-X-Film wurde in HC110 entwickelt.

Inside back cover

APRES LA COURSE von Raymonde Jarry

Ein sehr interessantes Bild. Aufnahmen von Menschenmengen aus der Vogelperspektive sind nicht leicht, da die Komponenten selten eine ausgeglichene Komposition ergeben oder sich zu oft wiederholen. In dieser Aufnahme verhindern die leeren Stühle eine monotone Wirkung, und die Rückansicht bewirkt eine ungewöhnliche Note.

Données Techniques

JAQUETTE par Martin Wolin Jr.

Très belle image, qui montre l'intérêt de la lumière matinale avant le lever du soleil. Elle engendre de délicates teintes pastel en couleurs. Cliché pris avec un appareil Pentax 6 x 7 équipé d'un objectif de 105 mm, sur pellicule Ektachrome High Speed; vitesse d'obturation: 1/60 s; ouverture de diaphragme: f/8. Reproduction à partir d'un tirage sur Cibachrome.

DEUXIÈME PAGE DE COUVERTURE

AU BÉGUINAGE DE BRUGES par Jean Berner

Cette photographie, due à un photographe français bien connu, traduit un sens aigu de la conception, dans laquelle la répétition rythmique et des contrastes puissants jouent un rôle prépondérant. Cliché pris en Belgique avec un appareil Nikkormat FT équipé d'un objectif de 20 mm, sur pellicule Tri-X développée au révélateur D76.

13

INDUSTRIE par John Davidson

Cette très belle image a été prise spécialement pour illustrer la couverture d'un supplément industriel du *Liverpool Daily Post*. Le photographe a utilisé un filtre Chromo comme filtre de densité neutre pour obtenir des contrastes fortement marqués. Cliché pris avec un appareil Nikon F équipé d'un objectif Nikkor de 28 mm, sur pellicule Tri-X développée au révélateur D76.

14

MARINE par José Torregrosa

Même les sujets les plus traditionnels peuvent être teintés de modernisme lorsqu'on défie les lignes directrices de la composition, qui, dans ce cas, auraient exigé que le bateau fût placé d'un côté au lieu d'être juste au centre. Cette façon de procéder a ajouté quelque chose à cette photographie tout empreinte d'une atmosphère vespérale. Cliché pris avec un appareil Nikkormat équipé d'un objectif de 24 mm, sur pellicule Tri-X.

15

VERCORS par J. J. Abassin

Très belle scène de neige, ayant presque un effet de carte de Noël, mise en relief par un ciel très sombre, qu'il est généralement possible d'obtenir en pareille circonstance au moyen d'un filtre clair. L'adjonction d'une minuscule silhouette donne l'échelle et la profondeur, et ouvre le champ visuel.

16

INDIENS À CALGARRY par George Webber

Les flèches au mur donnent une touche ironique au message transmis par cette photographie due à un jeune photographe canadien. Cliché pris à l'ombre avec un appareil Canon FT6N équipé d'un objectif de 50 mm, sur pellicule Ilford FP4 développée au révélateur ID11.

17

DANS LE MANTEAU DE PAPA par Raghu Rai
Amusante photographie qui fixe un moment heureux et montre, comme d'autres dans le présent album, qu'il y a place pour l'humour dans la photographie, même si celle-ci n'a pas de valeur esthétique durable. Cliché pris avec un appareil Nikon F équipé d'un objectif de 85 mm, sur pellicule Tri-X; vitesse d'obturation: 1/250 s; ouverture de diaphragme: f/5,6.

18

CARMEN par Josep María Ribas Prous
Utilisation extrêmement efficace du grain pour donner un impact artistique. Cet effet a été obtenu par agrandissement d'une très petite partie du négatif. Cliché pris sous un éclairage de studio au tungstène avec un appareil Nikon F2 équipé d'un objectif de 105 mm, sur pellicule Tri-X développée au révélateur Microdol X; vitesse d'obturation: 1/60 s; ouverture de diaphragme: f/5,6. Le photographe est un professeur espagnol de photographie.

19

INGRID par F. John Reid
Le traitement en clair a permis d'obtenir le meilleur résultat avec ce beau modèle de blonde. Cliché pris avec un appareil Mamiya C330 équipé d'un objectif Secor de 135 mm, sur pellicule FP4 développée au révélateur D76. L'éclairage du studio était assuré par deux flashes Multilec braqués sur le sujet, et deux autres sur l'arrière-plan. L'agrandissement a été rendu légèrement diffus au moyen d'une gaze de soie.

20

AU SECOURS par David Bearne
Photographie prise durant la finale de la Coupe de rugby du Hampshire disputée entre Basingstoke et Havant. Un dynamique jeune photographe a saisi un incident qui n'est pas dénué d'humour. David a utilisé un appareil Nikon F2 équipé d'un objectif de 135 mm, sur pellicule Tri-X développée au révélateur D76; vitesse d'obturation: 1/250 s; ouverture de diaphragme: f/5,6.

21

PÉNALISATION par Frank Travers
Les photographes de sport ont maintes occasions de saisir des épisodes et des gestes significatifs, mais il faut habileté et expérience pour trouver le bon moment, et pour être prêt lorsqu'il survient. Frank travaille pour le *Sheffield Morning Telegraph* et il a utilisé un appareil Canon Ftb équipé d'un objectif Novaflex de 400 mm pour réussir cette photographie sur pellicule Tri-X développée au révélateur Qualitol.

22/23

ROLF HARRIS SUR PLACE par John Davidson
Un célèbre animateur en compagnie d'un groupe d'écoliers de Liverpool durant une séance d'enregistrement destinée à une série de télévision. Cette photographie montre l'enthousiasme communicatif de Rolf Harris pour le travail avec des jeunes. Cliché pris sous l'éclairage ambiant dans le grand hall d'une école avec un appareil Nikon F équipé d'un objectif de 28 mm, sur pellicule Tri-X développée au révélateur D76; vitesse d'obturation: 1/15 s; ouverture de diaphragme: f/3,5.

24

S. RICHTER par Laszlo Lajas
Magnifique portrait de ce grand pianiste russe, pris juste au moment voulu pour saisir une expression caractéristique. Le cadre authentique et l'audience qui applaudit donnent le ton. Photographie prise sous l'éclairage ambiant avec un appareil Minolta SRT 101 équipé d'un objectif de 55 mm, sur pellicule Tri-X développée au révélateur Acufine; vitesse d'obturation: 1/30 s; ouverture de diaphragme: f/2,8.

25

JACKIE ROBINSON par Monroe S. Frederick
Le premier joueur de baseball de couleur américain photographié, avec sa femme, juste avant sa mort. Les expressions et les gestes naturels, inconscients de la présence du photographe, font de cette image un souvenir émouvant. Cliché pris avec un appareil Mamiyaflex 220 équipé d'un objectif de 65 mm, avec flash électronique, sur pellicule développée au révélateur D76.

26

INTELLIGENCE par Robert Llewellyn
Photographie tirée d'un livre intitulé "Silver Wings" (Ailes d'argent), que l'auteur décrit comme des manifestations visuelles de son voyage terrestre vers la compréhension et l'exploration de la pensée et de l'intelligence, ce qu'il a tenté d'exprimer par des objets placés dans différents plans en interaction les uns avec les autres. Cliché pris avec un appareil Nikon F équipé d'un objectif de 20 mm.

27

LEVER DU JOUR SUR LE LAC par Asko Salmi
Prise à 7 heures du matin dans l'archipel de Vaasa, cette photographie montre que les bateaux qui hantent les lacs embrumés ne sont pas l'apanage de l'école de Hong Kong. En fait, cette manière de procéder est caractéristique des très belles photographies que nous avons reçues de Finlande ces dernières années. Cliché pris avec un appareil Canon AE-1 équipé d'un objectif de 20 mm, sur pellicule Tri-X développée au révélateur D76.

28

SANS TITRE par J. M. Oriola
Amusante photographie, qui montre que les vues de dos sont parfois aussi expressives que les vues de face. Cette photographie est certainement originale et paraît très naturelle, bien qu'elle soit peut-être le résultat d'une pose. L'intensité des contrastes et le caractère insolite de la composition appellent un second coup d'oeil.

29

YOGA par Brian Sutton
Photographie extraite d'une série destinée à aider un professeur de yoga à vérifier sa posture et sa position, mais qui est inévitablement empreinte d'une touche d'humour en raison de l'effet de perspective. Cliché pris avec un appareil Pentax SPF équipé d'un objectif de 28 mm, sur pellicule Tri-X développée au révélateur D76.

30

SANS TITRE par Jozef Vissel
Photographie aux contrastes insolites. Elle est empreinte d'une délicate touche d'humour en raison même de son absurdité. Bien qu'elle soit de toute évidence le résultat d'une pose, elle retient assurément l'attention. Cliché pris avec un appareil Hasselblad, sur pellicule Panatomic X développée au révélateur Rodinal.

31

MERLYN REES, MEMBRE DU PARLEMENT par Asadour Guzelian
Un ancien ministre de l'Intérieur photographié à un moment de détente, lors d'un dîner de Sikhs à Leeds. Outre son caractère hautement descriptif quant à l'homme et à l'événement, la composition est originale et la photographie est plus expressive que ne le sont généralement les portraits officiels d'hommes politiques. L'appareil était un Pentax SP100 équipé d'un objectif de 135 mm, et chargé d'une pellicule Tri-X.

32

HIVER EN MONTAGNE par Tom Dodd
L'utilisation d'un filtre orange 4x à une altitude d'environ 600 mètres dans les monts Moelwyn de Snowdonia a donné cette saisissante image. Cliché pris avec un appareil Canon 2 équipé d'un objectif de 28 mm, sur pellicule FP4 de sensibilité 164 ASA développée au révélateur Aculux. L'auteur a utilisé une ouverture de diaphragme de f/16 pour réduire la réverbération du soleil.

33

DANSEUSES DE BALLET par Rudolf Auer
Magnifique image qui saisit tout le mouvement d'une pirouette d'une façon très artistique. Le tourbillon des tutus crée le rythme par la répétition et l'éclat des paillettes produit un contraste saisissant par rapport à l'éclairage en bleu, la froideur qui pourrait se dégager de l'ensemble étant contrebalancée par les teintes chaudes des dos et des jambes.

34

PORTRAIT par Dieter Kraft
Portrait exécuté de manière saisissante par un photographe suisse, qui a été très remarqué lors d'une exposition de photographies en couleurs de grand format présentée au stand Kodak lors du dernier Photokina. L'utilisation hardie du rouge sur la chair colorée et la composition décalée ont un impact considérable.

35

SUE par Henry Michaels
Reproduction d'un magnifique tirage en couleurs provenant d'un négatif Kodak Vericolour pris avec un appareil Bronica de 6 x 6 cm. Le traitement en sombre, qui souligne l'éclairage arrière, traduit une manière artistique de traiter un sujet classique. L'éclairage était assuré par deux flashes à éventail Multilec, l'un en argent, l'autre en or, et par un troisième flash situé derrière. Le tirage a été réalisé sur papier Agfacolor type 4.

36 (Haut)

PAYSAGE par le Dr. Alexander Dunbar, membre de la Société royale de photographie de Grande-Bretagne (FRPS)
Paysage typique des Highlands d'Ecosse, prise par un membre éminent de la Edinburgh Photographic Society, qui croit que les meilleures photographies sont celles que l'on fait par temps de brouillard et de pluie, tout en reconnaissant que c'est un avantage supplémentaire si le soleil perce momentanément. Cliché pris avec un appareil Minolta sur pellicule Kodachrome 64; vitesse d'obturation: 1/125 s; ouverture de diaphragme: f/8.

36 (Bas)

PAYSAGE Par Roger Arrandale-Williams
Photographie extraite d'une série comprenant des "modèles masqués en blanc" dans un environnement naturel, combinaison qui donne des juxtapositions fantastiques et parfois discordantes. Photographie obtenue à partir d'une diapositive sur Kodachrome 64 prise avec un appareil Minolta XE7.

37

PAYSAGE BLEU par Erik Steen
Cette photographie insolite et saisissante a été réalisée sur pellicule Ektacolor Slide Duplicating développée au révélateur E4, et non selon le procédé C22 recommandé. Le premier révélateur a été omis et la durée d'action du révélateur de la couleur réduite de 1/4. Cliché pris près de la maison de l'auteur à Drammen, en Norvège, avec un appareil Nikon F2 équipé d'un zoom de 43-86 mm.

38/39

PLEUREUSES DE PRESLEY par le Dr. James Billimoria
Photographie qui caractérise l'hystérie engendrée dans le monde occidental par la mort d'une vedette de rock and roll, sur laquelle les pleureuses dansent plutôt qu'elles ne pleurent. Cliché pris avec un appareil Leica équipé d'un objectif de 50 mm un dimanche matin à Trafalgar Square. Le photographe a choisi un point de vue qui a permis d'obtenir une bonne composition dans une scène de foule.

40 (Haut)

CRAPAUD AGUA ET RAINETTE par John Walker
Cette fine étude de la nature, qui présente un double intérêt, a été réalisée au flash avec un appareil Nikon EL équipé d'un objectif Micro-Nikkor, sur pellicule Ektachrome 200. Le crapaud, originaire d'Amérique du Sud, pèse environ, 1,6 kg, tandis que la rainette verte, originaire d'Italie, ne pèse que 90 g. La photographie a été prise au Welsh Mountain Zoo, Colwyn Bay, et il a fallu plusieurs expositions du fait que la rainette prenait un malin plaisir à sauter sur l'objectif!

40 (Bas)

HIBOU ET SA PROIE par Xabi Otera
Interprétation très artistique d'un sujet d'histoire naturelle. Le hibou et le lézard qu'il tient dans son bec sont clairement présentés, tandis que l'arrière-plan est empreint d'une atmosphère de nuit et de mystère qui convient parfaitement au sujet. L'ensemble constitue une belle harmonie de couleurs.

41

GRENOUILLE VOLANTE DU COSTA RICA par Heather Angel, membre de l'Institute of Incorporated Photographers (FIIP), membre de la Société royale de photographie de Grande-Bretagne (FRPS)
Grenouille très rare, transportée en Angleterre pour les besoins du feuilleton télévisé "Life on Earth" (La vie sur la Terre), puis renvoyée dans sa forêt tropicale au Costa Rica. Auteur de près de trente livres sur l'histoire naturelle, Heather Angel a utilisé un appareil Hasselblad 5000 équipé d'un objectif de 80 mm et une pellicule Ektachrome E-3. Le sujet était éclairé par un flash Braun FZK80 à têtes jumelées.

42

CLOWN par Baron Baron
La vue montante de ce personnage de cirque souligne le monde fantastique que le cirque crée pour les enfants. La conception simple et hardie souligne cet aspect, et une partie suffisante de l'arrière-plan du cirque a été retenue pour compléter le tableau.

43

NU par Michael Gnade
Etude de silhouette très naturelle dans laquelle l'éclairage en contre-jour a joué un rôle des plus important. La pose est aussi naturelle que l'environnement, et la coloration générale est extrêmement agréable. Cette photographie est extraite d'une série publiée dans un livre dont le photographe est l'auteur, intitulé "Les gens et mon appareil photo".

44/45

COMBATIVITÉ par Wang Yue Lung
Les bras tendus et les jambes écartées de ces gymnastes engendrent une extraordinaire sensation d'action, et c'est véritablement un trait de génie du photographe que d'avoir gardé au premier plan un sujet aussi grand par rapport à la classe. Cliché pris avec un appareil Canon AE1 équipé d'un objectif de 28 mm, sur pellicule Kodacolor 400 tirée sur papier Ektacolor.

46

AIGLE DE STEPPE AMÉRICAIN par Robert Hallman
Une belle image prise au Bird of Prey Centre (Centre des oiseaux de proie) de Chilham Castle, alors que l'oiseau émettait une perçante protestation à la vue de l'appareil photographique. Cliché pris avec un appareil Kowa Super 66 équipé d'un objectif de 85 mm et d'un accessoire pour prises de vues en gros plan 3x; pellicule Agfa 50S de sensibilité 100 ASA.

47

HULOTTE par E. Exton
La plus grande chouette de Grande-Bretagne, exclusivement nocturne, est dangereuse, car elle n'hésite pas à attaquer un photographe de ses serres acérées. Au moment où l'auteur de cette photographie opérait avec un appareil Pentacon Six équipé d'un objectif de 180 mm, sur pellicule CPS120, à une distance d'environ trois mètres, l'oiseau a fondu sur lui, lui imprimant huit marques de griffes autour de l'oeil gauche. Eclairage au flash.

48

SANS TITRE par Les Mansfield
Impressionnant portrait qui saisit la dignité d'une danseuse andalouse de flamenco. C'est une double exposition réalisée en photographiant la guitare au moyen d'un objectif standard, puis en utilisant un zoom Tamron d'environ 135 mm pour l'exposition du portrait. Cliché pris avec un appareil Nikon Ftn, sur pellicule HS Ektachrome de sensibilité 800 ASA, pour chaque exposition, développée normalement au révélateur E6.

49

RUTH KENNEDY par Mervyn Rees
Photographie d'action véritablement saisissante et pleine de mouvement, qui sied parfaitement à ce coureur de relais international. Alliée au grain, la présence du sujet tout à droite souligne l'impression d'effort. Cliché pris avec un appareil Nikon F2 équipé d'un objectif de 135 mm, sur pellicule Tri-X; vitesse d'obturation: 1/15 s; ouverture de diaphragme: f/4.

50

SOUS L'EAU par Ferdinando Quaranta
Photographie de l'auteur, prise au large de la Corse dans la baie de Sainte-Florence. Spécialiste bien connu de la photographie sous-marine, avec pour sujets les poissons, Ferdinando utilise un appareil Konica Autoreflex avec un boîtier en Ikelite équipé d'un objectif de 24 mm. L'éclairage naturel est renforcé par un flash électronique automatique Braun F2000. L'original était tiré sur Kodachrome et a été reproduit sur pellicule Tri-X.

51

BAIN DE BOUE par John Jones
Photographie qui dépeint l'atmosphère heureuse d'un match de football entre garçons et filles sur le terrain boueux où se déroule la manifestation annuelle connue sous le nom de Old Leigh Regatta. Les garçons ont perdu! Cliché pris avec un appareil Canon Ftb équipé d'un zoom de 100-200 mm, sur pellicule Tri-X développée au révélateur D76.

52

SHERRIL HAGUE par Chris Haig
Excellent portrait du genre candide, pris sous l'éclairage ambiant, qui a saisi quelque chose du caractère de ce joyeux vendeur de voitures d'occasion. Cliché pris avec un appareil Mamiya C330, sur pellicule FP4 développée au révélateur Acutol.

53

CONTRAVENTION par Ian Torrance
Peu de gens auraient saisi la combinaison qu'offrent ce chien et cette "aubergine", à l'origine de cette image délicieusement drôle, qui sera appréciée par tous ceux qui ont été victimes d'une contravention. Elle a valu un prix à ce photographe du *Scottish Daily Record* dans le cadre du Concours du meilleur photographe de presse britannique de l'année.

54

DEUIL À TÉHÉRAN par Rolf M. Aagaard
Photographie prise dans le cimetière principal de la ville durant une manifestation dirigée contre l'Ayatollah Khomeini, qui vivait alors encore à Paris. L'auteur a développé la pellicule dans sa chambre d'hôtel, puis l'a transmise par bélinographie à son journal norvégien *Aftenposten*. Cliché pris avec un appareil Nikon F2 équipé d'un objectif de 85 mm, sur pellicule Tri-X développée au révélateur D76.

55

PORTRAIT par Peter Purtz
Photographie caractéristique des oeuvres d'imagination qui nous viennent de Tchécoslovaquie, dans lesquelles on utilise des poses non conventionnelles et non appréciées sur des arrière-plans lourds, souvent industriels. L'emplacement insolite du sujet, allié à un grain très marqué, force le regard. Cliché pris avec un appareil Exa 500 équipé d'un objectif de 25 mm, sur pellicule Orwo 27 développée au révélateur Formadon R.

56

ANKA par Kazimiers Czapinski
Les photographes polonais ne se laissent généralement pas arrêter par les règles conventionnelles de la composition, et l'action principale, presque à la limite, est peut-être criticable aux yeux des traditionalistes, mais on ne saurait lui dénier qu'elle a engendré force et mouvement. Le nez retroussé par la pomme ajoute à l'effet, et le grain n'est pas fait pour nuire.

57

ADA ROGIVIN par George Wedding
Remarquable et d'un naturel parfait, cette étude de caractère d'une joueuse de poker de 87 ans, de Miami Beach, a été prise pour *The Palm Beach Post*. Le photographe a attendu exactement le bon moment pour lui donner l'action voulue. Cliché pris avec un appareil Nikon équipé d'un objectif de 180 mm, sur pellicule Tri-X de sensibilité 1600 ASA développée au révélateur Acufine.

58 (Haut)

DEUX CABANES par Geri Della Rocca
Simplicité absolue et puissants contrastes ont donné beaucoup d'impact à cette photographie prise au Nevada par un photographe italien. La conception est puissante et l'atmosphère d'isolement bien représentée. L'appareil était un Nikon F équipé d'un objectif de 20 mm et d'un filtre rouge, et la pellicule était une HP5 de sensibilité 600 ASA, développee au révélateur ID11.

58 (Bas)

CIMETIÈRE par J. L. Young, correspondant de la Société royale de photographie de Grande-Bretagne (ARPS)
Bon exemple de l'utilisation intelligente d'une pellicule infrarouge pour rehausser une scène banale. Partout où il y a différentes variétés d'arbres, l'infrarouge engendre des contrastes, en particulier sur un fond de ciel bleu. Cliché pris au cimetière Saint-Nicolas de Basildon avec un appareil Praktica LTL3 équipé d'un objectif de 35 mm et d'un filtre rouge foncé, sur pellicule infrarouge Kodak High Speed de sensibilité 50 ASA développée au révélateur Perceptol.

59

CHATEAU DE BELCASTEL, DORDOGNE par Jack Rufus, membre de la Société royale de photographie de Grande-Bretagne (FRPS)
Malheureusement, l'auteur de cette photographie est décédé peu après nous l'avoir envoyée, mais il laisse un héritage de magnifiques paysages tant dans le style traditionnel que dans le style contemporain. Cliché pris un soir de septembre avec un appareil Hasselblad équipé d'un objectif de 250 mm, sur pellicule Tri-X développée au révélateur Microdol X. Voir aussi à la page 196.

60

ISOLEMENT par Asad Ali
Tirage obtenu en assemblant la photographie du petit oiseau sur un fond de ciel nu et un arrière-plan photographié dans la campagne de Lahore. Cliché pris avec un appareil Kowa équipé d'un objectif de 200 mm et d'un 2x convertisseur, sur pellicule Agfa Super-Pan 200 développée au révélateur D76; vitesse d'obturation: 1/250 s; ouverture de diaphragme: f/8.

A great match for any photographer

What a superb combination from KJP.

The ARCA-Swiss mono-rail studio camera offers the still life specialist, the large format portrait photographer, the forensic & scientific photographer, or indeed any photographer regularly using the larger formats, the advantages once the exclusive province of the 35mm SLR user – Light Weight, High Precision camera with a NIKKOR lens.

KJP. offer you the best of both worlds with Swiss precision camera manufacture coupled with NIKON lens know how.

Why not phone or send in the coupon for further details of this great match.

KEITH JOHNSON PHOTOGRAPHIC
Ramillies House, 1-2 Ramillies Street,
London W1V 1DF
Telephone: 01-439 8811 Telex: 24447

NAME..

ADDRESS...

....

ARCA

61 (Haut)

HÉRON PÊCHANT par Donald A. Smith
Excellente photographie d'oiseau, pleine d'intérêt en raison de la manière dont les détails sont rendus et de l'environnement authentique du héron, qui a été "pris sur le fait". Cliché pris avec un appareil Nikon F2 équipé d'un objectif de 400 mm, sur pellicule Ilford FP4.

61 (Bas)

EFFRAIE ET MUSARAIGNE par Donald A. Smith, correspondant de la Société royale de photographie de Grande-Bretagne (ARPS)
Magnifique leçon d'histoire naturelle que cette photographie d'une effraie rentrant au nid avec sa proie. Cliché pris au flash avec un appareil Nikon F2 équipé d'un objectif de 35 mm, sur pellicule FP4.

62

NU par Frank Peeters
Photographie due à un jeune photographe belge spécialisé dans les études de nus, qui utilise de violents contrastes et une interprétation graphique, généralement obtenus par l'éclairage ambiant. Pour cette photographie, il a utilisé un appareil Nikkormat FT3 équipé d'un objectif de 28 mm, sur pellicule Tri-X de sensibilité 1600 ASA développée au révélateur Neutol S.

63

DANSE par Andrej Krynicki
Ce photographe polonais très éclectique et très prolifique utilise largement la solarisation de manière à donner aux aspects fantastiques à des sujets familiers. Ses idées sont toujours originales et il utilise le personnage d'une manière artistique et créatrice, comme on peut le voir sur cet exemple. Le contraste entre la vitalité d'une danseuse nue et la grisaille des toits des maisons est stimulant.

64

**TROIS RELIGIEUSES
par Montserrat V. Barraquer**
Les religieuses sont des sujets de prédilection pour les photographes, mais il n'est pas facile de réaliser un arrangement comme celui-ci. Cliché pris sur la place de la Cathédrale de Tarragone avec un appareil Leicaflex SL équipé d'un objectif de 180 mm, sur pellicule Tri-X développée au révélateur Rodinal.

65

MINU par Raghu Rai
Portrait bien posé d'une séduisante présentatrice de la télévision indienne, avec une photographie en arrière-plan utilisée pour constituer une composition intéressante mais insolite. Cliché pris avec un appareil Nikkormat équipé d'un objectif de 85 mm, sur pellicule Tri-X; vitesse d'obturation: 1/60 s; ouverture de diaphragme: f/5,6 sous l'éclairage ambiant.

66

DEUX BAISERS par Vladimir Filinov
Photographie prise par un des plus grands photographes d'URSS, spécialisé depuis de nombreuses années dans les techniques de dérivation des lignes. Le moment émotionnel fixé sur cette image évite tout excès de sentimentalité grâce au choix judicieux du traitement, mais la présence de l'insecte sur la joue de l'homme ne laisse pas d'intriguer.

67

AUTOPORTRAIT par Vladimir Filinov
L'une des meilleures photographies d'une série, considérable, qui nous vient d'URSS et qui comprend de multiples compositions imaginatives et exaltantes. Ici le message est non seulement clair, mais encore présenté avec une force et une originalité extraordinaires. L'un des négatifs a été pris avec un appareil de 6 x 7 cm, l'autre avec un objectif de 35 mm complété par un convertisseur 2x.

68

SANS TITRE par Frantisek Dostal
Photographie tout empreinte d'une délicate touche d'humour. L'auteur a suivi cet homme dans Prague pendant un certain temps jusqu'à ce qu'il fut arrêté à un feu de circulation. Elle montre l'intérêt qu'il y a à avoir toujours un appareil photographique avec soi. Cliché pris avec un appareil Minolta SR-T303 équipé d'un objectif de 50 mm, sur pellicule Orwo NP20 développée au révélateur A49; vitesse d'obturation: 1/250 s; ouverture de diaphragme: f/11.

69

SANS TITRE par Mike Hollist
Amusante photographie, qui paraît naturelle bien qu'elle soit nécessairement le résultat d'un montage. Elle montre le nouveau petit chien de l'émission de télévision "Blue Peter" arrivant à une répétition. Cliché pris pour *The Daily Mail* avec un appareil Nikon équipé d'un objectif de 105 mm, sur pellicule Tri-X développée au révélateur D76; vitesse d'obturation: 1/250 s; ouverture de diaphragme: f/5,6.

70 (Haut)

AMOURS D'ENFANTS par Frantisek Dostal
Délicieuse photographie d'une petite fille qui récompense son jeune "amoureux" d'un baiser après que celui-ci lui a cueilli une fleur. Elle a été prise tôt le matin sur le bord du fleuve, à Prague, avec un appareil Minolta ST-T303 équipé d'un objectif de 50 mm, sur pellicule Orwo NP20 développée au révélateur A49 (ex Atomal); vitesse d'obturation: 1/250 s; ouverture de diaphragme: f/5,6.

70 (Bas)

**EXPRESSION DE L'AMOUR
par Virender Mahajan**
Deux couples vus au zoo de Delhi ont donné au photographe l'idée du message que veut transmettre cette image. Elle montre que, si l'on a "un oeil qui sait voir", il n'y a pas que des animaux à observer dans un zoo... Cliché pris sous un ciel couvert avec un appareil Canon FX équipé d'un objectif de 400 mm, sur pellicule Orwo NP55 développée au révélateur D76; vitesse d'obturation: 1/125 s; ouverture de diaphragme: f/5,6.

71

AMOUR par L. B. Feresovi
Image extraite d'une série de photographies délicieusement expressives qui dépeignent l'émotion humaine – une photographie parmi de nombreuses autres du même genre qui nous viennent de Tchécoslovaquie. Cliché pris à la lumière du jour avec un appareil Minolta SRT équipé d'un objectif de 80-200 mm, sur pellicule Forma 21 développée au révélateur Métol-pyrocatéchine.

72/73

ECOLE PRÉPARATOIRE par Frank Loughlin
Prise par un photographe du *Liverpool Daily Post*, cette photographie synthétise l'image d'une école préparatoire, sur laquelle les canotiers sont presque symboliques de la classe moyenne. Cliché pris dans une école de Liverpool avec un appareil Nikon F équipé d'un objectif de 24 mm et d'un flash utilisé par réflexion, sur pellicule Tri-X développée au révélateur D76.

74

**CHAPEAU BAS DEVANT UNE DAME
par Bill Carden, membre de la Société royale de photographie de Grand-Bretagne (FRPS)**
Cette délicieuse image d'une dame qui transporte tout ce qu'elle possède dans des sacs en vagabondant dans les rues de Londres a été prise, lors d'une parade annuelle de cavalerie, avec un appareil Mamiyaflex C330F équipé d'un objectif de 80 mm, sur pellicule HP4 développée au révélateur ID11.

75

LE GRAND CYRIL SMITH, MEMBRE DU PARLEMENT par Stephen Shakeshaft
Photographie prise sur le vif, lors d'une conférence politique, d'un personnalité très en vue qui semble y avoir connu quelques moments de détente. L'auteur de cette photographie, qui a remporté par deux fois le prix du "Meilleur photographe de l'année", travaille pour *The Liverpool Daily Post and Echo*. Cliché pris sous l'éclairage ambiant avec un appareil Nikon F2 équipé d'un objectif de 28 mm, sur pellicule Tri-X développée au révélateur D76.

76

CONTRASTE par Roland Herpin
Il faut souvent un étranger pour voir ce que l'on a chez soi, et nous avons ici un exemple intéressant de "l'oeil qui sait voir" d'un photographe français en visite à Southampton. Cliché pris avec un appareil Leica M5 équipé d'un objectif de 90 mm, sur pellicule Tri-X. Le contraste a été obtenu en chambre noire en ombrant sur papier Agfa BH111-5.

77

**TOUR DE REFROIDISSEMENT D'EAU
par Wolfgang Volz**
Une tour de refroidissement d'eau de 20 mètres située près d'une centrale nucléaire d'Allemagne de l'Ouest a permis d'obtenir cette saisissante photographie industrielle, qui est également artistique en raison des contrastes très marqués dans les tons entre la tour et le minuscule pavillon. Cliché pris avec un appareil Nikon F2 et un objectif macro de 55 mm, sur pellicule Tri-X développée au révélateur D76.

78

**LA AMISTAD (L'AMITIÉ)
par Josep María Ribas Prous**
Photographie caractéristique des oeuvres très soignées de ce célèbre photographe espagnol, qui est professeur dans une école de photographie et organisateur de groupes de jeunes photographes à des fins culturelles. Il apporte sa contribution à des magazines photographiques du monde entier. Cliché pris avec un appareil Nikon F2 équipé d'un objectif de 28 mm, sur pellicule Tri-X développée au révélateur Microdol; vitesse d'obturation: 1/1000 s; ouverture de diaphragme: f/2.

79

BALLET par Leslie E. Spatt
Deux photographies, dues à un expert dans ce domaine très particulier, prises au cours d'une représentation. L'une montre Richard Cragum, du Ballet de Stuttgart, interprétant le rôle du Prince Siegfried dans le *Lac des Cygnes,* tandis que l'autre le représente avec Egon Madsen dans *Songs of a Wayfarer* (chansons d'un voyageur). Cliché pris avec un appareil Leica M3 équipé d'un objectif de 90 mm, sur pellicule Tri-X de sensibilité 100 ASA développée au révélateur Microdol.

80

VIEUX TURC, USKÜDAR par Jean Berner
Fine étude de caractère, très naturelle, avec un sens prononcé de profondeur et de mouvement résultant de l'utilisation d'un grand angulaire à une distance assez rapprochée pour donner une perspective diminuant rapidement. Cliché pris dans le vieux quartier d'Istanbul avec un appareil Nikkormat FT équipé d'un objectif de 20 mm, sur pellicule Tri-X développée au révélateur D76.

81

MAMAN par Ilmar Apkalns
Comme de nombreuses autres photographies qui nous viennent d'URSS, cet exemple traduit d'une manière moderne et imaginative un sentiment vieux comme le monde. La distance entre la mère et l'enfant, soulignée par une perspective exagérée, exprime le désir ardent que suggèrent les mains tendues. Le halo artificiel derrière la mère pourrait avoir un sens encore plus profond.

82

LUMINAIRE par John P. Delaney, membre de la Société royale de photographie de Grande-Bretagne (FRPS)
Prise au Derwentwater, dans le District des lacs anglais, cette photographie exprime l'atmosphère habituelle de cette région durant les mois d'hiver. Cliché pris avec un appareil Rolleiflex f/3,5 équipé d'un filtre jaune X2, sur pellicule Plus X Professional développée au révélateur Microdol; vitesse d'obturation: 1/500 s; ouverture de diaphragme: f/4,5.

Development's easy when you've got your heads together.

When designing our high quality range of enlargers, we decided to put our heads together.

After all, if you're starting on black and white, you don't want to buy a completely new enlarger when experimenting with colour later on.

With Berkey-Omega enlargers, you simply buy a new head. Because each column takes both black and white and colour heads.

Choose from the B600 or B66-XL Range. Then there's the C67 enlargers or the Concept Six System, with a choice of baseboards offering paper storage, Comparator Timer or Integrator Timer versions.

Berkey-Omega have established quite a reputation as innovators in darkroom technology. And interchangeable enlarger heads are just one of the many design features we've perfected over the years.

Send for full details of the Berkey range by simply filling in the coupon.

By putting our heads together, you could find your darkroom skills developing much easier than you expected.

Please send me information on the Berkey-Omega range.

Name _____

Address _____

_____

_____

BTC Berkey Technical Co UK., 22 Concord Road, London W3 0TQ. Tel: 01-992 0104.

rk y-Omega

83

CABANE SUR LA PLAGE par Victor J. Attfield, membre de la Société royale de photographie de Grande-Bretagne (FRPS)
La forme trapue de la cabane de pêcheur, qui se profile alors que le soleil perce dans un ciel d'orage, a donné cette image saisissante, tandis que le goémon que l'on voit au premier plan sur une étendue de plage donne une profondeur extraordinaire à cette composition. Cliché pris avec un appareil Nikkormat équipé d'un objectif de 28 mm et d'un filtre orange, sur pellicule Tri-X développée au révélateur D76.

84

MODÈLE PHOTOGRAPHIQUE SOUS-MARIN par Ferdinando Quaranta
Photographie prise au large de l'île de Ventovene, près de Naples, à une profondeur d'une dizaine de mètres, le modèle et le photographe participant à la réalisation d'un projet de recherche scientifique sur les poissons locaux. Ce photographe amateur italien bien connu a utilisé un appareil Konica Autoreflex monté dans un boîtier sous-marin en Ikelite équipé d'un objectif de 55 mm. Cliché original sur Kodachrome 64, reproduit sur pellicule Tri-X.

85

UN AS DE LA PLANCHE À ROULETTES par Clive Harrison, membre de la Société royale de photographie de Grande-Bretagne (FRPS)
Belle photographie d'action prise sur une piste de planche à roulettes de Paddington, construite par une entreprise communautaire sur un terrain vague pour les enfants de la localité. Cliché pris avec un appareil Olympus OM-1 équipé d'un objectif Zuiko de 100 mm, sur pellicule HP5 développée au révélateur ID11.

86

LA REINE AU DERBY par Mike Hollist
Tout photographe de presse s'efforce de montrer l'enthousiasme de la reine pour les courses de chevaux en saisissant ses expressions de joie, d'excitation ou de déception selon que son favori gagne ou non. Cet exemple, au reste peu flatteur, a assurément saisi un moment de tension. Cliché pris avec un appareil Nikon équipé d'un objectif de 1000 mm, sur pellicule Tri-X développée au révélateur D76.

87

SAINTE FUMÉE par Howard Walker
Photographie empreinte d'une délicieuse touche d'humour, qui a été posée par un acteur amateur interprétant le rôle d'un curé. Il a fallu trois heures pour que le rond de fumée atteigne la dimension et l'endroit voulus! Cliché pris avec un appareil Nikon F2 à moteur équipé d'un objectif de 85 mm et d'un flash utilisé par réflexion, sur pellicule Tri-X.

88/89

LA BANQUE ET L'ÉGLISE par Cleland Rimmer
Tentative réussie visant à symboliser le progrès en montrant le reflet d'une architecture ancienne dans un bâtiment moderne. Les séduisants policiers en jupon que l'on voit ici avaient été persuadés d'inclure l'établissement bancaire dans leur ''ronde'', de façon à évoquer l'idée de la sécurité de la banque pour laquelle la photographie avait été demandée. Le photographe est professeur de photographie au College of Higher Education de Hull, et il a utilisé un appareil Speed Graphic de 5 x 4 pouces équipé d'un objectif de 150 mm et d'un filtre jaune; la pellicule était une FP4 développée au révélateur Autophen; vitesse d'obturation: 1/60 s; ouverture de diaphragme: f/8.

90

CHRIS BARBER par Rudolf Bieri
Le célèbre tromboniste de jazz et de blues a été bien vu sur cette photographie, qui saisit également l'atmosphère du Casino de Berne, où il a été photographié durant un concert. Cliché pris sous l'éclairage ambiant avec un appareil Leicaflex SL2 équipé d'un objectif Apo-Telyt de 180 mm, sur pellicule Tri-X développée au révélateur Tetanal Emofin pendant deux fois 10 minutes à 30°C.

91

SAMMY DAVIS JR par Erwin Kneidinger, membre de la Fédération internationale de l'art photographique (FIAP)
Photographie qui exprime la vitalité de ce personnage dynamique et où l'atmosphère est soulignée tant par l'éclairage ambiant que par le grain. Cliché pris avec un appareil Nikon F équipé d'un objectif de 105 mm, sur pellicule Tri-X développée au révélateur Neutol; vitesse d'obturation: 1/250 s; ouverture de diaphragme: f/2,5.

92

SANS TITRE par J. R. Rudin
Les gens de couleur connaissent bien la valeur des contrastes, et le vêtement blanc sur la peau est imaginatif en même temps qu'il constitue un tour de force technique. La composition est originale, et même hardie, mais très réussie. L'auteur est propriétaire d'une galerie d'art antillais et a pris cette photographie avec un appareil Pentax, sur pellicule Tri-X de sensibilité 1600 ASA, sous la lumière tombant d'une fenêtre.

93

REGARD MAGNÉTIQUE par Virender Mahajan
Portrait d'un vieux ''momden phase'' caractéristique, pris, alors qu'il se rendait à la Cité du festival de Garh-Ganga-Mela, en Inde, sous un faible angle de prise de vue, de façon à donner en arrière-plan un ciel blanc accentué par le tirage sur papier dur. Cliché pris avec un appareil Canon FX équipé d'un objectif de 50 mm, sur pellicule Orwo NP55 développée au révélateur D76.

94 (Haut)

PAS DE SIGNAUX MANUELS par Stanley Matchett
Un jeune amateur de poneys, visiblement doué du sens de l'humour, a réalisé cette amusante photographie dans un centre équestre de County Down. L'auteur, photographe du *Daily Mirror* de Belfast, a utilisé un appareil Nikon F2 équipé d'un zoom de 80-200 mm, sur pellicule HP5 développée au révélateur D76; vitesse d'obturation: 1/250 s; ouverture de diaphragme: f/8.

94 (Bas)

RIEN DANS LES MAINS, RIEN DANS LES POCHES par Stanley Matchett
Le jeune prestidigitateur Darren Swann (dix ans) est en train de réaliser avec succès sa première illusion en matière de lévitation, avec l'assistance de Hilary Thompson. Il s'agit d'une photographie directe, qui montre la perfection du tour de passe-passe. Cliché pris avec un appareil Nikon F2 équipé d'un objectif de 80-200 mm, sur pellicule HP5, sous l'éclairage ambiant.

95

PIERRE, LE CLOWN par Martyn Hayhow
L'auteur de cette image, qui est photographe au *Evening Post*, a saisi l'atmosphère entourant un clown qui amuse une foule en vacances avec sa voiture de comédie, et cela lui confère, de surcroît, une valeur artistique incontestable. Cliché pris avec un appareil Nikon F2 équipé d'un zoom de 70-210 mm, sur pellicule HP5 développée au révélateur ID11; vitesse d'obturation: 1/250 s; ouverture de diaphragme: f/8.

96

AMOUREUX par Wilhelm Mikhailovski
Ces dernières années, les photographes soviétiques ont démontré qu'ils sont passés maîtres dans l'art d'exprimer les sentiments humains dans un contexte moderne. Le puissant contraste dans les tons que l'on voit ici entre le jeune homme et la jeune fille souligne la masculinité de celui-là par rapport à la féminité de celle-ci, et cela nous a valu une excellente composition. Voir aussi aux pages 116 et 117.

97

SANS TITRE par Michael Barrington Martin
Ce photographe de mode londonien bien connu ne cesse d'expérimenter des idées nouvelles et utilise des pellicules de grandes dimensions de façon à pouvoir éprouver des combinaisons de deux ou davantage. Les résultats sont généralement saisissants de ce q̇, ainsi qu'on peut s'en convaincre du seul fait q̇ nombre de ses travaux servent à illustrer des calendriers et des couvertures de magazines. Nous voyons ici un ton simplifié et filtré en noir et blanc, qui a été efficacement mis en sandwich avec une photographie floue.

98

PIETRO ALBERTELLI par Tony Duffy
Spectaculaire démonstration de ski, due à l'un des plus grands photographes de sport britanniques, qui a remporté de nombreux prix dans des concours de photographie tant nationaux qu'internationaux. Cet exemple est extrêmement saisissant en raison de la faible hauteur de prise de vue et de la teinte sombre du ciel, et c'est aussi un extraordinaire exploit technique d'avoir rendu les yeux et le visage derrière le masque tout en maintenant le ton dans les teintes claires.

99

JOUEUSE DE TENNIS par Leo Mason
Un point de vue très graphique, très haut au-dessus du court de tennis du stade de Flushing Meadow, a donné une photographie très insolite de Virginia Wade en action. L'appareil Nikon F2 équipé d'un objectif de 200 mm avait été laissé sur un support spécial pendant deux semaines, et l'obturateur était télécommandé. Cliché pris sur une pellicule Ektachrome Professional; vitesse d'obturation: 1/500 s; ouverture de diaphragme: f/8.

100 (Haut)

PIERRES par Lars Oddvar Lovdahl
Un type de photographie qui rend beaucoup mieux lorsqu'elle est projetée que lorsqu'elle est reproduite, et ce en raison des teintes marron subtiles des feuilles d'automne, qui sont alors mises en valeur. La présence de champignons traduit un sens aigu de la composition chez ce photographe norvégien indépendant. Appareil Nikon F2 équipé d'un objectif de 20 mm, sur pellicule photomicrographique Kodak 2483.

100 (Bas)

Foule par Nigel Stone
Les scènes de foule donnent généralement de bonnes compositions en couleur lorsqu'elles sont prises d'en haut, mais elles peuvent aussi être monotones à moins de présenter un élément particulier d'intérêt ou de contraste. Comme la photographie du dessus, cet exemple est basé sur un point rouge constitué par un homme stratégiquement placé sur l'image et dont la tête et les épaules émergent nettement au-dessus de la mêlée.

101 (Haut)

LAC SOUS LA LUNE par le Dr A. Farquhar
Photographie résultant d'un sandwich de deux diapositives, – l'une représentant un yacht après le coucher du soleil sur le lac Okanagan en Colombie Britannique, l'autre la lune – toutes deux prises avec un appareil Canon EF sur pellicule Kodachrome 64, la première avec un objectif de 100 mm, la seconde avec un objectif de 400 mm. Le cliché ayant été pris avec l'appareil en fonctionnement automatique, il n'est pas possible de préciser les conditions de prise de vue. Le sandwich a été reproduit sur Ektachrome 5071.

101 (Bas)

TOMBE par Mark Woolstencroft
Les cimetières semblent être des sujets particulièrement populaires auprès des photographes de cette année, mais il s'agit ici d'une composition beaucoup plus originale et imaginative que la plupart de celles qui nous ont été soumises dans ce genre. La remarquable composition en couleur est complétée par la configuration des points blancs qui conduisent l'œil à la croix tout en donnant à l'ensemble un effet quelque peu éthéré.

102/103

SOIR DE SEPTEMBRE À MILAN par Trevor Fry, membre de la Société royale de photographie de Grande-Bretagne (FRPS)
Cette impression de conte de fée des pinacles de la cathédrale de Milan a été saisie, d'un escalier à quelque distance en face, avec un appareil Leicaflex SL équipé d'un objectif de 90 mm, sur pellicule au tungstène Ektachrome de sensibilité 160 ASA. L'exposition a été de l'ordre de 1 seconde pour une ouverture de diaphragme de f/8, et la reproduction a été réalisée à partir d'un tirage sur Cibachrome.

104

KALÉIDOSCOPE par C. H. J. Martin, diplômé de la Société royale de photographie de Grand-Bretagne (LRPS)
Photographie reproduite à partir d'un original constitué de huit tirages identiques sur papier Kodak 37RC. Oeuvre d'imagination qui a valu à son auteur de remporter plusieurs prix. Le négatif original Kodacolor a été pris avec un appareil Pentax Spotmatic équipé d'un objectif de 55 mm.

105

ST THOMAS, ABOYNE par Francis Tocher Jr
L'atmosphère créée par la lumière qui filtre au travers d'un vitrail a été habilement rehaussée en photographiant au zoom pendant 25 des 30 secondes d'exposition. Cliché pris avec un appareil Nikkormat FT2 équipé d'un zoom Tamron de 70–150 mm, sur pellicule Ektachrome 64; ouverture de diaphragme: f/11.

106

AUTOPORTRAIT par Hektor Krome
Amusante juxtaposition de sujets réels réfléchis dans la porte peinte d'une fourgonnette, qui donne un puzzle autant qu'une photographie. Cliché pris avec un appareil Olympus OM-2 équipé d'un objectif de 28 mm et reproduit à partir d'un tirage en Ektacolor.

107

MOSAÏQUE 2 par A. R. Pippard, Officier de l'Ordre de l'Empire britannique (OBE), membre de la Société royale de photographie de Grande-Bretagne (FRPS)
Photographie extraite d'une série de tirages expérimentaux dont les négatifs ont été imprimés avec interposition de différents écrans de couleur. L'écran utilisé ici avait été réalisé en projetant de la teinture sur un morceau de pellicule fixée. Le photographe est le distingué chimiste créateur de la pellicule Photocolor II et d'autres procédés chimiques de traitement en couleur.

108/109

EXPOSITIONS MULTIPLES
Expérience intéressante en matière d'expositions à recouvrement par l'emploi de divers filtres, due à un photographe hollandais. Cette photographie est reproduite à partir d'un tirage Polaroïd de 10 x 8 pouces.

110 (Haut)

S.A.R. LE PRINCE CHARLES par Terry Fincher, membre de la Société royale de photographie de Grande-Bretagne (FRPS)
Photographie, d'un naturel inhabituel, de ce prince très populaire, prise sur les rives du fleuve Negro à Manáus, au Brésil, juste avant le coucher du soleil par un des journalistes photographes indépendants le plus en vue de Grande-Bretagne. Cliché pris avec un appareil Olympus équipé d'un objectif de 28 mm et d'un flash.

110 (Bas)

VIEILLARD par Francisco Hidalgo
L'auteur, un Espagnol établi à Paris, est connu surtout pour ses photographies allongées de gratte-ciel et non pas tant pour ses portraits pris sur le vif. Cependant, son génie n'en transparaît pas moins, et l'extraordinaire impact de ce visage intéressant souligne un caractère renforcé par la focale différentielle, ce qui n'est pas toujours facile à réaliser avec un objectif de 35 mm dans une foule.

sur pellicule Ektachrome E6; vitesse d'obturation: 1/15 s; ouverture de diaphragme: f/5,6.

111 (Haut)

TRAVESTIS par Alain Verdier
Saisissant double portrait extrait du livre publié par le photographe sous le titre "Messieurs, Mesdames", qui est une étude sur les extravagances d'artistes d'homosexuels du monde entier, certains tristes et d'autres exhuberants, et que son auteur, qui est également musicien, dit inspiré par le peintre René Magritte. Cliché pris avec un appareil Nikon F équipé d'un objectif de 20 mm.

111 (Bas)

RÊVES DE LOUVETEAUX par le Dr M. D. Constable, correspondant de la Société royale de photographie de Grande-Bretagne (ARPS)
Sandwich de deux diapositives réalisées sur pellicule Agfa CT18 avec un appareil Canon Ftb équipé d'un objectif de 80 mm. Le garçon est le jeune fils du photographe qui souhaitait ardemment rejoindre son frère aîné chez les Louveteaux, de sorte que, la voyant endormi, le Dr Constable a pensé que tel pouvait être le sujet de ses rêves. Cliché pris au flash.

112

NEUROPOLIS par Luciano Pestarino, membre de la Fédération internationale de l'art photographique (FIAP)
Photographie qui traduit indiscutablement une atmosphère de névrose, caractéristique de l'homme en milieu urbain. Le photographe a eu recours à son fils comme élément symbolique qu'il a placé dans le coin d'une place de Buenos Aires. M. Pestarino est un photographe amateur, qui expose beaucoup dans le monde entier.

113

IAN SMITH par Rolf M. Aagaard
Photographie prise à l'aéroport de Salisbury alors que le Premier ministre de Rhodésie était sur le point de s'envoler pour les Etats-Unis après une longue attente pour l'obtention de son visa. Par pure coïncidence, l'auteur de la photographie, qui venait de Johannesburg, se trouvait sur le même appareil à destination de New York, et c'est ce qui nous vaut aujourd'hui cette image. Cliché pris avec un appareil Nikon F2 équipé d'un objectif de 180 mm, sur pellicule Tri-X développée au révélateur D76.

114/115

IMAGES par David Bailey, membre de la Société royale de photographie de Grande-Bretagne (FRPS)
La plupart des photographes envieront les occasions qu'a ce célèbre photographe de travailler pour de prestigieux magazines de mode et avec les meilleurs modèles du monde. Sa technique est toujours impeccable, et qu'il travaille sur commande ou pour son plaisir, il est original. Il défie avec beaucoup de succès les poses et les compositions conventionnelles, ainsi qu'en témoignent ces deux photographies. Le cadrage avec un parasoleil effraierait un photographe plus timide, et bien peu oseraient insérer de tels éléments domestiques ou le relief qui leur est donné.

116/117

PARALLÈLE par Wilhelm Michaelovsky
Photographie d'une extraordinaire puissance d'un maître russe, rehaussée par une saisissante perspective, de puissants contrastes et du grain. L'expression des visages stimule l'imagination de l'observateur et la très insolite composition rompt brillamment avec toutes les "règles". Voir aussi à la page 96.

118

DANS LA PARC AUX SAFARIS DE WINDSOR par Mike Hollist
Les animaux retiennent toujours l'attention, et cette rencontre insolite entre un zèbre et une jeune girafe est en outre teintée d'humour. Cliché pris avec un appareil Nikon équipé d'un objectif de 400 mm à point focal

déformant, qui a permis de maintenir l'arrière-plan hors du champ; pellicule Tri-X développée au révélateur D76; vitesse d'obturation: 1/500 s; ouverture de diaphragme: f/5,6.

119

FILS ET ANIMAUX DOMESTIQUES par Andrew McGlynn
Les animaux domestiques retiennent toujours énormément l'attention, et ce touchant moment saisi par un photographe irlandais est un petit chef-d'oeuvre. La relation entre les sujets est évidente et l'éclairage arrière a aidé le groupe à se détacher de l'arrière-plan. Cliché pris avec un appareil Leica M4 équipé d'un objectif de 50 mm, sur pellicule FP4 développée au révélateur Rodinal; vitesse d'obturation: 1/125 s; ouverture de diaphragme: f/5,6.

120

VIEILLARD FRANÇAIS par E. Chambré Hardman
Etude sensible due à un célèbre photographe professional de Liverpool, qui se distingue d'autre part par l'excellente qualité du tirage original. Cliché pris avec un appareil SLR à plaque de 8,3 x 10,7 cm équipé d'un objectif Tessar de 6⅜ pouces, sur pellicule Super XX; vitesse d'obturation: 1/100 s; ouverture de diaphragme: f/8.

121

JEUNE FILLE HAUTAINE par Vlatislar Machacek
Pose très insolite, probablement prise pour accentuer la grosseur, bien que ce ne soit pas évident dès l'abord. Comme tant d'autres travaux qui nous viennent de Tchécoslovaquie, cette photographie ignore les problèmes de grain, les lignes verticales et les poses traditionnelles, pour s'attarder à mettre tout le "punch" possible dans le message. L'éclairage arrière donne un effet de halo très efficace.

122/123

FOOTBALL À EDGE HILL par John Davidson
Prise par un photographe renommé du *Liverpool Daily Post*, cette photographie synthétise l'amour du football, qui se manifeste à un âge précoce dans cette ville. Une rue pavée dans une zone abandonnée, un vieux ballon et quelques briques, voilà tout ce dont ces enfants ont besoin pour se lancer à la conquête de Wembley! Cliché pris avec un appareil Nikon F équipé d'un objectif de 28 mm, sur pellicule Tri-X développée au révélateur D76; vitesse d'obturation: 1/60 s; ouverture de diaphragme: f/3,5.

124

MARIAGE par Hans-Jorge Anders
Prise à la demande du magazine *Stern*, cette photographie, qui montre un mariage mennonite au Paraguay, est extraite d'une série illustrant cet événement et la vitalité des participants. Cliché pris avec un appareil Leicaflex SL2 équipé d'un objectif de 19 mm, sur pellicule Tri-X.

125

VERS LA MAISON par Leon Balodis
Cette simple noce de campagne dans un village soviétique a été bien illustrée par la présence d'invités et de spectateurs courant en avant de la mariée et créant beaucoup de mouvement. Le ciel tourmenté donne du relief à la mariée, qui est le centre d'attraction, et la photographie présente dans l'ensemble un grand intérêt, tout au moins pour un étranger.

126

SANS TITRE par Francisco Aszmann
Photographie qui n'a besoin d'aucun titre parce que tout en elle dit "Printemps". L'éclairage arrière a permis d'obtenir le cadre magnifique des arbres en fleurs et donné à l'image profondeur et éclat, ce qui convient parfaitement au sujet. Bien qu'elle ait été prise au Brésil, elle pourrait exprimer le printemps n'importe où dans le monde.

127
PAS DE L'OIE par Bernhard Heinz
Photographie exposée à Photokina, primée dans le cadre du Concours des lecteurs de journaux allemands "Aperture", qui a attiré plus de 30 000 visiteurs. C'est une composition surprenante, qui se signale notamment par une gradation habile des tons. Cliché pris sur pellicule FP4.

128
LA NATURE ET LA BEAUTÉ
par Mogens Lerche Madsen
Cette photographie est le résultat du tirage sur pellicule lithographique d'un négatif représentant un arbre, le dos du modèle ayant été utilisé comme écran lors de la projection de l'image légèrement adoucie. Cliché pris avec un appareil Leica équipé d'un objectif Summicron, sur pellicule HP4 développée au révélateur Rodinal.

129
SUZANNE par Jozef Tichy
Les études de silhouettes ne sont pas si courantes cette année, mais nous en avons là un très bon exemple dans le style traditionnel, qui nous vient de Tchécoslovaquie. Bien que son charme lui vienne pour une bonne part de la beauté du sujet, la douce lumière qui tombe de la fenêtre y a grandement contribué, et l'aspect sombre de l'image est très agréable. Cliché pris avec un appareil Pentacon Six équipé d'un objectif Biometer, sur pellicule Orwo 20 développée au révélateur Atomal; vitesse d'obturation: 1/15 s; ouverture de diaphragme: f/8.

130
M. LINCOLN, JE PRÉSUME? par Achim Sperber
Cette photographie, due à un photographe hambourgeois, est extraite d'une série intitulée "New York – Up and Down" (New York de long en large). Cliché pris avec un appareil Pentax équipé d'un zoom de 85-210 mm, sur pellicule Tri-X développée au révélateur D76; vitesse d'obturation: 1/500 s; ouverture de diaphragme: f/4.

131
EN CONFÉRENCE par Stephen Shakeshaft
Photographie prise au cours d'une conférence politique, à un moment particulièrement "chaud" pour le sujet, que le photographe a saisi dans une expression pensive. Ce photographe (voir aussi à la page 75) est devenu l'un des journalistes photographes les plus en vogue d'Angleterre, et il a battu tous les records en obtenant pour la septième fois la publication d'une photographie dans le *Photography Year Book*. Cliché pris avec un appareil Nikon F2 équipé d'un objectif de 28 mm, sur pellicule Tri-X.

132
PORTRAIT DE FAMILLE par Martin Wolin Jr
Photographie qui illustre bien l'intérêt que présente le brouillard de l'arrière-plan pour isoler le sujet. Les trois vaches semblent presque poser tandis que les arbres et le poteau forment un écho rythmique. Cliché pris avec un appareil Minolta XE7 équipé d'un objectif de 50 mm, sur pellicule Plus X développée au révélateur Rodinal; vitesse d'obturation: 1/60 s; ouverture de diaphragme: f/8.

133
PROMENADE Á SKIS par Vladimir Filinov
Un objectif à courte distance focale et un traitement de séparation des tons ont donné à cette image un impact très puissant, voire même agressif. La composition arrête le regard et la minuscule silhouette que l'on aperçoit dans le lointain y contribue pour une large part, un peu comme l'insecte de la photographie de la page 66. Cliché pris avec un appareil de 35 mm et un grand angulaire, sur pellicule de sensibilité 300 ASA.

134
BAILLEMENT par Pak Nin Yam
Caractéristique de maints puissants photographes de jeunes d'Extrême-Orient, cette photographie a remporté un succès considérable et a été présentée au Salon de Londres. Il ne fait aucun doute que l'aspect sombre et la composition intéressante y ont contribué, mais on ne saurait passer sous silence l'excellente qualité d'impression de l'original.

135
COUP DE VENT par Kin-Pong Chan
Comme la photographie précédente, qui nous vient de Singapour, cet exemple, qui nous vient de Hong Kong, est traditionnel mais vivant et si bien présenté qu'il a également atteint les murs du Salon. Les cheveux qui voilent le visage apportent une note insolite, tandis que le magnifique et riche original sur papier glacé déborde de vitalité.

136/137
BATAILLE DE MOTS par Don McPhee
Cette vue, qui n'est que trop familière en ces jours de conflits sociaux, a été saisie exactement au moment voulu par un photographe du *Guardian*. Elle a été prise à l'usine Chrysler alors que des épouses s'efforçaient d'arrêter une grève. L'appareil était un Minolta SRT 101, équipé d'un objectif de 28 mm, et la pellicule une FP4 développée au révélateur Microphen.

138
GESICHT EINES HAUSES (Visage d'une maison)
par W. H. Gratt
Conception simple, qui a été bien vue par ce photographe allemand, et point de vue soigneusement choisi pour donner une composition bien équilibrée qui est séduisante du fait de ses lignes nettes et du minimum de détail. Cliché pris avec un appareil Bronica 6 x 6 équipé d'un objectif de 50 mm, sur pellicule Plus-X développée au révélateur HC110; vitesse d'obturation: 1/60 s; ouverture de diaphragme: f/8.

139
ANGELS-ANGLES par Arthur Perry
La simplicité de ligne et de forme engendrée par le puissant contraste et le point de vue bien choisi ont donné beaucoup d'impact à ce toit d'église photographié en Californie. Cliché pris avec un appareil Rolleiflex 3,5 équipé d'un filtre jaune-vert, sur pellicule FP4; vitesse d'obturation: 1/60 s; ouverture de diaphragme: f/16.

140
APRÈS L'ORAGE par Ilmars Apkalns
Paysage extrêmement saisissant d'Union soviétique, empreint d'une atmosphère wagnérienne. Les rochers découpés par la lumière constituent un premier plan qui s'adapte parfaitement au tumulte de l'arrière-plan et au relief de la lumière du soleil qui perce à travers un ciel menaçant.

141
PAYSAGE DE PIERRES par Asko Salmi
Photographié sur l'île de Norrskari, sur la côte ouest de la Finlande, ce paysage est caractéristique de l'arrivée en force que l'on observe chez la jeune génération de photographes amateurs. Un grand angulaire et des tons puissants ont engendré cette saisissante photographie, prise avec un appareil Canon AE-1 équipé d'un objectif de 20 mm et d'un filtre rouge, sur pellicule Tri-X développée au révélateur D76.

142
DIANE par Ian Stewart
Photographie, due à un photographe australien indépendant, de Diane Minchin, modèle professionnel, dans une pose provocante cadrée dans la fenêtre d'une ferme déserte, de sorte que le contraste porte tant sur le sujet que sur les tons. Cliché pris avec un appareil Hasselblad 500 équipé d'un objectif de 150 mm, sur pellicule Tri-X développée au révélateur D76.

143
SANS TITRE par George Martin Jr.
Saisissant portrait de profil d'un modèle professionnel, dû à un photographe de studio new yorkais, dont l'original se signale par la remarquable qualité de son impression. Cliché pris sous un éclairage au tungstène avec un appareil Nikon équipé d'un objectif de 105 mm, sur pellicule Plus X développée au révélateur D76. Le tirage a été réalisé sur papier Poly-contraste développé au révélateur Dektol.

144
KINGS ROAD par Harm Botman
Photographie prise par un photographe hollandais lors d'une visite dans une rue animée bien connue de Chelsea à Londres, où Lord Snowdon a eu plusieurs photographies de grandeur nature affichées à un mur extérieur de théâtre. Cliché pris avec un appareil Rollei 35, sur pellicule de sensibilité 800 ASA développée au révélateur Promicrol.

145
SANS TITRE par David Burrows, correspondant de l'Institute of Incorporated Photographers (AIIP)
Photographie prise par un jeune photographe de télévision pour faire connaître un jeu de "snooker". Le groupe est très bien composé et la fusion des personnages les moins importants dans un arrière-plan sombre ne laisse pas d'intriguer. Cliché pris avec un appareil Hasselblad équipé d'un objectif de 150 mm, sur pellicule Ilford FP4, et éclairé par un flash orienté sur le personnage se trouvant au centre.

146
HENLEY ROYAL REGATTA (RÉGATES ROYALES DE HENLEY) par Steve Hartley
Le Révérend Gillen W. Craig, vicaire de l'église Saint-Marc de la Old Marylebone Road, à Londres, brave les intempéries d'une manière typiquement britannique, déterminé à maintenir l'atmosphère edwardienne traditionnelle de cette semaine de régates à l'aviron qui se déroule une fois l'an. Cliché pris avec un appareil Nikkormat équipé d'un objectif de 85 mm, sur pellicule HP5 développée au révélateur ID11; vitesse d'obturation: 1/250 s; ouverture de diaphragme: f/5,6.

147
SANS TITRE par Michael Gnade
Emouvante photographie d'enfant, qui retient l'attention en raison tant de la grande hauteur de prise de vue que de l'expression effrontée et de la pose. Extraite d'une série d'instantanés non posés publiée dans le livre du professeur bavarois intitulé "Les gens et mon appareil photo".

148
ORATEUR LONDONIEN par Vladimir Birgus
Photographie extraite d'une série prise à Londres par un professeur de photographie artistique de Prague. Il a saisi le point culminant d'un dialogue animé entre un orateur religieux et un spectateur. Cliché pris avec un appareil Pentax Spotmatic équipé d'un objectif de 28 mm, sur pellicule Orwo NP27 développée au révélateur Formadon N.

149
BLOUSON NOIR par Ricardo Gomez Perez
Photographie prise au Crystal Palace par un étudiant du College of Printing de Londres, qui est déjà en passe de se distinguer tant par des expositions que par des publications dans plusieurs pays. Photographie extraite d'une collection consacrée aux "blousons noirs", prise avec un appareil Leica OL équipé d'un objectif de 40 mm, sur pellicule Tri-X développée au révélateur D76.

150
SANS TITRE par Alberto H. Jordé
Les portraits en clair ont généralement un effet enchanteur en raison de la délicatesse des tons, mais ils sont rarement réussis lorsqu'ils sont grenus. Cet exemple, qui nous vient d'Espagne, est une exception à la règle; de plus, la pose, autant que les lignes ondulantes au-dessous du personnage, donnent de l'ambiance et de l'expression. Cliché pris avec un appareil Leica équipé d'un objectif de 35 mm, sur pellicule Tri-X; vitesse d'obturation: 1/100 s; ouverture de diaphragme: f/8.

Test Rollei's new SL35E

An exciting new concept in high technology expertise from Rollei. Fully automatic with manual over-ride.

Multi-exposure facility.

The automatic and manually operated shutter control with 'memory lock.'

Electronic delayed action setting with LED action light and battery check.

Flash hot shoe with shutter speed synchronisation up to 1/125 second also auto flash cut-out on faster speeds.

The film speed selector up to 6,400 ASA. with exposure correction + or − 2 stops.

Co-axial Flash Socket.

Provision for motor winder.

Depth of Field preview button.

50mm f1.8 HFT Planar lens of Zeiss design and quality.

The unique fully-automatic aperture priority electronic shutter system.

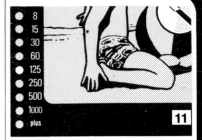

The viewfinder demonstrates to perfection Rollei's advanced technology in action.

Half-depressing the shutter control gives a 16 LED readout of the correct shutter speed for a preselected aperture.

A second depression of the button operates a 'memory' which will store a pre-measured light value (ideal for back-lit shots).

For focusing, the screen has no less than 3 aids: a split-image range-finder segment, a microprism circle, and a matt area surrounding both.

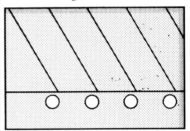

The multi-blade shutter is unique. Manufactured in hard-wearing steel, it runs vertically to cope with exposure times of from 1/1000 sec to 16 secs.

It's controlled by the SL35E's electronic brain: a maze of conductor lines, IC's, transistors, and silicon photo diodes with their own unique high sensitivity to low light levels.

It covers a range of film speeds from 25 to 6,400 ASA, plus a flash sync setting of 1/125, and a 'B' for long time exposures.

If for any reason the battery runs down the camera remains operational.

A range of 19 lenses including the famous Zeiss designs, Distagon, Planar, Tessar, Sonnar, in lengths from 16mm to 200mm with HFT coating match perfectly a truly professional system.

A recently introduced range of Rolleinar lenses add a further dimension, combining excellent quality with competitive prices made possible by technological break-throughs in lens manufacture.

Owning a Rollei says something about you.

151

LE GARDIEN par John Williams

Photographie prise, lors d'une visite au Louvre, à Paris, par un photographe australien qui avait été intrigué par l'indifférence apparente du gardien à l'égard de l'inestimable portrait de Mona Lisa et de la foule de visiteurs utilisant un flash, interdit, tout autour de lui. Cliché pris avec un appareil Olympus OM-1 équipé d'un objectif de 35 mm, sur pellicule Tri-X développée au révélateur Acufine; vitesse d'obturation: 1/60 s; ouverture de diaphragme: f/2.

152/153

**L'HEUREUX TEMPS DE L'ENFANCE
par Tsang-Chi Yen**

A en juger par le nombre de photographies qui nous en viennent, Formose se dégage comme un centre actif de photographie d'amateur en Extrême-Orient, et cette image en est un bon exemple. La vitalité de ces enfants attachants est rehaussée par la faible hauteur de prise de vue, qui engendre un arrière-plan bien dégagé de ciel. L'idée de leur faire battre des mains était géniale. Cliché pris avec un appareil Minolta SR 101, sur pellicule PX125; vitesse d'obturation: 1/125 s; ouverture de diaphragme: f/11.

154

SCÈNE DE NEIGE par W. Biggs

Les Chiltern Hills offrent de nombreuses occasions au photographe de paysages doué de sens artistique, et nous avons ici un exemple intéressant et parfaitement composé de haies se détachant de la neige. Cliché pris avec un appareil Mamiyaflex équipé d'un objectif de 180 mm, sur pellicule FP4 développée au révélateur ID11.

155

GLACIER BLANC par Vera Weinerstrova

Photographie pleine d'espace et de profondeur, due à une faible hauteur de prise de vue, bien choisie, qui a souligné la menace de ce phénomène naturel, tandis que les lignes des crevasses conduisent l'oeil dans le lointain et dans le ciel tourmenté. Cliché pris avec un appareil Praktisix équipé d'un objectif de 50 mm, sur pellicule Orwo NP20; vitesse d'obturation: 1/125 s; ouverture de diaphragme: f/16.

156

ETUDE DE SILHOUETTE par Valdis Brauns

Un nu dans le style traditionnel, presque daté, qui a été sorti de l'ordinaire par le ton hardi au lieu de l'image lumineuse qui est de règle pour les études en studio. Les lignes du châle constituent une intéressante juxtaposition avec les formes des bras qui leur font écho.

157

EN FORÊT par Andrej Krynicki

Exemple d'une série d'études de silhouettes en extérieur soumises par ce prolifique photographe polonais (voir aussi à la page 63) mais, dans le cas présent, non solarisées ou simplifiées. Comme toutes ses photographies, celli-ci est d'une conception originale, et l'éclairage arrière (pas la lumière dans le dos!) a engendré une agréable luminosité.

158

**HÔTEL DE VILLE DE TORONTO
par Jean Berner**

Un traitement très inhabituel pour une étude architecturale, qui rappelle une certaine école de peinture, a souligné les lignes claires. Les contrastes entre l'ancien et le moderne sont intéressants, tandis que l'enfant donne l'échelle et la profondeur. Cliché pris avec un appareil Nikkormat FT équipé d'un objectif de 105 mm, sur pellicule Tri-X développée au révélateur D76.

159

CENTRALE ÉLECTRIQUE EN NOUVELLE-ZÉLANDE par P. G. Gale

Une fine image de l'industrie, sur laquelle les cheminées donnent une impression de grande hauteur, due à la faible hauteur de prise de vue et au format vertical. La hardiesse des contrastes et la fumée créent une atmosphère authentique. Cliché pris avec un appareil Exa équipé d'un objectif de 50 mm, sur pellicule Adox KB21 développée au révélateur Microphen.

160

DIRECTEUR par Jiri Horak

Stimulante photographie, qui visait probablement à tracer le portrait d'un dirigeant agressif sur un arrière-plan industriel. Quelle que soit la manière dont l'observateur interprète la combinaison et le poing serré, son attention ne peut manquer d'être arrêtée par cette composition artistique. Cliché pris avec un appareil Petri FT équipé d'un objectif de 28 mm, sur pellicule Orwo 27 développée au révélateur Atomal.

161

UN FERVENT DE LA PLANCHE À ROULETTES par Peter Gant, correspondant de la Société royale de photographie de Grande-Bretagne (ARPS)

Extraordinaire image de mouvement soulignée par une faible vitesse d'obturation, extraite d'une série qui a remporté le premier prix du concours du Meilleur photographe de sport de l'année" du magazine *Amateur Photographer.* Cliché pris à la Skate City, à Londres, avec un appareil Olympus OM-1 équipé d'un objectif de 200 mm, sur pellicule Kodachrome 64; vitesse d'obturation: 1/15 s.

162 (Haut)

DELTAPLANE par Gordon Ratcliffe

Excellente photographie de deltaplane prise dans les Pennines, qui donne une bonne impression d'espace à ce ciel tourmenté. Le deltaplane est un appareil "Sunspot" piloté par Len Gabriels. Cliché pris avec un appareil Pentax Spotmatic équipé d'un objectif de 200 mm et d'un filtre cristal, sur pellicule Kodachrome 64; vitesse d'obturation: 1/125 s; ouverture de diaphragme: f/11.

162 (Bas)

SANS TITRE par David R. MacAlpine

Paysage qui démontre sans conteste qu'un éclairage à effet est tout aussi efficace en couleur qu'en noir et blanc, et peut imprégner un paysage ordinaire d'une puissante atmosphère. Cliché pris avec un appareil Pentax SIA équipé d'un objectif de 55 mm, sur pellicule Kodachrome II; vitesse d'obturation: 1/125 s; ouverture de diaphragme: f/5,6.

163 (Haut)

TURBULENCE par John L. Cawthra

Cette photographie a été prise dans l'intention déclarée de donner une impression futuriste de voyage dans l'espace. C'est un sandwich constitué d'une diapositive sur pellicule Agfa CT21 prise au travers du fond d'une bouteille à lait et d'une photographie d'un deltaplane prise avec un appareil Canon AT1 équipé d'un objectif de 135 mm, sur pellicule Fuji 100.

163 (Bas)

IN MEMORIAM par Tony Howard

Photographie prise un soir d'été, à une heure tardive, dans un cimetière anglais alors que le soleil se reflétait dans le marbre de la croix. Cliché pris avec un appareil Nikkormat FTN équipé d'un objectif de 50 mm, sur pellicule Ektachrome X développée dans le commerce; vitesse d'obturation: 1/30 s; ouverture de diaphragme: f/5,6.

164/165

MOTO-CROSS par Woot Gilhuis

Photographie d'action dynamique due à l'auteur de "Between sharp and unsharp" publié par Argus Books Ltd. Woot est un photographe indépendant en même temps qu'un membre éminent de l'Association néerlandaise des photographes professionnels. Cliché pris avec un appareil Canon F1 équipé d'un objectif de 400 mm, sur pellicule Kodachrome 64. Le mouvement a été obtenu en panoramiquant au 1/8 s.

166

SANS TITRE par Patrick Lichfield

Ce portrait de la duchesse de Roxburghe et de la comtesse de Lichfield a été tiré pour le magazine *Vogue,* et il est reproduit avec l'aimable autorisation de Condé Nast. Il traduit une pose agréable et originale, qui convient parfaitement à deux soeurs, tandis que le traitement sensible de la couleur dans des teintes claires est des plus artistique. Cliché pris avec un appareil Olympus OM-2, sur pellicule Ektachrome.

167

CARON par James Elliott

Portrait tout empreint de charme et de beauté grâce à une belle combinaison de teintes pastel parfaitement harmonisées, tandis que la position haute de la tête traduit la dignité. Cliché pris avec un appareil de 35 mm équipé d'un zoom de 70-210 mm et d'un flash électronique, sur pellicule Ektachrome.

168

VOITURE VUE AU TRAVERS D'UN VERRE CANNELÉ par John F. Percy

Photographie extraite d'une série dans laquelle le photographe a exploré le monde au travers du panneau de verre cannelé de 23 cm de largeur de sa porte d'entrée. La voiture se trouvait de l'autre côté de la route, de sorte que l'appareil Olympus OM-1 équipé d'un objectif de 50 mm et d'un convertisseur Komura 2x a été pratiquement utilisé avec une ouverture de diaphragme de f/16. Cliché pris sur pellicule Kodachrome 64.

169

SANS TITRE par D. J. Bellham

Photographie insolite obtenue par la double exposition, sur le même châssis, d'un paysage pris au coucher du soleil et d'un motif sur une surface ondulée noire à la lumière du soir. Cliché pris avec un appareil Canon EF équipé d'un objectif de 50 mm, sur pellicule Kodachrome 25.

170

PORTRAIT par Ray Williamson

Recours délibéré à la perspective déformée créée en se rapprochant du sujet avec un objectif standard de façon à renforcer une atmosphère étouffante, voire même énigmatique, que l'auteur décrit comme "la vision d'un peintre". Cliché pris à l'aide d'un flash à éventail utilisé par réflexion sur pellicule Kodachrome 25 avec un appareil Contax RTS équipé d'un objectif de 50 mm; ouverture de diaphragme: f/5,6.

171

PORTRAIT par K. Amil

Photographie sur laquelle la couleur domine et où l'auteur a fait preuve d'un réel sens artistique en se concentrant sur le turban au lieu de faire un portrait direct. Le reste de la couleur engendre l'harmonie sans être lourd.

172/173

TRISUL par Frank Martin, membre de l'Institute of Incorporated Photographers (FIIP)

Cette photographie du mont himalayien qui s'élève à quelque 7 200 m montre une moraine formée par le retrait d'un glacier; elle a été prise par un photographe professionnel qui s'était rendu sur place durant un congé pour faire de l'alpinisme. Il a utilisé un appareil Petri TTL équipé d'un zoom de 70-230 mm, et une pellicule Kodachrome 64.

174 (Haut)

PORTRAIT par C. Nutman
Il est aujourd'hui admis de recourir à des filtres de couleur pour certains types de photographies en couleur, à condition que leur utilisation ajoute quelque chose à l'atmosphère. Dans ce cas, la chaleur et l'effet de coucher de soleil, obtenus en photographiant l'arrière-plan séparément au zoom pendant l'exposition, ont donné un portrait artistique.

174 (Bas)

SANS TITRE par Joan Wakelin, membre de la Société royale de photographie de Grande-Bretagne (FRPS)
Le photographe, qui a parcouru en tous sens la Zambie et le Sri Lanka pour s'y livrer à des études photographiques sur les gens, a ici trouvé un sujet dans un jardin de Sheffield. Cliché pris avec un appareil Pentax SV équipé d'un objectif de 28 mm, sur pellicule Agfa CT18, reproduite à partir d'un tirage sur Cibachrome.

175

VISION par le Dr Surendra Sahai
Intéressant sandwich de deux diapositives, l'une représentant un feu d'artifice et l'autre des adorateurs du soleil sur la plage de Konorak, en Inde. La composition a donné une image qui stimule l'imagination. Les deux clichés ont été pris avec un appareil Pentax SPII, sur pellicule Kodachrome 64, dont un double a été tiré sur pellicule Kodak Special.

176

PORTRAIT par Maurice Braun
Portrait très séduisant d'enfant, qui a quelque chose de la qualité d'une peinture en raison de l'atténuation des couleurs et du sombre arrière-plan. Il s'agit d'un spécimen de portrait de grand format, extrait d'une magnifique collection présentée au stand Kodak à Photokina. Voir aussi à la page 34.

177

MANNEQUIN par Carlos Canovas
Expression vivante d'un visage en plastique dans lequel la texture de chair naturelle a été rendue par le grain. La hardiesse de la composition, ajoutée au gros plan, augmente le réalisme et engendre un puissant effet tridimensionnel. Cliché pris avec un appareil Nikon F2 équipé d'un objectif de 135 mm, sur pellicule Tri-X développée au révélateur HC100.

178

ETUDE DE NU par Frank Peeters
Etude expressive, qui traduit une interprétation artistique de la silhouette humaine utilisée comme base d'une conception puissante. Cliché pris avec un appareil Nikkormat FTN équipé d'un objectif de 28 mm, sur pellicule Tri-X de sensibilité 1600 ASA développée au révélateur Neutol S.

179

NU par Hideki Fujii
Etude qui traduit l'individualité caractéristique que l'on trouve dans l'art japonais en général. Cela tient en partie à la pose très insolite du personnage, qui est presque suspendu dans l'espace, et en partie au masque.

180

PAYSAGES par Signe Drevsjo
Deux agréables paysages de Norvège – celui du haut pris à Gomsoy dans les îles Lofoten. La formation particulièrement heureuse de nuages conduit l'oeil dans le lointain et donne une impression marquée de profondeur. La photographie du bas constitue une excellente image. L'une et l'autre ont été prises avec un appareil Canon F1 muni d'un filtre rouge, sur pellicule Tri-X développée au révélateur D76. Le photographe a utilisé un objectif de 17 mm pour le panorama du haut et un Macro de 50 mm pour la photographie du bas.

181

CHÂTEAU MYSTÉRIEUX par Vera Weinerstrova
L'utilisation d'un grand angulaire pour les paysages, alliée à l'adjonction d'un objet hardi au premier plan, est devenue très à la mode. Associée à des tons puissants et contrastés, avec beaucoup de grain et des noirs riches, cette technique est assurément impressionnante, comme on peut le voir sur cet exemple. Appareil Praktisix et pellicule Orwo NP20.

182

PLONGEUSE par Mervyn Rees, membre de la Société royale de photographie de Grande-Bretagne (FRPS)
Cette merveilleuse photographie d'action a été prise au Crystal Palace de Londres au cours d'une séance d'entraînement pour les Jeux du Commonwealth. Cliché pris avec un appareil Nikon F2 équipé d'un objectif de 50 mm, sur pellicule Tri-X développée au révélateur D76; vitesse d'obturation: 1/250 s; ouverture de diaphragme: f/3,5.

183

KARIN FITZNER par Mervyn Rees
Photographie dramatique d'une lanceuse de poids est-allemande, prise au moment de lâcher le poids. Le grain, inévitable lorsqu'on force une pellicule rapide, ajoute en fait à l'atmosphère de force et d'effort tandis que la diagonale très marquée suggère le mouvement. Cliché pris avec un appareil Nikon F2 équipé d'un objectif de 500 mm, sur pellicule Tri-X; vitesse d'obturation: 1/1000 s; ouverture de diaphragme: f/8.

184

VILLE DES AILES par Jiri Horak
Photographie caractéristique des oeuvres d'imagination qui nous viennent de Tchécoslovaquie. Il y a une similarité d'idées entre cette photographie et celle de la page 160, du même photographe, mais l'une et l'autre sont très élaborées. L'appareil était un Petri FT équipé d'un objectif de 28 mm; le cliché a été pris au 1/125 s, sur pellicule Orwo NP27 développée au révélateur Atomal.

185

EDDY BOYD par Reijo Porkka
L'auteur de cette photographie a bien vu la silhouette intéressante formée par l'éclairage arrière et l'a judicieusement soulignée par une simplification des tons, de façon à donner une impression intense d'atmosphère de night-club. Cliché pris avec un appareil Nikon équipé d'un objectif de 50 mm, sur pellicule Tri-X de sensibilité 1600 ASA.

186

SANS TITRE par Jim Barker
Nombre de personnes ont dû passer par cette situation amusante résultant du contraste entre la jeune fille de l'affiche et la dame assise. Elle montre l'intérêt qu'il y a à rester en alerte et à avoir toujours un appareil photographique avec soi. Cliché pris avec un appareil Hasselblad, sur pellicule FP4 développée au révélateur Unitol.

187

AU CHÔMAGE par E. Chambré Hardman
Très belle étude industrielle montrant une chaudière désaffectée dans une mine de houille galloise. Cliché pris avec un appareil Rolleiflex, sur pellicule HP3; le négatif a été agrandi sur une pellicule ordinaire à grain fin Ilford, de façon à donner une diapositive qui a ensuite été tirée sur papier dur au bromure.

188

HYDE PARK par F. Russell, membre de l'Institute of Incorporated Photographers (FIIP), membre de la Société royale de photographie de Grande-Bretagne (FRPS)
Photographie extraite d'une série décrivant les parcs et les gens de Londres, due à un jeune photographe industriel, qui s'est déjà distingué dans ce domaine. Cette série a été réalisée exclusivement durant ses loisirs. Cliché pris avec un appareil Nikkormat équipé d'un zoom de 43-86 mm, sur pellicule HP5 de sensibilité 800 ASA.

189

AUTOMNE par Lazslo Lajas
La présence de feuilles sur la jeune fille endormie a un effet légèrement macabre, mais cela augmente assurément l'atmosphère d'automne et nous vaut une image stimulante dans un paysage par ailleurs assez terne. Le traitement souligne la similarité d'approche entre les photographes hongrois et les photographes tchèques.

190

LA TÊTE ENTRE LES MAINS par Howard Walker
Ce photographe bien connu, du *Sunday Mirror*, s'est assurément diverti lorsqu'il a photographié son beau-père dans un miroir concave à raser de la salle be bain, mais il a engendré également une curieuse dimension abstraite. Cliché pris sous l'éclairage ambiant avec un appareil Nikon F2 équipé d'un objectif de 50 mm, sur pellicule Tri-X surdéveloppée au révélateur D76.

191

JANVIER par Vladimir Filinov
Autre photographie qui nous vient d'URSS, surprenante en ce qu'elle traite de manière inhabituelle un sujet assez banal en isolant un élément du groupe. Le garçon donne le ton tandis que les autres forment le décor. Cliché pris avec un appareil de 35 mm équipé d'un objectif standard et d'un convertisseur 3x, tiré sur une pellicule lignée au format 6 x 9 cm.

192

L'ONCLE JEAN par V. Sonta
Photographie extraite d'une série représentant des paysans lithuaniens, pour laquelle l'auteur a judicieusement choisi de prendre le sujet de profil et où la pose ajoute un élément de stabilité et de force. Cliché pris avec un appareil Konica A3 équipé d'un objectif de 50 mm, sur pellicule Tri-X développée au révélateur Microphen.

193

SANS TITRE par David Burrows, correspondant de l'Institute of Incorporated Photographers (AIIP)
Photographie prise lors d'un récital de piano à Manchester, dont il n'est pas nécessaire de nommer le sujet, même si son visage est en partie caché. On connaît les liens de M. Heath avec la musique, et le point de vue choisi a donné une composition insolite et surprenante. Cliché pris avec un appareil Nikon F2 équipé d'un objectif de 135 mm, sur pellicule Tri-X développée au révélateur D76.

194/195

PETER BONETTI par Mike Hollist
Le célèbre gardien de but de Chelsea, surnommé "Cat", est accompagné, durant son entraînement, de son fils âgé de neuf ans qui espère succéder à son père! Mike, qui travaille pour *The Daily Mirror,* a utilisé un appareil Nikon F2 équipé d'un objectif de 180 mm, sur pellicule Tri-X développée au révélateur D76; vitesse d'obturation: 1/500 s; ouverture de diaphragme: f/5,6.

196

FENÊTRE À LONDRES par Jack Rufus, membre de la Société royale de photographie de Grande-Bretagne (FRPS)
Lorsqu'il n'était pas en safari dans l'Est africain, le regretté Jack Rufus adorait flâner à Londres avec son appareil photographique, et il trouvait généralement l'interprétation artistique tant de l'architecture moderne que de l'architecture ancienne, telle celle-ci, prise dans le quartier du Barbican. Cliché pris avec un appareil Hasselblad équipé d'un objectif de 80 mm, sur pellicule Tri-X développée au révélateur Microdol. Voir aussi à la page 59.

197

TOUR par Geri Della Rocca
Vue très insolite du World Trade Centre à New York, qui montre que, lorsque les circonstances empêchent de garder les lignes à la verticale, c'est un avantage certain de photographier de très près de façon à exagérer la sensation de hauteur et à donner une composition puissante. Cliché pris avec un appareil Nikon F équipé d'un objectif de 20 mm, sur pellicule HP5 de sensibilité 600 ASA.

198

TENDRESSE par Serge de Sazo
L'émotion de l'amour peut être projetée de nombreuses manières, mais il faut un artiste pour utiliser des nus des deux sexes sans tomber dans l'indécence. Les Français sont passés maîtres en la matière dans le domaine de la sculpture et de la peinture, et cette image nous montre qu'ils y réussissent également bien en photographie. Cette photographie permet une comparaison intéressante avec celles des pages 71 et 211.

199

KALHAMA ET GUTTA par K. Szebessy
Photographie qui saisit l'atmosphère d'un studio d'artiste en raison du papier qui sert d'arrière-plan et des supports, mais elle sort de l'ordinaire du fait de la silhouette qui s'avance vers l'appareil photographique, en donnant un mouvement et un équilibre parfaits à la composition.

200

BRIAN BECK par Geoffrey Tyrer
Photographie prise exactement à la vitesse voulue de ce gymnaste olympique exécutant un saut périlleux. Non seulement l'action a été saisie au summum de son intensité, mais le tableau est très complet. Cliché pris pour le *Sheffield Star* avec un appareil Canon FT équipé d'un objectif de 50 mm et d'un flash utilisé par réflexion, sur pellicule Tri-X; ouverture de diaphragme: f/5,6.

201

GYMNASTE par Luis Arteaga Cerdain
Comme celle de la page opposée, cette photographie est le résultat d'un temps de pose très précis, qui a permis de saisir l'action à son apogée. Elle complète également le tableau en montrant un arrière-plan authentique, et la vue de dos est d'une touche inhabituelle. Cliché pris avec un appareil Nikon F2A équipé d'un objectif de 105 mm, sur pellicule Tri-X développée au révélateur Rodinal.

202

UNE ENFANT DES RUES À RIO par Henning Christoff
Photographie extraite d'une série consacrée aux enfants sans foyer d'Ipanema, contraints de dormir dans les rues après avoir été expulsés de chez eux. Cliché pris avec un appareil Leica M4 équipé d'un objectif Summilux de 35 mm et d'un flash, sur pellicule Tri-X développée au révélateur D76.

203

VISIONS par Vlado Bača
Photographie extraite d'une série due à ce jeune photographe indépendant slovaque, prise pour le magazine *Slovensko*. Les tirages ont été obtenus à partir de réflexions sur des plaques chromées avec un appareil Pentacon Six équipé d'un objectif de 50 mm, sur pellicule Orwo NP27 développée au révélateur D76.

204

UN SOIR DANS LE VALLON par David Dalby
L'atmosphère menaçante d'un orage dans les Highlands a été parfaitement saisie et restituée par l'utilisation de noirs lourds. Les différentes couches et la trouée de lumière dans le lointain donnent une bonne impression de profondeur. Cliché pris avec un appareil Hasselblad équipé d'un objectif de 80 mm, sur pellicule Tri-X développée au révélateur D76; vitesse d'obturation: 1/250 s; ouverture de diaphragme: f/16.

205

MON AMIE par V. Sonta
Photographie qui plairait à ceux qui combattent ce qu'ils appellent la "menace de la motocyclette". L'éclairage à effet et la place inhabituelle du personnage donnent une impression de vitesse menaçante pour l'observateur. Le photographe a utilisé un filtre rouge et un appareil Pentacon Six équipé d'un objectif de 80 mm. Pellicule Photo 65 développée au révélateur D76; vitesse d'obturation: 1/60 s; ouverture de diaphragme: f/5,6.

206

AU BORD DE L'ABÎME par John Woodhouse
Autoportrait pris dans le Peak District National Park, à l'aide d'un trépied et d'un déclencheur à retardement, par un ascensionniste/alpiniste bien connu, qui a déjà remporté plusieurs prix. Cliché pris avec un appareil Olympus OM-1 équipé d'un objectif de 35 mm et d'un filtre orange, sur pellicule FP4 développée au révélateur Aculux.

207

DELTAPLANE par T. G. Edwards
Photographie qui permet une comparaison intéressante avec son homologue de la page 162, et qui soulève la question, très discutée dans les clubs, de savoir qui de la couleur ou du noir et blanc engendre le plus d'ambiance ou d'intensité dramatique. Cliché pris à Devils Dyke avec un appareil Nikon F2 équipé d'un objectif de 85 mm et d'un filtre polarisant, sur pellicule FP4.

208

A DOS par Min Shik Choi
Le thème de l'amour d'un enfant pour un animal domestique est émouvant et a de nombreux adeptes, mais il est inhabituel de voir un renard aussi apprivoisé que celui-ci en Corée. La démarche et l'expression résolues ajoutent du piquant et du mouvement. Cliché pris avec un appareil Leica M3 équipé d'un objectif de 200 mm, sur pellicule Tri-X développée au révélateur Microdol X; vitesse d'obturation: 1/120 s; ouverture de diaphragme: f/4.

209

A DOS par David Wilding
Photographie prise sur le vif lors du *Tattoo* d'Edimbourg, alors que le sujet était à la recherche d'un siège. Autre photographie qui montre qu'il y a toujours intérêt à avoir un appareil photographique avec soi. Cliché pris avec un appareil Pentax Spotmatic équipé d'un objectif de 135 mm, sur pellicule Tri-X de sensibilité 650 ASA.

210

MODÈLE DE SCULPTEUR par Frank Peeters
Prise dans une école des Beaux-Arts belge sous l'éclairage normal des tubes, cette photographie a retenu l'atmosphère d'une classe des Beaux-Arts — ce qui aurait été perdu avec un flash. Cliché pris avec un appareil Nikkormat FT3 équipé d'un objectif de 105 mm, sur pellicule Tri-X de sensibilité 1600 ASA développée au révélateur Neutol S.

211

RETRATO DE DOS ENAMORADOS (PORTRAIT DE DEUX AMOUREUX) par Josep María Ribas Prous
La représentation d'un homme et d'une femme nus sur la même photographie a été traitée avec goût et tact compte tenu de la difficulté du sujet. Le résultat est artistique et expressif. Cliché pris sous l'éclairage ambiant avec un appareil Nikon F2 équipé d'un objectif de 105 mm, sur pellicule Tri-X développée au révélateur Microdol X; vitesse d'obturation: 1/30 s; ouverture de diaphragme: f/2.

212

MITSUO TSAKAHARA par Sven Simon
Les photographies de sport sont toujours un grand défi pour les photographes en raison du temps de pose très précis nécessaire pour saisir l'action à son apogée. Le résultat paraît toujours facile, mais il faut beaucoup d'expérience. L'adjonction des barres parallèles complète le tableau.

213 (Haut)

FIONA ROGERS par Mervyn Rees, membre de la Société royale de photographie de Grande-Bretagne (FRPS)
Cette photographie d'un sauteur d'obstacles a été prise au Crystal Palace de Londres pendant une séance d'entraînement. L'effet dramatique a été obtenu par l'utilisation d'un *fish eye* Sigma monté sur un appareil Nikon F2; cliché pris sur pellicule Tri-X développée au révélateur D76; vitesse d'obturation: 1/1000 s.

213 (Bas)

UNE BOULISTE par Terry Cooper
Scène typiquement anglaise, prise dans le cadre d'une opération "Communauté et Environnement", qui a remporté un prix décerné par la South Eastern Arts Association. Cliché pris au Preston Park de Brighton avec un appareil Olympus OM-1 équipé d'un objectif de 50 mm, sur pellicule FP4 développée au révélateur ID11.

214

DANS UN MUSÉE D'ATHÈNES par Jean Berner
Amusante photographie de la fille du photographe, qui manifeste sa réticence à développer sa culture! Initialement prise sur pellicule Fujichrome 100 avec un appareil Nikkormat équipé d'un objectif de 20 mm, cette image a été rephotographiée et tirée sur pellicule Tri-X pour obtenir l'agrandissement et isoler le sujet par ombrage.

215

MÉTRO par Achim Sperber
Prise dans le métro de New York pour une série intitulée "New York — Up and Down" (New York de long en large), cette photographie a saisi l'atmosphère de ce moyen de transport très décrié. Cliché pris avec un appareil Leica équipé d'un objectif de 35 mm, sur pellicule Tri-X développée au révélateur D76; vitesse d'obturation: 1/125 s; ouverture de diaphragme: f/2,8.

216

SANS TITRE par Signe Drevsjo
Double portrait pris sur le vif, qui exprime un moment de bonheur d'une façon que seule la photographie peut restituer. Le contraste de la jeunesse et de la vieillesse porte son propre message, et les deux têtes sont judicieusement placées pour donner une composition d'une grande vitalité. Cliché pris avec un appareil Canon F1 équipé d'un objectif de 50 mm, sur pellicule Tri-X développée au révélateur D76.

217

DOUBLE PORTRAIT par Egons Spuris
Portrait qui défie tous les manuels prétendant qu'il doit toujours y avoir un lien physique ou suggéré entre deux personnes dans un portrait et, en outre, "que l'une doit être plus saillante que l'autre". Il n'en reste pas moins que cette composition inhabituelle est là, et que l'intensité des expressions stimule l'imagination.

218

SANS TITRE par Karin Szekessy
Remarquable arrangement de personnages par un photographe qui, de toute évidence, met tout en oeuvre pour présenter une idée et ne se soucie pas des considérations techniques à prendre en compte pour équilibrer l'éclairage. En fait, la lumière qui tombe de la fenêtre semble ajouter de l'authenticité. Voir aussi à la page 199.

219

SANS TITRE par Michael Gnade
Photographie qui permet une intéressante comparaison avec celle de la page opposée. La délicate touche féminine est remplacée par des contrastes très accusés, non seulement en ce qui concerne le sujet, mais aussi les tons, et la composition est remarquablement cohérente en dépit d'un aussi grand nombre d'éléments.

220

CALELLA par Ferran Artigas
Un faible angle de prise de vue et des contrastes marqués ont permis au photographe de renforcer l'impression que les appartements risquent de s'effondrer lors du prochain orage par suite de l'érosion sous-jacente. Cliché pris avec un appareil Minolta SRT équipé d'un objectif de 28 mm, sur pellicule Tri-X.

221

PAYSAGE DE SKYE par Chris Peet, membre de la Société royale de photographie de Grande-Bretagne (FRPS)
Photographie due à un exposant qui a abandonné la couleur pour le noir et blanc. Le tirage original était d'un ton sépia marqué, obtenu par deux développements dans une solution sulfurée concentrée. Présentée au Salon de Londres, elle a été prise avec un appareil Praktica équipé d'un objectif de 20 mm et d'un filtre orange sur pellicule FP4.

222 (Haut)

LES DÔMES par Roland Herpin
Intéressante photographie tout empreinte d'atmosphère grâce à l'utilisation d'un écran et à l'ombrage du ciel lors du tirage. Cliché pris en Tunisie avec un appareil Minolta SRT 101 équipé d'un objectif de 135 mm, sur pellicule Tri-X tirée sur papier Agfa dur.

222 (Bas)

COMPOSITION par Ilmar Apkalns
Il s'agit presque d'un exercice de manuel, qui ne semble pas avoir de sens ou de message caché, mais qui dénote un sens remarquable de la composition. L'original présentait une qualité d'impression irréprochable.

223

ARCHITECTURE DE PLAGE par Michael Scott
Extraite d'une série due à un professeur d'art, cette photographie illustre la manière dont "l'oeil qui sait voir" cherche l'interaction intéressante du modèle, de la texture et du ton chez les sujets les plus banals. Cliché pris avec un appareil Praktica LTL équipé d'un objectif de 50 mm sur pellicule HP5, tirée en sépia pour souligner le caractère et l'âge de l'édifice.

224

NU par José Torregrosa
Le recours à une silhouette féminine pour une conception abstraite ou semi-abstraite n'est pas inhabituel, mais le puissant effet des formes simples et d'un modèle hardi fait de cette photographie un exemple supérieur à beaucoup d'autres. Cliché pris avec un appareil Nikon F équipé d'un objectif de 24 mm, sur pellicule Tri-X développée au révélateur HC110.

TROISIÈME PAGE DE COUVERTURE

APRÈS LA COURSE par Raymonde Jarry
Photographie de formes très intéressantes. Les prises de vues d'une grande hauteur de foules ne sont pas faciles parce que les composants forment rarement une composition équilibrée, ou sont par trop répétitifs. Dans le cas présent, les chaises vides remédient à la monotonie et la vue de dos apporte une touche inhabituelle.

Datos Technicos

CUBIERTA DE POLVO por Martin Wolin Jr.
Bella fotografía que nos muestra el valor estético de la luz matinal antes de la aparición del sol. Produce unos delicados colores pastel y una bella composición de color. Pentax de 6 x 7 cm con objetivo de 105 mm; 1/60 de sugundo, a f/8, en película Ektachrome High Speed. Reproducción es de una copia en Cibachrome.

Portada: parte interior

AU BEGUINAGE DE BRUGE, por Jean Berger
La foto, obra de un famoso fotógrafo francés, muestra una brillante capacidad de diseño en la que juegan un gran papel el ritmo, la repetición y el fuerte contraste. Tomada en Bélgica con una cámara Nikkormat FT y objetivo de 20 mm. Película Tri-X revelada en D-76.

13

INDUSTRIA de John Davidson
Esta fotografía fue tomada con objeto de situarla en la cubierta de un suplemento dedicado a la industria por parte del *Liverpool Daily Post*. Para reducir el extremado contraste se utilizó un cromofiltro como filtro de densidad neutra. Se empleó una Nikon F con un objetivo Nikkor de 28 mm. y una película Tri-X revelada en D76.

14

PAISAJE MARINO, por José Torregrossa
Hasta a los temas más tradicionales se les puede dar cierta modernidad desafiando las reglas de la composición, reglas que en este caso hubiesen obligado a situar la barca a un lado, en lugar de al centro. Esto ha aportado mucho a esta foto, que está llena de la atmósfera del atardecer. Nikkormat con objetivo de 24 mm. película Tri-X.

15

VERCORS, por J. Abassin
Hermoso paisaje nevado, que parece una postal de Navidad, dramatizado por el oscuro cielo; es fácil de obtener, en las circunstancias apropiadas, con un filtro suave. La inclusión de la diminuta figura le da proporción y profundidad, a la vez que dirige la vista.

16

INDIOS EN CALGARRY de George Webber
Las flechas de la pared proporcionan un toque irónico al mensaje contenido en esta instantánea de un joven fotógrafo canadiense. Tomada en la sombra con una Canon FT6N y un objetivo de 50 mm. en una película Ilford FP4 revelada en ID11.

17

CON EL TRAJE DEL PADRE, por Raghu Rai
Agradable foto que relata un momento feliz, a la vez que muestra, como otras de este libro, el hecho de que hay un lugar para el humor en la fotografía, incluso cuando ésta no tenga un valor estéticamente perdurable. Nikon F con objetivo de 85 mm. Película Tri-X; 1/250 de segundo, diafragma f/5,6.

18

CARMEN de Josep Maria Ribas Prous
Eficacísima utilización del grano para obtener un impacto artístico. El autor, un profesor español de fotografía, obtuvo el efecto mediante la ampliación de una pequeña zona del negativo. Se sirvió de una lámpara de tungsteno, una Nikon F2 con un objetivo de 105 mm. y una película Tri-X revelada en Microdol X. 1/60 seg. a f/5,6.

19

INGRID, por F. John Reid
El tratamiento en clave alta saca buen provecho de esta bella modelo rubia. Mamiya C330 con objetivo Sekor de 135 mm. Película FP4 revelada en D76. La luz de estudio se logró a base de dos unidades de flash Multilec dirigidas hacia el modelo y dos unidades más hacia el fondo. La ampliación se difuminó un poco por medio de una gasa de seda.

20

SOCORRO de David Bearne
Instantánea tomada en la final de la Copa Hampshire de rugby disputada por el Basingstoke y el Havant. El fotógrafo ha conseguido captar un incidente al que no le falta su toque humorístico. Se sirvió de una Nikon F2 con un objetivo de 135 mm. y una película Tri-X revelada en D76. Exposición de 1/250 seg. a f/5,6.

21

ENTENDIENDO DE QUÉ VA EL ASUNTO, por Frank Travers
Los reporteros fotográficos a menudo tienen la oportunidad de captar episodios significativos y ciertos gestos; pero se necesita mucha maestría y experiencia para anticiparse al hecho y saber disparar en el momento preciso. Frank, que trabaja por el *Sheffield Morning Telegraph*, utilizó una cámara Canon Ftb con objetivo Novaflex de 400 mm. para esta instantánea. Película Tri-X revelada en Qualitol.

22/23

ROLF HARRIS EN ACCIÓN de John Davidson
Un famoso comediante con un grupo de escolares de Liverpool durante la grabación de una serie televisiva. En la imagen se recoge el gran entusiasmo que despierta en Rolf Harris el trabajo con niños. El escenario es una gran sala de la escuela y el fotógrafo se sirvió de la luz natural, una cámara Nikon F con un objetivo de 28 mm. y una película Tri-X revelada en D76. Exposición de 1/15 seg. a f/3,5.

24

S. RICHTER, por Laszlo Lajas
Magnífico retrato de este gran pianista ruso hecho en el momento exacto para captar una expresión típica. El ambiente que le rodea y el público que aplaude lo explican todo. Tomado con la luz disponible. Minolta SRT 101 con objetivo de 55 mm. Película Tri-X revelada en Acufine; 1/30 de segundos, diafragma f/2,8.

25

JACKIE ROBINSON, por Monroe S. Frederick
El más grande jugador de color de béisbol de América, fotografiado momentos antes de morir por su propia mujer. La expresión natural y el gesto, ambos ignorando la cámara, hacen que sea un recuerdo emocionante. Mamiyaflex 220 con objetivo de 65 mm. Revelador D-76. Flash electrónico.

26

INTUICIÓN de Robert Llewellyn
Esta instantánea forma parte de un libro titulado "Alas plateadas" al que el autor describe como una manifestación visual de su "viaje" hacia la comprensión y exploración del pensamiento y la percepción interna. Para expresar sus sensaciones se ha servido de la interacción de varios objetos situados en distintos planos. Nikon F, objetivo de 20 mm.

27

AMANECER EN EL LAGO de Asko Salmi
Tomada a las 7 de la mañana en el archipiélago UAASA, esta fotografía nos demuestra que la captación de embarcaciones en lagos neblinosos no constituye una prerrogativa exclusiva de la escuela de Hong-Kong. De hecho este tratamiento se repite a menudo en algunas de las mejores obras que hemos recibido de Finlandia en los últimos años. Canon AE-1 con un objetivo de 20 mm. Película Tri-X revelada en D-76.

28

SIN TÍTULO, por J. M. Oriola
Fotografía cómica que muestra cómo a veces la espalda es tan expresiva como el frente. Esta instantánea es sin duda alguna muy original y parece natural aunque podría ser artificial. La fuerza del contraste obliga a contemplarla otra vez.

29

YOGA, por Brian Sutton

Fotos de una serie creada para ayudar al profesor de yoga a controlar la postura y la posición. No le falta sentido del humor debido al escorzo. Tomada con un objetivo de 28 mm; cámara Pentax SPF. Película Tri-X revelada en D-76.

30

SIN TÍTULO, por Jozef Vissel

Una foto de contrastes fuera de lo corriente, y que tiene un toque de humor gracias a que es absurda. Aunque se trata de una foto preparada, no hay duda que se trata de un ''stopper''. Hasselblad. Película Panatomic-X revelada en Rodinal.

31

MERLYN REES M.P., por Asadour Guzelian

El antiguo ministro del interior fotografiado en un momento agradable durante un banquete de los Sikh en Leeds. Además de decirnos mucho sobre el hombre y el momento, la composición es original y la foto es mucho más expresiva que otras hechas con todas las formalidades. Cámara Pentax SP100 con objetivo de 135 mm. Película Tri-X.

32

INVIERNO EN LA MONTAÑA, por Tom Dodd

La utilización de un filtro naranja, a una altura aproximada de 600 metros en las montañas Moelwyn de Snowdonia (Gales), ha dado como resultado una fotografía dramática. Canon F2 con objetivo de 28 mm. Película FP4, a 164 ASA, revelada en Aculux. El autor usó una abertura de f/16 para reducir el resplandor del sol.

33

DANZARINES DE BALLET, por Rudolf Auer

Magnífica foto que recoge de modo artístico el movimiento de la pirueta. El remolino del faldellín crea un ritmo por su repetición, y el destello de las lentejuelas contrasta con las luces azuladas, mientras que los colores cálidos de la espalda y de las piernas restan sensación de frialdad al conjunto.

34

RETRATO de Dieter Kraft

Un retrato dramáticamente ejecutado por un fotógrafo suizo cuyas extraordinarias fotografías en color fueron muy admiradas en el stand que Kodak situó en la última Photokina. La atrevida utilización del color rojo en la piel y la composición descentrada dan un fuerte impacto a la foto.

35

SUE de Henry Michaels

Reproducción de una extraordinaria copia en color obtenida a partir de un negativo Kodak Vericolor tomado con una cámara Bronica de 6 x 6 cm. Los tonos bajos dan énfasis a la iluminación posterior y proporcionan un tratamiento plenamente artístico a este sujeto convencional. La iluminación se obtuvo por medio de dos paraguas de flash Multilex, uno plateado y el otro dorado, con un tercer flash situado detrás. La copia se obtuvo con papel Agfacolor tipo 4.

36

PAISAJE del Dr. Alexander Dunbar, FRPS

Un típico paisaje de las Highlands escocesas fotografiado por uno de los miembros más activos de la Sociedad fotográfica de Edimburgo, que está convencido de que las mejores instantáneas se obtienen con tiempo lluvioso y neblinoso, el cual posee todavía una mayor eficacia en los momentos en que el sol hace una tímida aparición. En este caso empleó una cámara Minolta y una película Kodachrome 64; 1/125 seg. a f/8.

37

PAISAJE AZUL de Erik Steen

Esta instantánea efectiva e insólita se obtuvo mediante el uso de una película duplicadora de diapositivas que se reveló a través de un proceso E4 en lugar de utilizarse el C22 recomendado. Se omitió el primer revelador y se redujo en una cuarta parte el tiempo del revelado cromógeno. Este paisaje se halla cerca de la población donde reside el autor (Drammen, en Noruega), que empleó una Nikon F2 con un objetivo zoom de 43-86 mm.

38/39

LAS PLANIDERAS DE PRESLEY por de doctor James Billimoria

Esta foto muestra la histeria que produjo en el mundo occidental la muerte de la gran esterella del ''rock and roll''. Los acompañantes del entierro más bien bailan que lloran. Tomada con una Leica, objetivo 50 mm, un domingo por la mañana en Trafalgar Square. El autor ha escogido un punto de vista que hace buena composición de esta escena de muchedumbre.

40 (arriba)

MOCHUELO Y PRESA por Xabi Otera

Artística representación de un tema de la naturaleza. El mochuelo que ha logrado aprisionar un lagarto está bien representado, mientras que el fondo ofrece un efecto nocturno y misterioso que se adapta al tema. El conjunto forma una bella armonía de colores.

40 (abajo)

SAPO MARINO Y RANA por John Walker

Este estudio de la naturaleza, con doble interés, se tomó con flash, con una Nikon EL y objetivo Micro-Nikkor, en película Ektachrome 200. El sapo, procedente de América del Sur, pesa unos 1600 gramos; y la rana verde de árbol, que procede de Italia, solamente pesa 85 gramos. La foto está tomada en el parque zoológico de las montañas de Gales, Colwyn Bay. Se hicieron varias exposiciones porque la rana saltaba sobre el objetivo.

41

RANA VOLADORA COSTARRICENSE de Heather Angel, FIIP

Extraña rana llevada a Inglaterra para el rodaje de la serie televisiva ''Vida en la Tierra'' y devuelta luego a la selva costarricense. Heather Angel es autora de casi 30 libros de fotografía sobre temas de historia natural. Aquí utilizó una Hasselblad 500C con un objetivo de 80 mm y una película Ektachrome E-3. La iluminación fue proporcionada por un flash de dos cabezas Braun FZK80.

42

PAYASO por Baron Baron

La vista a ras del suelo hace aún más fantástico para los niños el mundo del circo. El diseño sencillo y audaz del decorado del circo aumenta y complementa la historia.

43

DESNUDO por Michael Gnade

La iluminación a contraluz juega un papel muy importante en este natural estudio de figura. La ''pose'' y el ambiente, así como el color en general, son muy agradables. Una de las fotos del libro de este autor titulado ''Fotografía de gente''.

44/45

COMBATIVOS de Wang Yue Lung

En esta imagen se ha introducido una tremenda acción a través de la perfecta captación del movimiento de brazos y piernas de los gimnastas, obteniéndose un excelente subrayado artístico por medio del gran tamaño dado a la figura del primer plano. El fotógrafo utilizó una Canon AE1 con un objetivo de 28 mm, una película Kodacolor 400 y papel de copiado Ektacolor.

46

AGUILA DE ESTEPA AFRICANA por Robert Hallman

Hermosa foto tomada en el ''Centro de aves de presa'' en Chilham Castle, en el momento que el ave protestaba airadamente por la presencia de la cámara (una Kowa Super 66 con objetivo de 85 mm, más una lente de aproximación de 3 dioptrías). Película Agfa 50S valorada en 100 ASA.

47

LECHUZA LEONADA, por E. Exton

La lechuza mayor de la Gran Bretaña es un ave nocturna peligrosa, porque podría atacar al fotógrafo con sus afiladas garras. La lechuza le dejó ocho marcas alrededor del ojo izquierdo cuando pretendía tomar la foto. Pentacon Six con objetivo de 180 mm. Película CPS120; distancia 2,70 metros. Illuminación con flash.

48

SIN TITULO, por Les Mansfield

Expresivo retrato que ha sabido captar la dignidad de un ''bailaor'' de flamenco. Se trata de una exposición doble que consiste, por un lado, en fotografiar la guitarra con un objetivo estándar, y por otro lado, disparar con un objetivo Tamron Zoom ajustado a unos 135 mm para el retrato. Tomada con una Nikon Ftn y Ektachrome High Speed, a 800 ASA para cada exposición, revelado normalmente con E6.

49

RUTH KENNEDY, por Mervyn Rees

Foto dramática, llena de acción y de movimiento, que resulta muy apropiada para esta carrera de relevos internacional. El situar la figura en el lado derecho, junto con el grano, pone de relieve la sensación de esfuerzo. Cámara Nikon F2 con objetivo de 135 mm. Película Tri-X; 1/15 de segundo a f/4.

50

BAJO EL AGUA de Ferdinando Quaranta

Una imagen de la esposa del autor tomada en la bahía de Sta. Florencia, isla de Córcega. Conocido especialista en fotografía subacuática, normalmente de peces, Ferdinando utiliza una Konica Autoreflex con un objetivo de 24 mm protegida por una caja Ikelite. Reforzó la luz natural por medio de un flash electrónico automático Braun F2000. La película utilizada originalmente fue la Kodachrome 64, pero luego se duplicó la imagen en una Tri-X.

51

BAÑO DE BARRO, por John Jones

Esta foto nos muestra el feliz ambiente que reina durante el encuentro anual de fútbol entre chicos y chicas, en el fangoso campo del Old Leigh Regatta. ¡Perdieron los chicos! Tomada con una Canon Ftb, ''zoom'' de 100-200. Película Tri-X revelada en D-76.

52

SHERRIL HAGUE, por Chris Haig

Excelente retrato espontáneo tomado con la luz del lugar, que ha sabido captar algo del vivo carácter de este vendedor de automóviles usados. Cámara Mamiya C330. Película FP4 revelada en Acutol.

53

PESCADO, por Ian Torrance

Pocos se habrían percatado de esta combinación de perro y de policía de tráfico para hacer esta fotografía deliciosamente cómica, como puede apreciar todo aquel que haya sido ''pescado''. Ganó un premio para el reportero del *Scottish Daily Record* en el concurso anual británico de periodismo.

54

DUELO EN TEHERÁN de Rolf M. Aagaard

Esta instantánea fue tomada en el cementerio principal de Teherán en el curso de una manifestación contra el ayatollah Jomeini, por entonces todavía en París. El autor reveló la película en la habitación del hotel donde residía y luego la envió al periódico noruego ''Aftenposten''. Utilizó una cámara Nikon F2 con un objetivo de 85 mm y una película Tri-X revelada en D76.

55

RETRATO, por Peter Purtz
Típico trabajo propio de la labor imaginativa procedente de Checoslovaquia, en el que las "poses" nada convencionales aparecen ante fondos a menudo de naturaleza industrial. La situación poco común del modelo, junto con el grano tan ausano, producen un impacto seguro. Cámara Exa 500 con objetivo de 25 mm. Película Orwo revelada en Formadon R.

56

ANKA, por Kazimierz Czapinski
Los fotógrafos polacos suelen apartarse de las normas de composición usuales y presentan la acción primordial casi siempre en los límites; los tradicionalistas pueden criticarlo, aunque no se puede ignorar lo que ha aportado en cuanto a fuerza y movimiento. La nariz, empujada hacia arriba por la manzana, aumenta el efecto, y el grano no le daña tampoco.

57

ADA ROGOVIN, por George Wedding
Estudio expresivo y natural de un viejo jugador de poker, de ochenta y siete años de edad, en Miami Beach, captado para el "The Palm Beach Post". El autor supo escoger el momento preciso para captar el punto álgido de la acción. Cámara Nikon con objetivo de 180 mm con película Tri-X, a 1600 ASA, revelada en Acufine.

58 (arriba)

CEMENTERIO, por J. L. Young, ARPS
Este es un buen ejemplo del uso inteligente de la película infrarroja para dramatizar una escena corriente. Allí donde haya diferentes clases de árboles, los rayos infrarrojos dan lugar a un contraste, especialmente contra el cielo azul. Cementerio de la iglesia de San Nicolás en Basildon. Praktica LTL3, con objetivo de 35 mm y filtro rojo fuerte. Película Kodak High Speed Infra-red, a 50 ASA, revelada en Perceptol.

58 (abajo)

DOS CABAÑAS, por Geri Della Rocca
La pura simplicidad y los fuertes contrastes causan el impacto de esta fotografía tomada en Nevada por el fotógrafo italiano. El diseño es poderoso y la atmósfera de aislamiento está bien representada. Cámara Nikon F; objetivo de 20 mm y filtro rojo. Película HP5 forzada hasta 600 ASA y revelada en ID-11.

59

CHÂTEAU EN BELCASTEL, DORDOÑA, por Jack Rufus, FRPS
Desgraciadamente, el autor murió poco tiempo después de haber remitido esta foto, pero nos dejó un rico legado de bellos paisajes de tipo clásico y moderno. Tomada con una Hasselblad, con objetivo de 250 mm, una tarde de septiembre. Película Tri-X revelada en Microdol X. (Ver también la página 196.)

60

AISLAMIENTO de Asad Ali
Una copia obtenida mediante la combinación de una foto del pájaro contra el cielo inhóspito y la del fondo expuesto en los campos cercanos a Lahore. El fotógrafo utilizó una cámara Kowa con un objetivo de 200 mm más un convertidor 2x y una exposición de 1/250 seg. a f/8 en una película Agfa Super-Pan 200 revelada en D76.

61 (arriba)

GARZA REAL PESCANDO, por Donald A. Smith
Excelente fotografía del ave, llena de interés debido al detalle y al contorno auténtico de la garza real, que han sido atrapados en el preciso instante. Tomada con una Nikon F2 con objetivo de 400 mm. Película FP4.

61 (abajo)

LECHUZA CON MUSARAÑA de Donald A. Smith ARPS
Una soberbia instantánea en la que vemos a una lechuza regresando al nido con una presa. Tomada con luz de flash y una Nikon F2, con un objetivo de 35 mm, en una película Ilford FP4.

62

DESNUDO de Frank Peeters
Una instantánea de un joven fotógrafo belga que se ha especializado en estudios de figuras, a las que proporciona, mediante atrevidos contrastes, interpretaciones de gran riqueza gráfica, producidas normalmente por la propia luz disponible. Se sirvió de una Nikkormat FT3 con un objetivo de 28 mm y de una película Tri-X, utilizada a 1600 ASA y revelada en Neutol S.

63

DANZA, por Andrej Krynicki
Este versátil y prolífico fotógrafo polaco usa la solarización para dar fantasía a objetos corrientes. Sus ideas son siempre originales, como también lo es el modo de emplear la figura con creatividad y maestría, como se puede ver en este ejemplo. El contraste entre la vitalidad de la bailarina desnuda y la monotonía del tejado de la casa es estimulante.

64

TRES MONJAS, por Montserrat V. Barraquer
Las fotografías de monjas son populares, pero no es fácil lograr composiciones tan buenas como ésta. Tomada en el patio de la catedral de Tarragona. Leicaflex SL con objetivo de 180 mm. Película Tri-X revelada en Rodinal.

65

MINU, por Raghu Rai
Un retrato muy bien logrado de una bellísima presentadora de la TV india. El cuadro que aparece al fondo que le da interés y originalidad. Nikkormat con objetivo de 85 mm. Película Tri-X; 1/60 segundos, a f/5,6, con la luz disponible.

66

DOS BESOS, por Vladimir Filinov
Filinov, uno de los fotógrafos más importantes de la URSS, se ha especializado durante muchos años en las técnicas de la derivación de líneas. La foto de este momento es emocionante, peso evita el dramatizar por medio del tratamiento que le da. El insecto en la mejilla del hombre produce más bien curiosidad.

67

AUTORRETRATO, por Vladimir Filinov
Una de las mejores fotos de la copiosa serie procedente de la URSS, que incluye gran cantidad de trabajos llenos de imaginación. El mensaje, en este caso, no es tan sólo claro sino que además está presentado con fuerza y originalidad. Se tomó un negativo con una cámara de 6 x 7 y el otro con un objetivo de 35 mm más un duplicador de focal.

68

SIN TÍTULO de Frantisek Dostal
He aquí una imagen de tono humorístico. El autor siguió a este hombre a través de Praga hasta que el semáforo lo obligó a detenerse. Aquí vemos, pues, la importancia de llevar siempre una cámara consigo. En este caso se trata de una Minolta SR-T303 con un objetivo de 50 mm y una película Oswo NP20 revelada en A49. Exposición: 1/250 seg. a f/11.

69

SIN TÍTULO, por Mike Hollist
Una foto cómica que a primera vista parece natural, pero que indudablemente se preparó de antemano. Esta foto nos muestra la llegada al ensayo del nuevo perrito del programa de TV "Blue Peter". Tomada para el "Daily Mail" con una Nikon; objetivo de 105 mm, película Tri-X revelada en D76; 1/250 de segundo con diafragma f/5,6.

70 (arriba)

AMOR JOVEN de Frantisek Dostal
Una deliciosa imagen en la que vemos a una niña besando a su "amado" como compensación por haberle dado una flor. Fue tomada por la mañana temprano junto al río que pasa por Praga, por medio de una Minolta ST-T303 con un objetivo de 50 mm y una película Oswo NP20 revelada en A49 (anteriormente Atomal). 1/250 seg. a f/5,6.

70 (abajo)

EL AMOR SE PROPAGA, por Virender Mahjan
Dos parejas que vio en el zpo de Delhi inspiraron en el autor la idea del mensaje que transmite la foto. Ello nos indica que en el zoo, además de las fotos de los animales, también se puede hacer otras diferentes, siempre que se tenga buena vista. Canon FX con objetivo de 400 mm. Película Orwo NP55, revelada en D-76; 1/125 de segundo a f/5,6. Luz diurna en día nublado.

71

AMOR de L. B. Feresovi
Otra deliciosa imagen en la que se recogen las emociones humanas; varias fotos de este tipo nos han llegado de Checoslovaquia. Tomada con una Minolta SRT, con un objetivo de 80-200 mm, aprovechando la luz natural. La película fue una Forma 21 y se la reveló en metol pirocatequina.

72/73

ESCUELA PREESCOLAR, por Frank Loughlin
Esta foto, obra de un reportero gráfico del "Liverpool Daily Post", resume el ambiente de una escuela preparatoria. Los sombreros de paja se convierten casi en un símbolo de los privilegios de la clase media. Tomada en una escuela de Liverpool. Nikon F con objetivo de 24 mm. Película Tri-X revelada en D-76. Flash rebotado.

74

DESCUBRIOS ANTE LA SEÑORA, por Bill Cargen, FRPS
Esta deliciosa foto de una dama que lleva sus pertenencias particulares en paquetes, deambulando por Londres, se tomó con una Maxiflex C330F con objetivo de 80 mm. Película HP4 revelada en ID11.

75

BIG CYRIL SMITH, M.P., por Stephen Shakeshaft
Retrato espontáneo de un personaje importante en una conferencia política, en la cual parece que tuvo momentos de inspiración. El autor, que ganó dos veces el premio "El fotógrafo del año", y trabaja para el "Liverpool Daily Post and Echo". Tomada con la luz disponible. Nikon F2, con objetivo de 28 mm. Película, Tri-X revelada en D-76.

76

CONTRASTE, por Rolan Herpin
A menudo es un forastero quien percibe una fotografía en nuestra propia casa. Esta foto es un ejemplo interesante del modo de ver de un fotógrafo francés de visita en Southampton. Leica M5 con objetivo de 90 mm. Película Tri-X. El contraste se aumentó en el laboratorio "quemando" el papel Agfa BH111-5.

77

UNA TORRE DE REFRIGERACIÓN DE AGUA, por Wolfgang Volz
Esta torre de refrigeración de agua de 180 metros de altura, de una central nuclear de la República Federal Alemana, ha dado lugar a una dramática fotografía industrial y también artística, por el fuerte contraste en tono y tamaño de la torre y la casita. Nikon F2 con objetivo Micro-Nikkor de 55 mm. Película Tri-X revelada en D-76.

78

LA AMISTAD, de Josep Maria Ribas Prous
He aquí una muestra de los excelentes trabajos realizados por este conocido fotógrafo español, profesor de una escuela de fotografía y organizador de experiencias culturales para grupos de jóvenes fotógrafos. Sus obras se publican en revistas de todo el mundo y en este caso se sirvió de una Nikon F2 con un objetivo de 28 mm y de una película Tri-X revelada en Microdol. Exposición de 1/1.000 seg. a f/2.

79

BALLET, por Leslie E. Spatt

Las fotos, que pertenecen a un experto especializado en este campo se tomaron durante una representación. Una muestra a Richard Cragum, del Ballet de Stuttgart, interpretando el papel del princípe Sigfrido en *El Lago de los cisnes;* la otra nos lo muestra en el papel de Egon Madsen en *Las canciones del caminante.* Leica M3, con objetivo de 90 mm. Película Tri X, a 100 ASA, revelada en Microdol.

80

VIEJO TURCO, USKÜDAR, por Jean Berner

Estudio de carácter bello y natural, con gran sentido de movimiento y de profundidad, conseguido mediante el empleo de un objetivo gran angular y lo suficientemente cerca como para que se produzca una compresión abrupta de la perspectiva. Tomada en el barrio viejo de Estambul con una Nikkormat FT, objetivo de 20 mm. Película Tri-X revelada en D76.

81

MADRE, por Ilmar Apkalns

Como muchas fotografías de la URSS, este ejemplo muestra un tratamiento moderno e imaginativo del sentimiento eterno. La distancia entre la madre y el hijo, puesta de relieve por la perspectiva exagerada, expresa el deseo que sugieren las manos extendidas. El halo artificial detrás de la madre podría tener un significado aun más profundo.

82

ILUMINACIÓN, por John P. Delaney, FRPS

Tomada en Derwentwater, en el Distrito de los Lagos en el norte de Gran Bretaña, esta foto nos muestra el ambiente que prevalece en esta zona durante los meses de invierno. Cámara Rolleiflex f/3,5; filtro X2 amarillo y película Plus X Professional, revelada en Microdol. Exposición 1/500 de segundo a f/4,5.

83

LA CABAÑA EN LA PLAYA, por Victor J. Attfield, FRPS

La silueta de la cabaña del pescador, producida por los rayos del sol al atravesar el cielo tormentoso, da lugar a una dramática foto, y las algas marinas en la playa dan gran profundidad a la composición. Nikkormat con objetivo de 28 mm. Filtro naranja. Película Tri-X revelada en D-76.

84

FODOMODELLA SUB, de Ferdinando Quaranta

Fotógrafo y modelo formaban parte de una expedición científica que se dedicaba al estudio de las especies piscícolas de las aguas de la isla Ventotene, situada cerca de Nápoles, cuando se obtuvo esta foto. El conocido fotógrafo italiano se sirvió de una Konica Autoreflex equipada con un objetivo de 55 mm y protegida por una caja Ikelite. La imagen original se obtuvo en una película Kodachrome 64 y luego se trasladó a una Tri-X.

85

PISTA DE PATINAJE, por Clive Harrison, FRPS

Esta bella foto llena de acción se tomó en una pista de patinaje sobre hielo construida para una empresa, en beneficio de los niños del pueblo en un terreno yermo. Olympus OM-1 con objetivo Zuiko de 100 mm. Película HP5 revelada en ID11.

86

LA REINA EN EL DERBY, por Mike Hollist

Todos los fotógrafos de la prensa intentan reflejar el entusiasmo de la Reina de Inglaterra por los caballos de carreras y atrapar sus expresiones, sean de gozo, de excitación o de desencanto, de acuerdo a cómo haya actuado su favorito. Este ejemplo, que no tiene nada de adulador, se captó sin duda en un momento tenso. Cámara Nikon con objetivo de 1000 mm. Película Tri-X revelada en D-76.

87

HUMO SAGRADO, por Howard Walker

Esta foto llena de humor nos muestra a un actor aficionado interpretando el papel de un sacerdote. Nada menos que tres horas fueron necesarias para conseguir que el humo fuese suficiente y que tomara la forma deseada. Tomada con una cámara Nikon F2 con motor y objetivo de 85 mm. Flash rebotado. Película Tri-X.

88/89

BANKING ON THE LORD, por Cleland Rimmer

Un logrado intento de simbolizar el progreso captando las reminiscencias de la arquitectura antigua en un edificio moderno. Se consiguió persuadir a la atractiva mujer policía para que incluyese el edificio en su ronda para sugerir la sensación de seguridad del banco que había encargado la fotografía. El autor, un profesor de fotografía en la universidad de Hull, se sirvió de una Speed Graphic de 5 x 4" con objetivo de 150 mm y filtro amarillo. Película FH4 revelada en Autophen; 1,60 segundo, diafragma f / 8.

90

CHRIS BARBER, por Rudolf Bieri

Un excelente retrato del famoso músico de "jazz" y "blues" en que además se capta el ambiente del Kursaal en Berna, donde se tomó durante una actuación. Luz disponible Leicaflex SL2 con objetivo Apo-Telyt de 180 mm. Película Tri-X revelada en Tetenal Emofin 2 x 10 min. a 30°C.

91

SAMMY DAVIS JR., por Erwin Kneidinger, EFIAP

La instantánea consigue expresar bien la vitalidad y el dinamismo de su carácter, y la atmósfera se pone de de relieve por la luz disponible y también por el grano. Nikon F con objetivo de 105 mm. Película Tri-X revelada en Neutol; 1/250 de segundo a f/2.5.

92

SIN TÍTULO, por J. R. Rudin

La gente de color conoce el valor del contraste y un adorno blanco sobre la piel tiene imaginación al mismo tiempo que supone un *tour de force* técnico. La composición es original y atrevida y al mismo tiempo buena. El autor es propietario de una galería de arte en el Caribe. La foto se tomó con una Pentax. Película Tri-X, a 1600 ASA, con la luz de la ventana.

93

MIRADA MAGNÉTICA, por Virender Mahajan

Retrato de un viejo típico de la "momden phase" hecho durante la peregrinación a la ciudad del Festival de Garh-Ganga-Mela en la India, tomada desde un punto de vista bajo para producir un cielo blanco que acentúa el positivado en papel duro. Camara Canon FX con objetivo de 50 mm. Película Orwo NP55 revelada en D-76.

94 (arriba)

NO HAGA SEÑALES CON LA MANO, por Stanley Matchett

Un autor aficionado con buen sentido del humor da como resultado una divertida foto en una escuela de equitación en County Down. El autor, que trabaja en el *Daily Mirror* en Belfast, empleó una Nikon F2 con objetivo 80–200 mm. Película HP5 revelada en D-76; 1/250 segundo, y diafragma f/8.

94 (abajo)

¿VES? SIN TOCARLO, por Stanley Matchett

El niño de diez años Darren Swan , actuando como mago, efectúa su primera levitación, mientras le asiste Hilary Thompson. Es una fotografía que muestra bien el truco de que se trata. Tomada con una Nikon F2, con objetivo 80–200, en película HP5, con la luz existente.

95

PIERRE, EL PAYASO, por Martyn Hayhow

El autor ha sabido captar el ambiente de la actuación de un payaso ambulante que divierte a la gente durante las vacaciones. El autor, que es reportero gráfico del *Evening Post,* también ha sabido darle calidad artística. Nikon F2 con objetivo "zoom" 70–210. Película HP5 revelada en ID11; 1/250 de segundo, a f/8.

96

ENAMORADOS, por Wilhelm Mikhailovsky

En estos últimos años los fotógrafos de la URSS se han mostrado maestros en la capacidad de expresar los sentimientos humanos en el contexto moderno. El poderoso contraste entre el hombre y la joven pone de relieve la masculinidad frente a la femineidad, de lo que resulta una buena foto. Ver también las páginas 116 y 117.

97

SIN TÍTULO, por Michael Barrington Martin

Este conocido fotógrafo captador de las bellezas de Londres, que siempre experimenta con nuevas ideas, trabaja con formatos grandes, por lo que puede mezclar dos o más imágenes. Los resultados pueden ser sorprendentes, como el hecho de que a menudo se reproduzcan en calendarios y portadas de revistas. Esta muestra simplificada y filtrada en blanco y negro está perfectamente combinada con una instantánea desenfocada.

98

PIETRO ALBERTELLI, por Tony Duffy

Esta espectacular instantánea de un esquiador es obra de uno de los primeros fotógrafos deportivos británicos, que ha ganado muchos premios en concursos de fotografías deportivas, tanto en Inglaterra fuera de ella. Este ejemplo resulta tan dramático debido al punto de vista bajo que ha sabido captar, manteniendo las luces altas, los ojos y la cara que se escondían detrás de la máscara.

99

TENISTA, por Leo Mason

Esta fotografía tomada desde un punto de vista elevado sobre el campo de tenis de Flushing Meadow Stadium, de Nueva York, nos muestra una instantánea fuera de lo corriente, a Virginia Wade en acción. Una cámara Nikon F2, con objetivo de 200 mm, se mantuvo colocada en posición durante dos semanas y se disparó por control remoto. Película Ektachrome Professional; exposición de 1/500 segundo, diafragma f/8.

100 (arriba)

ROCAS, por Lars Oddvar Lovdahl

Es un tipo de fotografía que resulta mejor proyectada que reproducida, porque el sutil color castaño de las hojas otoñales se pone de relieve. La posición de los hongos da muestra de una buena capacidad de composición de parte del fotógrafo noruego. Nikon F2 con objetivo de 20 mm. Película Kodak photomicrography 2483.

100 (abajo)

MUCHEDUMBRE de Nigel Stone

Las instantáneas en color de muchedumbres presentan normalmente formas equilibradas al tomarlas desde arriba, pero se convierten en monótonas sino existe un punto de interés o contraste. Al igual que la situada encima, esta imagen deriva su fuerza de la mancha roja que presenta un hombre situado de forma estratégica dando la impresión de que su cabeza y hombros se proyectan por encima de los demás.

101 (arriba)

LAGO BAJO LA LUNA del Dr. A. Farquhar
He aquí un "sandwich" de dos siapositivas, en una de las cuales se captó un pequeño yate navegando en el lago Okaganan de la Columbia británica, mientras que en la otra se hizo la propio con la luna. En ambos casos se empleó una película Kodachrome 64 y una cámara Canon EF, con objetivos de 100 mm. y 400 mm. respectivamente. La exposición se determinó automáticamente, por lo que no tenemos los datos. El "sandwich" se duplicó en una Ektachrome 5071.

101 (abajo)

LÁPIDA FUNERARIA, por Mark Woolstencroft
Parece ser que este año los cementerios se han convertido en tema favorito para los fotógrafos, pero esta foto es mucho más original e imaginativa que la mayor parte de las presentadas. El sorprendente esquema de colores está complementado por la red de puntos que hacen que la mirada se dirija hacia la cruz, produciendo un efecto etéreo.

102/103

ATARDECER DE SEPTIEMBRE, EN MILAN, por Trevor Fry, FRPS
Los pináculos de la catedral de Milán, que producen la impresión de brotar de un cuento de hadas, se fotografiaron desde las escaleras opuestas. Película Ektachrome 160 ASA para luz artificial. Leicaflex SL con objetivo de 90 mm. Exposición de aproximadamente un segundo a f/8; reproducción de una copia Cibachrome.

104

CALEIDOSCOPIO, por C. H. J. Martin, LRPS
Reproducida de un original compuesto por ocho fotos idénticas en papel Kodak 37RC. Con esta imaginativa concepción el autor ha ganado varios premios. Negativo original en Kodacolor. Cámara Pentax Spotmatic con objetivo de 55 mm.

105

ST. TOMAS, ABOYNE, por Francis Tocher Jr.
La atmósfera que crea la luz al atravesar un vitral fue sabiamente puesta de relieve por medio del "zooming" durante 25 segundos (en una exposición total de 30 segundos de un objetivo "zoom"). Nikkormat FT2 con "zoom" Tamron 70–150 mm. Ektachrome 64, diafragma f/11.

106

AUTORRETRATO de Hektor Krome
Divertida yuxtaposición de varios sujetos reflejados en la puerta de una furgoneta constituyendo una especia de rompecabezas. Obtenida con una Olympus OM-2 y un objetivo de 28 mm. y reproducida de una copia Ektacolor.

107

MOSAICO 2, por A. R. Pippart, OBE, FRPS
Pertenece a una serie de copias experimentales impresionadas a través de varios filtros de color obtenidos esparciendo colorante en un trozo de película fijada sin impresionar. El autor es un distinguido químico responsable del Photocolor II y otros procesos de la química del color.

108/109

EXPOSICION MULTIPLE
Un interesante experimento llevado a cabo por un fotógrafo holandés por medio de la superposición de las exposiciones obtenidas con filtros distintos. Se trata de una reproducción de una copia Polaroid de 18 x 24 cm.

110 (arriba)

S.A.R. EL PRINCIPE CARLOS de Terry Fincher, FRPS
Fotografía tomada por sorpresa al príncipe Carlos a la orilla del Río Negro en Manans poco antes de la puesta del sol por el más conocido reportero británico. La cámara utilizada fue una Olympus, con un objetivo de 28 mm. seleccionándose una exposición de 1/15 seg. a

f/5,6 aumentada con flash en una película Ektachrome E6.

110

ANCIANO de Francisco Hidalgo
Al autor, un español residente en París, se le conoce por sus representaciones de alargados rascacielos, por lo que este retrato constituye una agradable sorpresa. Sin embargo, su fuerza artística se manifiesta en la perfecta captación del carácter del retratado a través del uso de un enfoque diferencial, no siempre fácil de conseguir cuando se fotofrafía en una muchedumbre con un objetivo de 35 mm.

111 (arriba)

TRANSVERSITIES, por Alain Verdier
Retrato doble tomado del libro del autor "Messieurs, Mesdames" que viene a constituir un estudio de los "gay" en todas las partes del mundo. Unos están apagados y otros son exuberantes. El autor, que también es músico, dice haber hallado inspiración en el pintor René Magritte. Tomada con una Nikon F con objetivo de 20 mm.

111 (abajo)

SUEÑOS DE CACHORRO, por el Dr. M. D. Constable, ARPS
Un sandwich de dos transparencias en película Agfa CT18. Cámara Canon Ftb con objetivo de 80 mm. El chico, que es el hijo pequeño del autor, ansía formar parte de la pandilla de su hermano mayor. De verle dormido, el Dr. Constable pensó que éste podía ser el asunto de sus sueños. Foto con flash.

112

NEUROPOLIS, por Luciano Pestarino, EFIAP
En esta foto se pone de relieve la fuerza de la neurosis como una característica del hombre que vive en las grandes aglomeraciones urbanas. El autor usó a su propio hijo como figura simbólica en el ángulo de una plaza de Buenos Aires. Pestarino es un fotógrafo amateur que ha expuesto en muchas partes del mundo.

113

IAN SMITH de Rolf M. Aagaard
Imagen tomada en el aeropuerta de Salisbury cuando el primer ministro rhodesiano Ian Smith estaba a punto de partir para los EE.UU. después de un largo retraso en proporcionarle un visado. Fue una coincidencia que el fotógrafo efectuara en el mismo avión al viaje Johannesburgo – Nueva York. La cámara utilizada fue una Nikon F2 con un objetivo de 180 mm y la película una Tri-X revelada en D-76.

114/115

FOTOS, por David Bailey, FRPS
La mayoría de fotógrafos envidian la oportunidad que tiene este famoso fotógrafo de trabajar para prestigiosas revistas de moda con las mejores modelos del mundo. Su técnica es siempre impecable, pero con trabajos de puro placer es muy original. No teme desafiar las "poses" convencionales ni la composición y con ello consigue las buenas imágenes que muestran estas fotos. El uso del encuadre con objetivo protegido asustaría al que fuese más tímido y muy pocos se atreverían a incluir accesorios domésticos o a darles el énfasis que él les da.

116/117

PARALELAS, por Wilhelm Michaelovsky
Sorprendente foto hecha por el gran maestro ruso. El impacto aumenta por la perspectiva dramática, el fuerte contraste y el grano. Las expresiones de los rostros estimulan la imaginación del espectador; y la extraordinaria composición rompe con éxito todos los moldes y reglas. Ver También la página 96.

118

EN EL SAFARI PARK DE WINDSOR, por Mike Hollist
Los animales nos atraen siempre, y este raro encuentro de una zebra y una jirafa joven tiene, además, humor. Tomada con una Nikon y objetivo de 400 mm. con lo cual

se ha desenfocado el fondo. Película Tri-X, revelada en D-76; 1/500 de segundo, diafragma f/5,6.

119

HIJOS Y MASCOTAS, por Andrew McGlyn
Los animales domésticos son muy atractivos, y este emocionante momento fue muy bien captado por un fotógrafo irlandés. La relación entre los modelos es obvia, y el contraluz hace que el grupo parezca separado del fondo de la foto. Leica M4 con objetivo de 50 mm. Película FP4, revelada en Rodinal. 1/125 de segundo, diafragma f/5,6.

120

UN VIEJO FRANCÉS, por E. Chambré Hardman
Un emotivo retato hecho por un famoso fotógrafo profesional de Liverpool, muy conocido además por la excelente calidad de sus ampliaciones. Tomada con una cámara réflex de 9 x 12 cm, con objetivo Tessar de 160 mm; 1/100 de segundo a f/8. Película Super XX.

121

CHICA ORGULLOSA, por Vlastislar Machacek
Extraordinaria "pose", tal vez tomada con el fin de poner de relieve que la muchacha está en cinta, lo que no se nota a primera vista. Como en muchos trabajos que nos vienen de Checoslovaquia, ignora por entero los problemas de grano, de verticales y de poses tradicionales y sólo se centra en la emotividad de la imagen. El contraluz le añade un efectivo halo.

122/123

FUTBOL EN EDGE HILL de John Davidson
Tomada por uno de los mejores fotógrafos del *Liverpool Daily Post*, en esta instantánea se refleja la temprana edad en que la afición por el fútbol se despierta en los habitantes de esta ciudad inglesa. ¡Todo lo que necesitan para "ponerse en camino" hacia Wembley es una calle poco transitada, una pelota vieja y un par de ladrillos!. El autor utilizó una Nikon F con un objetivo de 28 mm. y una película Tri-X revelada en D-76. La exposición fue de 1/60 seg. a f/3,5.

124

BODA, por Hans-Jorge Anders
Esta foto de una boda memnonita en el Paraguay nos muestra el acontecimiento y la vitalidad de los participantes. Se tomó para la revista alemana "Stern". Cámara Leicaflex SL2 con objetivo de 19 mm. Película Tri-X.

125

HACIA CASA, por Leon Balodis
Una sencilla boda en una aldea de la URSS bien completada con la inclusión de los invitados y el público que caminan ante la novia, quienes crean una sensación de movimiento. La fuerza dinámica del cielo hace convierte a la novia en el centro de interés y hace que todo resulte muy interesante, cuando menos para los forasteros.

126

SIN TITULO, por Francisco Aszmann
Esta foto no necesita título porque todo en ella está diciendo ¡primavera! La iluminación a contraluz pone de relieve la floración y da a la imagen profundidad y brillo, todo muy apropiado al asunto. Aunque fue tomada en el Brasil podría perfectamente ser de cualquier otro lugar del mundo.

127

PASO DE LA OCA, por Bernhard Heinz
Esta foto, presentada en la Photokina, ganó el premio del concurso "Apertura" de la asociación de lectores de periódicos de Alemania. La exposición atrajo a más de 30.000 concursantes. Es una composición, llamativa y muy notable por la maestría que demuestra la gradación de los tonos. Película FP4.

128

**NATURALEZA Y BELLEZA,
por Mogens Lerche Madsen**
Un positivo en película "lith", hecho de tres negativos, y donde la espalda de la modelo se utilizó como pantalla y se suavizó la imagen ligeramente. Cámara Leica con objetivo Summicron. Película HP4 revelada en Rodinal.

129

SUSAN, por Jozef Tichy
Este año abundan los estudios de figuras, pero este ejemplo de estilo tradicional checoslovaco es muy bueno. Aunque gran parte del encanto provenga de la belleza del modelo, la luz suave de la ventana, así como el tratamiento en clave baja, ayudan mucho. Tomada con una Pentacon Six con objetivo Biometar. Película Orwo 20 revelada en Atomal; 1/15 de segundo, diafragma f/8.

130

**SUPONGO QUE SE TRATA DEL SR. LINCOLN
de Achim Sperber**
Esta instantánea, obra de un fotógrafo hamburgués, pertenece a una serie titulada "Nueva York – Arriba y Abajo". Tomada con una Pentax y objetivo zoom de 85–210 mm. en una película Tri-X revelada en D-76. Exposición de 1/500 seg. a f/4.

131

EN LA CONFERENCIA, por Stephen Shakeshaft
Tomada en una conferencia política en un momento de controversia para el modelo; el fotógrafo ha sabido coger su expresión pensativa. El autor (también ver la página 75) es uno de los periodistas gráficos más conocidos de Inglaterra; ha batido todos los récords al haber obtenido que sus fotos fuesen publicadas en el "Photography Year Book" siete veces. Nikon F2 con objetivo de 28 mm. Película Tri-X.

132

RETRATO DE FAMILIA, por Martin Wolin Jr.
La niebla del fondo produce el aislamiento del tema. Parece como si las vacas estuvieran en el estudio, y los árboles y el poste le dan cierto eco rítmico. Minolta XE7 con objetivo de 50 mm. Película Plus-X revelada en Rodinal; 1/60 de segundo a f/8.

133

**ESQUIADORES EN MARCHA,
por Vladimir Filinov**
El objetivo gran angular y la separación de tonalidades dan a esta foto gran fuerza, en cierto modo agresiva. La composición es llamativa y la pequeña figura en la distancia juega un papel muy relevante: en cierto modo se parece al insecto que vemos en la página 66. Tomada con una cámara de 35 mm, con objetivo gran angular, en película de 300 ASA.

134

BOSTEZO, por Pak Nin Yam
Esta foto, expuesta en el London Salon, constituye una muestra del éxito obtenido por este joven fotógrafo del Lejano Oriente. No hay duda que los tonos oscuros y lo interesante de la composición han contribuido al éxito, pero tampoco se puede descontar la soberbia calidad de la ampliación original.

135

BLOW-UP, por Kin-Pong Chan
Lo mismo que la foto anterior, de Singapur, esta otra, que llega de Hong Kong, es de género tradicional, pero tan vivaz y tan bien presentada que también se expuso en el Salón. Es poco acostumbrado el toque del cabello que ondea ante el rostro, y la ampliación esmaltada rezuma vitalidad.

136/137

**LA BATALLA DE LAS PALABRAS,
por Don McPhee**
El fotógrafo del "Guardian" ha tomado una foto corriente, en el momento preciso, en estos días de enfrentamientos laborales, cuando las esposas de los trabajadores de la Chrysler trataban de impedir la huelga de sus maridos. La cámara era una Minolta SRT101 con objetivo 28 mm, y la película FP4, revelada en Microphen.

138

LA CARA DE UNA CASA, por W. H. Gratt
Un sencillo diseño bien captado por este fotógrafo alemán desde un punto de vista escogido con cuidado hasta conseguir una composición equilibrada, atractiva por la limpieza de las líneas y el mínimo detalle. Tomada con Bronica 6 x 6 con objetivo de 50 mm. Película Plus-X revelada en HC110; 1/60 de segundos, diafragma f/8.

139

ANGULOS ANGELICALES, por Arthur Perry
La simplicidad de la línea y de la forma procedente del contraste y de haber sabido escoger un buen punto de vista dan gran impacto al tejado de esta iglesia de California. Rolleiflex 3.5. Película FP4; filtro verde-amarillo; 1/60 segundos, diafragma f/16.

140

**DESPUES DE LA TORMENTA,
por Ilmars Apkalns**
Dramático paisaje de la URSS con una atmósfera wagneriana. Las rocas destacadas por la luz constituyen el primer plano para la tormenta, en la distancia, y un rayo de sol mitiga el amenazador aspecto del cielo.

141

PAISAJE PETREO de Asko Salmi
Fotografiado en la isla de Norrskari, situada en la costa occidental finlandesa. En este paisaje se recoge claramente la fuerza de exposición típica de la nueva generación de fotógrafos aficionados. El objetivo gran angular y los tonos enérgicos han producido una imagen de elevado contenido dramático. Canon AE-1 con un objetivo de 20 mm. más un filtro rojo y película Tri-X revelada en D-76.

142

DIANE, por Ian Stewart
Fotografía de Diane Minchin, famosa modelo australiana, realizada por un fotógrafo independiente que nos muestra una pose provocativa en la ventana de una casa de campo abandonada; por eso existe un contraste tanto del asunto como del tono. Hasselblad 500 con objetivo de 150 mm. Película Tri-X revelada en D-76.

143

SIN TITULO, por George W. Martin Jr.
Este sorprendente perfil de una modelo profesional, hecho por un fotógrafo en un estudio de Nueva York, destaca en el original por la chispeante calidad de la copia. Luz incandescente. Cámara Nikon con objetivo de 105 mm. Película Plus-X revelada en D-76. Ampliación en papel Poly-contrast revelado en Dektol.

144

KINGS ROAD, por Harm Botman
Fue tomada por un fotógrafo halandés durante su visita a un famoso "swinging" en la calle Chelsea, de Londres, donde Lord Snowdon tiene unos murales con fotos tamaño natural fuera del teatro. Tomada con una Rollei 35 en película Tri-X, a 800 ASA, revelada en Promicrol.

145

SIN TITULO, por David Barrows, AIIP
Esta foto fue tomada por un joven fotógrafo, especializado en vistas fijas para la televisión, para promocionar un nuevo juego de billar. El grupo está muy bien compuesto. La incorporación de los personajes menos importantes con el fondo oscuro es intrigante. Hasselblad, con objetivo de 150 mm. Película Ilford FP4; con destello de un flash dirigido hacia el centro.

146

HENLEY ROYAL REGATTA, por Steve Hartley
El reverendo Gillen W. Craig, cura de San Marcos en la vieja calle Marylebone de Londres, desafía el tiempo de una manera típicamente británica con el claro propósito de mantener el ambiente tradicional de la época eduardiana propio de esta semana de regatas. Nikkormat con objetivo de 85 mm. Película HP5 revelada en ID11; 1/250 de segundo, a f/5,6.

147

SIN TITULO, por Michael Gnade
Llamativa foto infantil que llama la atención debido al punto de vista alto y a las pícaras expresión y "pose". Esta foto pertenece a la colección del libro del maestro bávaro "Fotografía de gente".

148

PREDICADOR LONDINENSE de Vladimir Birgus
Una instantánea que forma parte de una serie tomada en Londres por un profesor de fotografía de Praga. En ella ha captado perfectamente el acalorado diálogo mantenido por un predicador religioso y un espectador. Se sirvió de una Pentax Spotmatic con un objetivo de 28 mm. y una película Orwo NP27 revelada en Formadon N.

149

TEDDY BOY de Ricardo Gómez Pérez
Instantánea tomada en el Crystal Palace por un estudiante del London College of Printing que empieza a ser conocido por haber publicado algunas de sus obras en revistas de varios países. La foto forma parte de una serie sobre "teddy boys" (muchachos con pinta de gamberro) y fue tomada con una Leica CL, con un objetivo de 40 mm., en una película Tri-X revelada en D-76.

150

SIN TITULO, por Albert Hernando Jordà
Los retratos en clave alta son muy llamativos, pero el uso del grano mitiga su éxito. Este ejemplo que proviene de España es una excepción a la regla; la "pose" y la línea ondulada tras la figura aportan tono y significado. Leica con objetivo de 35 mm. Película Tri-X; 1/1000 de segundo, diafragma f/8.

151

EL VIGILANTE, por John Williams
Un fotógrafo australiano tomó la foto cuando visitaba el Museo del Louvre en París. El autor se sintió intrigado por la aparente indiferencia del vigilante ante el cuadro de la Mona Lisa y por la gente que disparaba flashes a pesar de estar prohibido. Cámara Olympus OM-1 con objetivo de 35 mm. Exposición 1/60 de segundo, a f/2. Película Tri-X revelada en Acufine.

152/153

**DICHOSO TIEMPO DE LA NIÑEZ,
por Tsang-Chi Yen**
Esta foto es un buen ejemplo del progreso que se está desarrollando en Formosa por parte de los fotógrafos aficionados. La vitalidad de estos críos llenos de vida está realzada por el hecho de que se tomó la foto desde un punto de vista muy bajo. La inclusión de las manos que aplauden es el toque final. Tomada con una Minolta SR101. Película PX125; 1/125 de segundo a f/11.

154

ESCENA DE NIEVE, por W. Biggs
Las colinas de Chiltern ofrecen grandes oportunidades para los fotógrafos de paisaje con capacidad artística. Esta es una interesante representación de las formas de los setos, que contrastan con la nieve, compuesta con maestría. Mamiyaflex con objetivo de 180 mm. Película FP4 revelada en ID11.

155

GLACIAR BLANCO, por Vera Weinerstrova
Esta foto llena de espacio y profundidad es el resultado de haber sabido escoger un punto de vista bajo que pone de relieve la amenaza de los fenómenos naturales, mientras que el perfil de los acantilados desvía la mirada hacia la distancia y el cielo dramático. Cámara Praktisik con objetivo de 50 mm. Película Orwo NP20; 1/125 de segundos, diafragma f/16.

156

ESTUDIO DE FIGURA, por Valdis Braun
Este desnudo tiene un aspecto tan tradicional que casi resulta anticuado, pero se aparta de lo ordinario por el tratamiento atrevido del tono en lugar de la clave alta que antes se consideraba válida para este tipo de estudios. Las liness del chal producen una interesante yuxtaposición que sirven de eco a las formas de los brazos.

157

EN EL BOSQUE, por Andrej Krynicki
Esta ha sido escogida de una serie de estudios de figuras al aire libre presentados por este prolífico fotógrafo polaco (ver también la página 157). En este caso ni ha solarizado ni ha simplificado nada. Como en todas sus fotos, su originalidad reside en el contraluz, que le ha dado una encantadora luminosidad.

158

EL AYUNTAMIENTO DE TORONTO, por Jean Bernier
Original tratamiento para un estudio de tipo arquitectónico, con reminiscencias de cierta escuela de pintura, que pone de relieve las limpias líneas. El contraste entre lo nuevo y lo viejo resulta interesante, y la figura del niño le proporciona escala y profundidad. Nikkormat FT con objetivo de 105 mm. Película Tri-X revelada en D76.

159

CENTRAL DE ENERGIA EN NUEVA ZELANDA, por P. G. Gale
Bella foto de edificios industriales. Las chimeneas parecen muy altas por la utilización del punto de vista bajo y por el formato vertical; difícil de lograr sin una cámara técnica. El alusado contraste y el humo le dan una atmósfera genuína. Exa II con objetivo de 50 mm. Película Adox KB21 revelada en Microphen.

160

DIRECTOR, por Jiri Horak
Lo que posiblemente pretende esta llamativa foto es poner de relieve la agresividad del ejecutivo, situándole delante del complejo industrial. Sea cual sea la interpretación del observador, la combinación de los puños cerrados le llevará a reconocer que el conjunto es artístico. Petri FT con objetivo 28 mm. Película Orwo 27 revelada en Atomal.

161

WHEELIE, por Peter Gant, ARPS
Dramática foto de movimiento puesto de relieve por la exposición lenta. Pertenece a la serie que ganó para Gant el panel de periodista gráfico del año. Fue hecha en Skate City, Londres, con una cámara Olympus OM-1, objetivo de 200 mm., a 1/15 segundo. Película Kodachrome 64.

162 (arriba)

EASY GLIDER, por Gordon Ratcliffe
Excelente foto de vuelo sin motor, hecha en los Apeninos, que da una buena impresión del espacio y del cielo dramático. El planeador es un "Sunspot" pilotado por Len Gabriels. Pentax Spotmatic con objetivo de 200 mm. Película Kodachrome 64; 1/125 segundos a f/11.

162 (abajo)

SIN TITULO, por David MacAlpine
Este paisaje demuestra que las condiciones dramáticas de iluminación son tan efectivas en color como en blanco y negro y pueden dar un sentimiento poderoso a un paisaje ordinario. Pentax S1A con objetivo de 55 mm. Película Kodachrome II; 1/125 de segundo a f/5,6.

163 (arriba)

TURBULENCIA, por John L. Cawthra
Se hizo esta foto para sugerir un futuro viaje espacial. Se trata de un sandwich de una transparencia en película Agfa CT21, tomada a través del fondo de una botella de leche, y otra de un planeador suspendido en película Fuji 100. Cámara Canon AT1 con objetivo de 135mm.

163 (abajo)

RECORDADO, por Tony Howard
Final de una tarde de verano en el patio de una iglesia de Gran Bretaña cuando el sol se reflejaba en el mármol de la cruz. Cámara Nikkormat FTN con objetivo de 50 mm. Exposición 1/30 de segundo a f/5,6. Película Ektachrome X, procesado comercial.

164/165

MOTOCROSS de Woot Gilhuis
Una dinámica imagen obtenida por el autor de "Between sharp and unsharp" publicado por Argus Books Ltd. Woot es un fotógrafo "free-lance", uno de los miembros más activos de la Asociación de fotógrafos profesionales holandeses. En la obtención de esta foto utilizó una Canon F1 con un objetivo de 400 mm. y una película Kodachrome 64. El movimiento fue introducido mediante un barrido de 1/8 de seg.

166

SIN TITULO, por Patrick Lichfield
Este retrato de la Duquesa de Roxburghe y la Condesa de Lichfield, hecho para "Vogue" y reproducida con la amable autorización de Condé Nast, muestra una agradable y original "pose" que, sin embargo, resulta apropiada para las dos hermanas. El delicado empleo del color en clave alta resulta muy artístico. Cámara Olympus OM-2. Película Ektachrome.

167

CARON, por James Elliot
Un retrato que consigue darnos una sensación de belleza plástica y artística a base de una bella combinación de colores al pastel en perfecta armonía. La cabeza levantada le da dignidad. Cámara de 35 mm. con objetivo "zoom" de 70–210 mm. Película Ektachrome. Iluminación con flash electrónico.

168

AUTOS A TRAVES DE VIDRIO ESCARCHADO, por John F. Percy
De la serie en que el autor experimenta fotografiando a través del vidrio escarchado de la puerta de su casa. El automóvil estaba al otro lado de la calle. Cámara Olympus OM-1 con objetivo de 50 mm. y un duplicador de focal Komura. Kodachrome 64; diafragma f/16.

169

SIN TITULO, por D. J. Bellham
Insólita foto obtenida con doble exposición: un paisaje a la puesta del sol y las formas sobre una superficie negra ondulada usando la luz del atardecer. El resultado obtenido recuerda un poco un abanico japonés. Canon EF con objetivo de 50 mm. Kodachrome 25.

170

RETRATO de Ray Williamson
En la instantánea se muestra el uso deliberado de la perspectiva distorsionada creada a través de la aproximación al sujeto con un objetivo normal. El propósito del autor fue introducir una atmósfera sofocante y enigmática a la que califica de "visión pictórica". Se sirvió de un flash rebotado en un paraguas, película Kodachrome 25 y una cámara Contax RTS con un objetivo de 50 mm. a f/5.6.

171

RETRATO, por K. Amil
En esta foto domina el diseño de color. El autor muestra su percepción artística al concentrarse en el turbante en lugar de hacerlo en el rostro. También contribuye el hecho de que el color produce armonía sin que llegue a dominar.

172/173

TRISNL, de Frank Martin, FIIP
En esta instantánea de un pico de 7.100 m. situado en el Himalaya se muestra una morrena formada por un glaciar en retroceso. Su autor es un fotógrafo profesional que aprovechó sus vacaciones para desplazarse a aquella cordillera. Utilizó una cámara Petri TTL con un objetivo zoom de 70–230 mm. y una película Kodachrome 64.

174 (arriba)

RETRATO, por C. Nutman
El usar filtros de color se ha hecho aceptable, siempre claro está, que añada algo positivo al ambiente. En este caso lo cálido, más el efecto de la puesta del sol obtenido por el "zooming" del fondo durante la exposición le dan calidad artística.

174 (abajo)

SIN TITULO, por Joan Wakelin, FRPS
El autor ha viajado mucho por Zambia y Sri Lanka haciendo fotos de ensayo de sus habitantes; y ahora resulta que ha encontrado aquí, en Sheffield, un asunto interesante, precisamente en el jardín de una casa. Pentax SV con objetivo de 28 mm. Película Agfa CT18. Reproducida de una copia en Cibachrome.

175

VISION, por Surendra Sahai
Interesantes superposición de dos diapositivas; una de fuegos artificiales y la otra de los adoradores del sol en la playa de Konorak en la India. La combinación da lugar a una foto que espolea la imaginación. Cámara Pentax SPII y película Kodachrome 64 para ambas instantáneas; duplicado en película Kodak Special.

176

RETRATO, por Maurice Braun
Esta llamativa foto de un niño en cierto modo parece una pintura debido a que los tonos pastel contrastan con el fondo oscuro. Pertenece a la magnífica colección de grandes retratos mostrados en el stand de Kodak en Photokina. Ver también la página 34.

177

MANIKIN, por Carlos Canovas
El acabado granuloso consigue dar una impresión natural a esta cara de plástico. El atrevido tratamiento en primer plano aumenta aún más el realismo, y produce un impresionante efecto tridimensional. Tomada con una Nikon F2, con objetivo de 135 mm. Película Tri-X revelada en HC100.

178

ESTUDIO DE DESNUDO de Frank Peeters
Un expresivo estudio en que la forma del cuerpo humano se utiliza como base para obtener un diseño extraordinariamente enérgico. El fotógrafo se sirvió de una Nikkormat FTN con un objetivo de 28 mm. y de una película Tri-X, utilizada a 1600 ASA y revelada en Neutol S.

179

DESNUDO, por Hideki Fujii
Este estudio refleja las cualidades de individualismo que caracterizan al arte japonés. El efecto se debe a la "pose", nada corriente, con la figura casi suspendida en el espacio; y por otra parte, al efecto de la máscara.

180

PAISAJES, por Signe Drevsjo

Dos agradables paisajes de Noruega. El de arriba se fotografió en Gimsoy, en las islas Lofoten. La formación perpendicular de las nubes lleva la vista hacia la distancia y da una fuerte impresión de profundidad. El de abajo forma un diseño muy bello. Las dos fotos se tomaron con una Canon F1, con filtro rojo, en película Tri-X revelada en D-76. Se utilizó un objetivo de 17 mm. para obtener la amplia vista, y uno de 50 mm, macro, para la foto de la hierba (abajo).

181

CASTILLO MISTERIOSO, por Vera Weinerstrova

El uso de objetivos gran angulares para fotografiar paisajes, junto con la inclusión en primer plano de un objeto destacado se ha puesto de moda. El tratamiento con fuertes contrastes, más mucho grano y un río negro, resulta impresionante en este ejemplo. Cámara Praktisix. Película Orwo NP20.

182

BUCEADOR, por Mervyn Rees, FRPS

Esta maravillosa foto, llena de acción, fue tomada en el Palacio de Cristal de Londres durante los entrenamientos para el Campeonato del Commonwealth. Nikon F2 con objetivo de 50 mm. Película Tri-X revelada en D-76 Exposición 1 / 250 de segundo diafragma f / 3,5.

183

KARIN FITZNER, por Mervyn Rees

Dramática fotografía, procedente de Alemania Oriental, de un tirador a punto de disparar. El grano que inevitablemente se produce al forzar la sensibilidad del filme origina en éste una sensación de fuerza, mientras que la diagonal sugiese el movimiento. Nikon F2 con objetivo de 500 mm. Película Tri-X; 1 / 1000 segundo diafragma f / 8.

184

WINGS TOWN, por Jiri Horak

Trabajo típico y lleno de imaginación procedente de Checoslovaquia. Existe cierta similitud entre esta foto y la de la página 160, del mismo autor, y ambas estan llenas de expresividad. Cámara Petri Ft con objetivo de 28 mm; exposición 1/125 de segundo. Película ORWO NP27 revelada en Atomal.

185

EDDY BOYD, por Reijo Porkka

El autor supo ver las posibilidades del perfil formado por el contraluz y las puso relieve con el tratamiento de simplificación de tonos, lo que le da la impresión intensa del ambiente de una "Boîte". Cámara Nikon; objetivo de 50 mm. Película Tri-X forzada hasta 1600 ASA.

186

SIN TITULO, por Jim Barker

Mucha gente habrá pasado por aquí sin darse cuenta de la divertida situación que crea el contraste de la muchacha del cartel y la señora sentada. Esto reafirma la necesidad de tener los ojos abiertos y la cámara siempre a punto. Hasselblad. Película FP4 revelada en Unitol.

187

PARADOS, por E. Chambré Hardman

Un buen estudio de tipo industrial que muestra unas calderas abandonadas en una mina de carbón de Gales. Cámara Rolleiflex. Película HP3. Se amplió el negativo en película Ilford Fine Grain Ordinary para darle transparencia y luego se copió en papel brommo de gradación dura.

188

HYDE PARK, por F. Russell, FIIP, FRPS

Escogida de una serie de fotografías sobre los parques y la gente de Londres hechas por un joven fotógrafo industrial que se ha distinguido en este campo. La serie es un proyecto de tipo personal que realiza él mismo. Su cámera era una Nikkormat, con objetivo "zoom" 43-86; película HP5 valorada en 800 ASA.

189

OTOÑO, por Lazslo Lajas

El cubrir con hojas a la chica que está durmiendo produce cierto efecto macabro; no obstante, esto aumenta la sensación otoñal y convierte en interesante un paisaje que en sí no lo era. El tratamiento refuerza la sensación de similitud con que trabajan los fotógrafos húngaros y los checos.

190

LA CABEZA ENTRE LAS MANOS, por Howard Walker

Este famoso periodista gráfico del "Sunday Mirror" se lo estaba pasando muy bien cuando fotografió a su suegro en un espejo cóncavo del cuarto de baño; además ha conseguido un extraño cuadro abstracto. Nikon F2 con objetivo de 50 mm. Luz disponible. Película Tri-X revelada en D76.

191

ENERO, por Vladimir Filinov

Otra intrigante fotografía procedente de la URSS en la que se da un tratamiento original a un tema bastante corriente haciendo que una figura destaque del grupo. El chico impone el tema y los demás arreglan la escena. Tomada con una cámara de 35 mm, con objetivo estándar y un convertidor 3X, y luego copiada a 6 x 9 cm en película "lith".

192

TIO JUAN, por V. Sonta

Escogida entre una serie de fotos de campesinos lituanos, el autor ha escogido un tratamiento de perfil, al que en este caso la "pose" añade estabilidad y fuerza. Tomada con una Konica A3 con objetivo de 50 mm. Película Tri-X revelada en Microphen.

193

SIN TITULO, por David Burrows, AIIP

Tomada durante un recital de piano en Manchester. No hace falta decir quién es el modelo aunque la cara queda en parte escondida. El interés de Mr. Heath por la música es conocido de todos, y el punto de vista que se ha escogido hace que resulte una composición sorprendente. Nikon F2 con objetivo de 135 mm. Película Tri-X revelada en D-76.

194/195

PETER BONETTI, por Mike Hollist

El famoso guardameta del Chelsea, alias "Cat" (gato), se entrena junto con su hijo de nueve años. ¡Espera ser el sucesor de su padre! Mike, que trabaja en el "The Daily Mail", utilizó una cámara Nikon F2 con objetivo de 180 mm. Película Tri-X revelada en D-76. Exposición 1 / 500 de sugundo, diafragma f / 5,6.

196

VENTANA SOBRE LONDRES, por Jack Rufus, FRPS

Cuando no se encontraba de safari en el Africa oriental, el fallecido Jack Rufus gustaba de pasear por Londres con la cámara y se la arreglaba para encontrar interpretaciones artísticas tanto en la arquitectura moderna como en la antigua; como ésta, tomada en el Barbican. Hasselblad con objetivo de 80 mm. Película Tri-X, revelada en Microdol. Ver también la página 59.

197

RASCACIELOS, por Geri Della Rocca

Extraordinaria vista del "World Trade Centre" en Nueva York. Cuando las circunstancias hacen imposible mantener rectas las verticales, resulta positivo fotografiar desde muy cerca para exagerar la sensación de altura; esta foto nos muestra que si se hace con gran maestría mejora el diseño. Nikon F con objetivo de 20 mm. Película HP5 a 600 ASA.

198

TERNURA, por Serge de Sazo

Se puede expresar de muchas maneras el sentimiento amoroso; pero se precisa ser un hábil artista para saber utilizar desnudos de los dos sexos sin que el tono resulte lascivo. En esto siempre fueron maestros los franceses, tanto en escultura como en pintura; y esta foto demuestra que también pueden hacerlo en fotografía. Es aleccionador comparar esta foto con las de la páginas 71 y 211.

199

KALHAMA AND GUTTA, por K. Szebessy

Esta foto capta el ambiente de un estudio de artista debido a los posters que se ven en segundo plano; pero consigue expresar personalidad propia con la figura que se dirige a la cámara, dándole el movimiento y el equilibrio perfectos.

200

BRIAN BECK, por Geoffrey Tyrer

Una oportunísima instantánea de este atleta olímpico efectuando un salto mortal. Tyrer recogió el punto culminante de la acción y además supo narrar toda la historia. Fotografía tomada para el "Sheffield Star". Cámara Canon Ft con objetivo de 50 mm. Flash rebotado; diafragma f / 5,6; película Tri-X.

201

ATLETA, por Luis Arteaga Cerdain

Como la de la página anterior, también esta foto recoge el momento esencial de la acción. El escenario auténtico complementa la acción, y la vista posterior es atractiva. Nikon F2A con objetivo de 105 mm. Película Tri-X revelada en Rodinal.

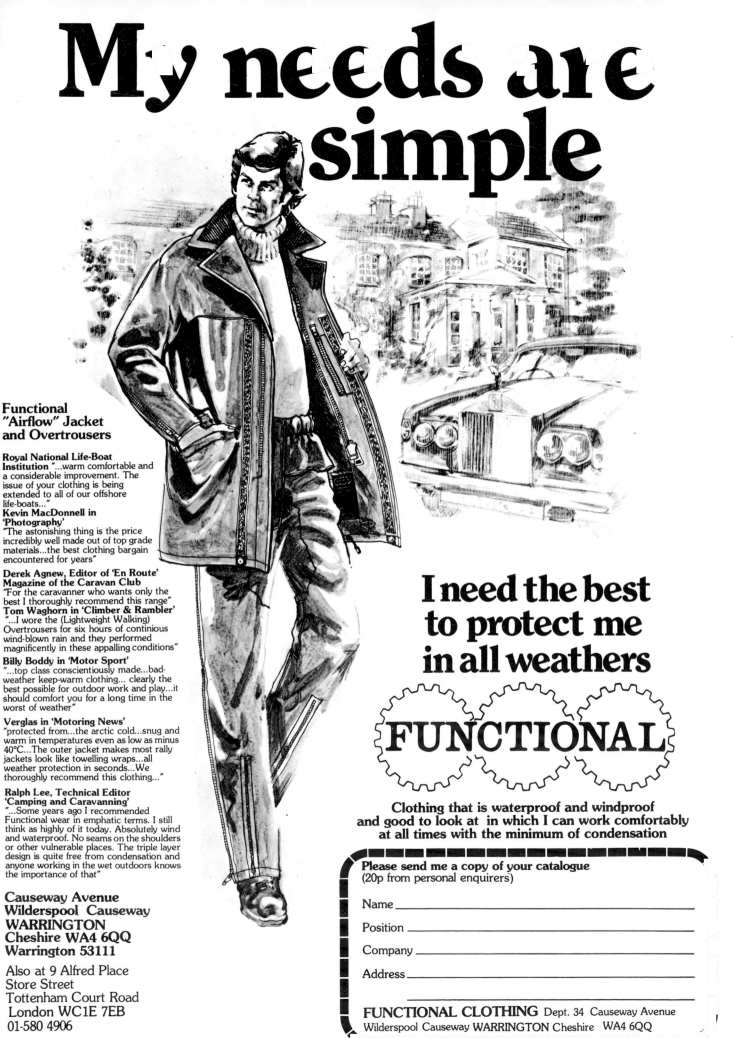

My needs are simple

Functional "Airflow" Jacket and Overtrousers

Royal National Life-Boat Institution "...warm comfortable and a considerable improvement. The issue of your clothing is being extended to all of our offshore life-boats..."

Kevin MacDonnell in 'Photography' "The astonishing thing is the price incredibly well made out of top grade materials...the best clothing bargain encountered for years"

Derek Agnew, Editor of 'En Route' Magazine of the Caravan Club "For the caravanner who wants only the best I thoroughly recommend this range"

Tom Waghorn in 'Climber & Rambler' "...I wore the (Lightweight Walking) Overtrousers for six hours of continious wind-blown rain and they performed magnificently in these appalling conditions"

Billy Boddy in 'Motor Sport' "...top class conscientiously made...bad-weather keep-warm clothing... clearly the best possible for outdoor work and play...it should comfort you for a long time in the worst of weather"

Verglas in 'Motoring News' "protected from...the arctic cold...snug and warm in temperatures even as low as minus 40°C...The outer jacket makes most rally jackets look like towelling wraps...all weather protection in seconds...We thoroughly recommend this clothing..."

Ralph Lee, Technical Editor 'Camping and Caravanning' "...Some years ago I recommended Functional wear in emphatic terms. I still think as highly of it today. Absolutely wind and waterproof. No seams on the shoulders or other vulnerable places. The triple layer design is quite free from condensation and anyone working in the wet outdoors knows the importance of that"

**Causeway Avenue
Wilderspool Causeway
WARRINGTON
Cheshire WA4 6QQ
Warrington 53111**

Also at 9 Alfred Place
Store Street
Tottenham Court Road
London WC1E 7EB
01-580 4906

Personal callers welcome

I need the best to protect me in all weathers

FUNCTIONAL

Clothing that is waterproof and windproof and good to look at in which I can work comfortably at all times with the minimum of condensation

Please send me a copy of your catalogue
(20p from personal enquirers)

Name _____

Position _____

Company _____

Address _____

_____

FUNCTIONAL CLOTHING Dept. 34 Causeway Avenue
Wilderspool Causeway WARRINGTON Cheshire WA4 6QQ

202

**PERDIDOS Y ABANDONADOS,
por Henning Christoff**

De una serie sobre "niños sin hogar" de Ipanema, que duermen en las calles después de haber sido evacuados de sus casas. Leica M4 con objetivo Summilux de 35 mm y flash. Película Tri-X revelada en D-76.

203

VISIONES, por Vlado Baca

Una de las fotos de la serie presentada por este joven fotógrafo independiente checoslovaco. se tomaron para la revista "Slovensko" fotografiando et reflejo de unas placas cromadas. Cámara Pentacon Six con objetivo de 50 mm. Película Orwo NP27 revelada en D-76.

204

GLENEVE, por David Dalby

La atmósfera ominosa de una tormenta en los Highlands está bien captada y representada gracias al empleo de fuertes tonos oscuros. Las diferentes capas de la atmósfera y las luces altas lejanas incrementan la profundidad. Cámara Hasselblad con objetivo de 80 mm. Película Tri-X revelada en Rodinal; f / 16, 1 / 250 de segundo.

205

MI AMIGO, por V. Sonta

Una fotografía que, sin duda, agradará a los que se oponen a lo que llaman "la amenaza de las motos". La dramática iluminación y la poco usual colocación de la figura dan una impresión de velocidad que sobrecoge al espectador. Cámara Pentacon Six; objetivo de 80 mm y filtro rojo. Película "Photo 65" revelada en D-76; 1/60 de segundo a f/5,6.

206

JUNTO AL CURBAR, por John Woodhouse

Un autorretrato en el Peak District National Park, hechó por un conocido alpinista ganador de diferentes premios, tomadó con la ayuda de un trípode y autodisparador retardado. La cámara era una Olympus OM-1 con objetivo de 35 mm. y filtro naranja. Película FP revelada en Aculux.

207

HANG GLIDING, por T. G. Edwards

Una foto interesante, para comparar con la titulada "Easy glider" de la página 162 y que nos obliga a hacernos también la pregunta que muchos clubs se hacen para saber si es el color o el blanco y negro lo que proporciona más ambiente o fuerza dramática. Tomada en el escondrijo del diablo "Devils Dyke" con una Nikon F2; objetivo de 85 mm., filtro polarizador, y película FP4.

208

PIGGY BACK, por Min Shik Choi

El sentimental tema del cariño de los niños hacia los animales se utiliza con frecuencia; pero no es corriente ver un zorro tan domesticado como éste de Corea, de paso firme y picaresca expresión. Leica M3 con objetivo de 200 mm. Película Tri-X revelada en Rodinal; 1/125 de segundo y diafragma f/4.

209

PIGGY BACK, por David Wilding

Instantánea hecha durante el Edinburgh Tattoo cuando el modelo buscaba sitio para sentarse. Esta foto muestra, una vez más, la conveniencia de llevar siempre con uno la cámara. Pentax Spotmatic con objetivo 135 mm. Película Tri-X valorada a 650 ASA.

210

MODELO DE ESCULTOR, de Frank Peeters

Tomada en una escuela artística belga con la luz fluorescente disponible, esta instantánea refleja fielmente la atmósfera de la escena original, la cual se habría perdido al utilizar un flash. La cámara fue una Nikkormat FT3 con un objetivo de 105 mm. y se utilizó una película Tri-X a 1600 ASA, revelándosela en Neutol S.

211

**RETRATO DE DOS ENAMORADOS,
de Josep Maria Ribas Prous**

He aquí una pareja desnuda tratada con un gusto excelente, obteniéndose un resultado de gran expresividad artística. El autor empleó una Nikon F2 con un objetivo de 105 mm., luz natural y una película Tri-X revelada en Microdol X. Exposición de 1/30 seg. a f/2.

212

MITSUO TSAKAHARA, por Sven Simon

La fotografía deportiva representa un gran desafío para el fotógrafo por la dificultad de calcular el momento justo del disparo y de captar el momento culminante de la acción. El resultado produce la impresión de que todo fue fácil, pero se necesitó mucha maestría para lograrlo. Las barras horizontales complementan el relato.

213 (arriba)

FIONA ROGERS, por Mervyn Rees, FRPS

Foto de la gran corredora de vallas tomada en el Palacio de Cristal de Londres durante los entrenamientos. El efecto dramático se obtuvo mediante el uso de un objetivo "ojo de pez" Sigma en una cámara Nikon F2. Exposición 1/1000 de segundo. Película Tri-X revelada en D-76.

213 (abajo)

LADY BOWLER, por Terry Cooper

Típica escena británica, tomada por motivo del "Community and Environment", que ganó un premio en la South Eastern Association. Tomada en el Preston Park de Brighton con una Olympus OM-1 con objetivo de 50 mm. Película FP4 revelada en ID11.

214

EN EL MUSEO DE ATENAS, por Jean Berner

Simpática foto en la que vemos a la hija del propio autor protestando de recibir tanta cultura. Película Fujichrome 100 y cámara Nikkormat con objetivo de 20 mm. Se copió la ampliación en papel inversible con película Tri-X para obtener un negativo y aislar al modelo con el sombreado.

215

METRO de Achim Sperber

Tomada en el metro de Nueva York para ser incluida en una serie titulada "Nueva York – Arriba y Abajo", en esta instantánea se refleja claramente la atmósfera típica de este vilipendiado medio de transporte. El fotógrafo se sirvió de una cámara Leica, con un objetivo de 35 mm. y una película Tri-X revelada en D76. La exposición fue de 1 / 125 seg. a f / 2,8.

216

SIN TITULO, por Signe Drevsjo

Un retrato doble, lleno de sinceridad, que capta un momento de felicidad como sólo puede hacer la fotografía. El contraste entre la juventud y la vejez encierra su propio mensaje; y las dos cabezas están situadas de tal modo que dan gran vitalidad a la composición. Canon F1 con objetivo de 50 mm. Película Tri-X revelada en D-76.

217

RETRATO DOBLE, por Egon Spuris

Este retrato es un desafío a todos los textos que afirman que ha de existir una conexión – aparente o sugerida – entre dos modelos; y aún más, que uno de ellos ha de destacar sobre el otro. Sea como sea, esta insólita composición refleja una expresión que sirve de estímulo para la imaginación.

218

SIN TITULO, por Karin Szekessy

Extraordinaria composición de figuras hecha por un fotógrafo que no se para en barras para presentar sus ideas y que no se preocupa por los problemas técnicos que plantea el equilibrio de las luces. De hecho, el halo de la ventana le añade realismo. Véase también la página 199.

219

SIN TITULO, por Michael Gnade

Es muy interesante comparar esta foto con la de la página opuesta. La delicadeza del toque femenino está reemplazada por el fuerte contraste no tan sólo del tema, sino también del tono. La composición es muy coherente a pesar de los muchos elementos que la componen.

220

CALELLA, por Ferrán Artigas

El punto de vista bajo y el fuerte contraste dan pie al autor para dramatizar y dar la impresión del riesgo de que los edificios se desplomen con la próxima tormenta, debido a la erosión del terreno sobre et que se asientan. Tomada con una Minolta SRT con objetivo de 28 mm. Película Tri-X.

221

**UN PAISAJE DEL CIELO,
por Chris Peet FRPS**

Fue tomada por un fotógrafo que ha dejado el color por el blanco y negro. La impresión original era de tono sepia oscuro obtenido a base de dos revelados en una fuerte solución de sulfato. Presentada en el London Salon. Cámara Praktica con objetivo de 20 mm. Filtro naranja y película FP4.

222 (arriba)

COMPOSICION, por Ilmar Apkans

Produce la impresión de ser un libro de enseñansa lleno de ejercicios y no parece que contenga un significado oculto ni un mensaje; sin embargo, muestra la percepción del fotógrafo para captar una composición interesante. El original era de gran calidad.

222 (abajo)

LAS CUPULAS, por Rolan Herpin

Una interesante foto de diseño, que al mismo tiempo tiene atmósfera porque se utilizó una trama y se sombreó el cielo al impresionar el positivo. Tomada en Túnez. Minolta SRT 101 con objetivo de 135 mm. Película Tri-X. Positivo en papel Agfa duro.

223

**ARQUITECTURA EN LA PLAYA,
por Michael Scott**

Una foto de la serie tomada por un artista, que nos muestra cómo hallar el juego reciproco de las formas, de las texturas y del tono, en el más corriente de los sujetos. Praktica LTL con objetivo de 50 mm. Película HP5. La copia tenía un tono sepia para poner de relieve los años y el carácter de la estructura.

224

DESNUDO, por José Torregrossa

No es desacostumbrado utilizar figuras femeninas en las representaciones abstractas o semiabstractas, pero el poderoso efecto de las formas simples y del modelado libre hacen que éste ejemplo sobresalga de los demás. Cámara Nikon F con objetivo de 24 mm. Película Tri-X revelada en HC110.

Cubierta posterior: interior

**DESPUES DE LA CARRERA, por
Raymonde Jarry**

Interesante foto de formas. El tomar fotos desde la altura, sobre la muchedumbre, no es fácil porque raras veces resulta una composición equilibrada, o puede más bien resultar repetitiva y monótona. En este caso, la silla vacía rompe la monotonía y la vista posterior le da un toque insólito.

RAYMONDE JARRY